The Politics of Trafficking

The Politics of Trafficking

The First International Movement to Combat

the Sexual Exploitation of Women

Stephanie A. Limoncelli

Stanford University Press
Stanford, California

Stanford University Press
Stanford, California

Printed in the United States of America on acid-free, archival-quality paper

Library of Congress Cataloging-in-Publication Data

Limoncelli, Stephanie A.
  The politics of trafficking : the first international movement to combat the sexual exploitation of women / Stephanie A. Limoncelli.
     p. cm.
  Includes bibliographical references and index.
  ISBN 978-0-8047-6294-6 (cloth : alk. paper)
  1. Human trafficking—Europe—Prevention—History. 2. Prostitution—Europe—History. 3. Women—Crimes against—Europe—Prevention—History. 4. Social movements—Europe—History. I. Title.
  HQ281.L55 2010
  306.3'62—dc22
                          2009029055

Typeset by Bruce Lundquist in 10/14 Minion

For my dad

Contents

Tables

Preface

WHEN I FIRST BECAME INTERESTED IN THE TOPIC OF TRAFFICKING, very little academic research had been done, and what research existed was dominated by an often vitriolic feminist debate over the normalization and legalization of prostitution. This literature often treated trafficking as a discursive construction or moral panic about prostitution, and drew broad conclusions about the repressive motivations of anti-trafficking reformers. Seeking to learn more about trafficking, I began to peruse the historical literature on prostitution, which, although small, provided a much richer, more complicated picture of the social organization of prostitution and the first anti-trafficking movement. It seemed important to me to situate trafficking for prostitution as a process intertwined with globalization and nation-state development, to look at the global and comparative reach of anti-trafficking activities, examining the rise of migratory prostitution, the development of the international anti-trafficking movement, and the specific implementation of anti-trafficking efforts within countries and empires.

Trafficking is now rapidly developing into a topic of widespread interdisciplinary interest, drawing scholars from law, political science, criminal justice, sociology, and women's studies. Although many of these scholars note the existence of the earlier anti-trafficking movement, historians have not yet fully documented it, and most scholars in other disciplines have overlooked the potential insights that an analysis of the movement could provide. Among other things, for sociologists, political scientists, and those interested in women's studies, a study of early anti-trafficking efforts could furnish information on the dynamics of international social movements and the origins of humanitarianism and human rights efforts; it could also offer possibilities for understanding the national and international politics of gender, race, class, and nationality. For legal scholars, it could not only supply a context for the origins of national and international anti-trafficking and prostitution law, but also offer lessons on how those laws were implemented and whether they worked as intended. Using primary data drawn from the archives of the League of Nations and the involved international voluntary associations, including uncatalogued material, this book provides a unique historical, ethnographic account of the first anti-trafficking movement that helps to illuminate all of the issues just listed, especially the role of gender and sexuality in international politics.

Acknowledgments

This project would not have gotten under way without assistance from a number of colleagues and friends. Gail Kligman discussed the project at length, read numerous drafts, provided sound scholarly and personal advice, and helped me to strengthen the contribution to the literature on gender and states and on trafficking. Michael Mann's exemplary macro-level comparative-historical sociology greatly inspired me. I benefited enormously from his vast knowledge of European history and I appreciated his constructive feedback and good humor during our meetings. Ruth Milkman could always be counted on for her conceptual clarity and her support for comparative-historical work. Kathryn Norberg provided historical expertise on prostitution, extremely valuable comments, cheerful optimism, and ongoing encouragement.

Several organizations and programs generously provided funding for different aspects of the project. The German Marshall Fund of the United States and the UCLA Center for the Study of Women provided a fellowship that supported the initial research. The UCLA International Institute was helpful at two stages of the process: the Institute's Global Fellows Program provided a supportive place for interdisciplinary, transnational research during the data analysis stage, and its Center for European and Eurasian Studies provided support during the writing of the manuscript.

The librarians and staff at the Women's Library in London provided a home away from home in their beautifully renovated facility, often teasing me for my keen manner when I arrived promptly in the reading room each morning. The staff of the British Library of Political and Economic Science at the London School of Economics and Political Science were always prompt and professional, as were those at the British Library. Marianne Tsioli-Bodenmann at the University and Public Library at Geneva, now known as the Geneva Library, graciously let me sit among the stacks in the basement leafing through the uncatalogued boxes of material from the International Abolitionist Federation's library. The staff kindly tolerated my daily presence in their workspace. Bernhardine Pejovic at the League of Nations archives in the library of the United Nations Office at Geneva was extremely helpful in locating League of Nations trafficking materials and answering questions, often while juggling the demands of several researchers, each speaking a different language. I also wish to thank the scholars I met in the archives and during my travels—Carole Moschetti, Karen Offen, Carole Pateman, and Jane Cowen—who provided friendly camaraderie along the way.

A number of people discussed the project with me, read various incarnations of chapters, or shared their valuable insights on particular aspects of the subject matter: Catherine Y. Lee, Peter Stamatov, David Cook-Martin, Sasha Milicevic, Bill Roy, Gabriela Fried, Stephen Legg, Andrew Abalahin, Leo Lucassen, Mara Loveman, Sidney Tarrow, and the faculty and visiting scholars that were part of the UCLA Global Fellows Program in 2004.

All of the staff at Stanford University Press have been wonderful, especially my editor, Kate Wahl. I have been impressed with their promptness, efficiency, and professionalism. I also wish to thank the reviewers for their thoughtful and constructive feedback on the manuscript, which has certainly helped to improve it.

My father, Fred Limoncelli, provided loving support that meant the world to me, as did my sisters, Stacy Moses and Anna-Maria Trimboli, and my mother and grandmother, Anna and Helen Koutouras. Tiffani Chin was unfailingly helpful, providing astute advice and friendship, as was Liana Grancea, with whom I spent much time at the UCLA International Institute. Liana also assisted me with translations of French material, for which I am grateful, and any errors are mine alone. Nona Glazer offered inspiration and empathy gained from her years of academic experience. My colleagues in the Department of Sociology at Loyola Marymount University, especially Nadia Kim and Anna Muraco, formed a great cheering section in the final revision stages of the manuscript. Finally, I wish to thank my family, Mark and Sophia, for everything.

Abbreviations

Archival materials are cited in the endnotes using the following abbreviations for the libraries where the materials are located:

WL: The Women's Library, London Metropolitian University

GL: Geneva Library (formerly Geneva Public and University Library)

LON: The League of Nations Archive, Library of the United Nations Office at Geneva

LSE: London School of Economica and Political Science

The Politics of Trafficking

1 Introduction

[T]here is a regular trade in young girls who are bought and sold, imported and exported, to and from the ports and cities of Europe. . . . It will naturally occur to remark that such a traffic involves slavery. . . . The business is an international trade, kept up very much by the movement of girls from one country to another, and in a very large number of cases the movement [does not have] the nature of emigration, or free voluntary movement of adults, but of export, that is, movement of persons under stress of fear or fraud, often minors incapable of consent.

—P. Bunting

We want to destroy this traffic. Well, a traffic consists of three parts; first, there is the supply; second, there are the traffickers; and third, there must be a demand. . . . [E]verything that can be done . . . to improve women's position . . . will cut off the supply. . . . [S]trike at the supply, strike at the traffickers, but strike also at the demand for the victims.

—Henry J. Wilson

THE TRAFFIC IN WOMEN AND GIRLS FOR PROSTITUTION has captured the attention of academics, activists, politicians, and reporters around the world, spurring an energetic movement to help those involved in the international sex trade. As the introductory quotes suggest, women and girls may be moved across borders into situations of coercive prostitution tantamount to slavery. What may surprise those who think of trafficking as a recent phenomenon, however, is that the introductory quotes are actually from reformers at an international anti-trafficking congress in 1899.[1]

It was well over a century ago, amid increasing globalization and the rise of nation-building and imperialism, that the emergence of traffic in women and girls for prostitution alarmed reformers and state officials in European and other countries throughout the world.[2] They formed anti-trafficking committees within countries and worked to incorporate anti-trafficking activities first into the League of Nations and then into the United Nations. They also developed a variety of international anti-trafficking accords from 1904 through 1949, before the movement began to lose momentum. Trafficking was actually the first women's issue taken up in international accords, well before other issues that were advocated during the same period, including suffrage, education, and married women's citizenship.[3]

This book traces the construction and diffusion of the first anti-trafficking movement from its beginnings in Great Britain to key European countries, including the Netherlands, France, and Italy, where local anti-trafficking movements varied in their agendas and in their successes. Initially conceived of as a global humanitarian effort to protect women from sexual exploitation, the movement's international feminist-inspired vision failed to achieve its universal goal. Instead, in both international settings and in local areas, it gradually gave way to nationalist concerns about protecting states from certain groups of "undesirable" migrants and led to increased social control of women.

Why did the movement lose its original vision and turn against the very women it sought to protect? The core theme and argument of this book is that the movement was limited by the central role of women's sexual labor in both nation/state- and empire-building. State officials sought to defend and preserve their right to maintain and regulate prostitution in metropolitan and colonial areas in support of militaries and migrant laborers, and as a means of maintaining ethnic hierarchies. They were able to do so largely because the international voluntary associations who initiated the first anti-trafficking movement were divided in their approaches to prostitution, in their views about the proper role of state involvement in sexual relations, and in their imperial and national biases.

Using archival and secondary historical sources, the first part of the book examines the overall development of the movement as it was promoted by two key international voluntary associations that competed to define the issue of trafficking in both international settings, such as at the League of Nations, and local areas. One of the associations, composed of emerging feminist groups, challenged state sovereignty in matters of prostitution; the other, which was organized by purity reformers, sought to reinforce that sovereignty. This broad level of analysis from a global vantage point allows us to see the workings of international governmental and nongovernmental organizations, and the often contradictory outcomes of humanitarian efforts in international governance. The anti-trafficking movement ended up reinforcing rather than challenging state power as state officials selectively used reforms as mechanisms to realize their own interests in maintaining and controlling women's mobility and sexual labor.

This process was mediated to some degree by the interactions of voluntary associations and state officials in particular locales, and by the importance of women's sexual labor in empire-building. In the second part of the book I highlight the efforts of the international voluntary associations in specific countries where their relative influence, along with the perceived importance of prostitution to nation-building and imperial projects, led to differences between specific anti-trafficking projects in the Netherlands, France, and Italy. Only the Netherlands applied anti-trafficking measures throughout its territories and addressed the traffic in non-European women. Officials in France, in contrast, sought to maintain the state's right to permit immigrant women in state-regulated prostitution and refused to apply anti-trafficking measures in colonial areas. In Italy, state officials used the issue of trafficking as a proxy for controlling migration as part of Fascist population policy, and tried unsuccessfully to import European, but not Italian, women for prostitution in colonial areas.

As early examples from an international humanitarian movement, these first anti-trafficking efforts need to be considered as part of global politics, replete with power struggles and contradictions of their own. To understand the dynamics and outcomes of the movement, then, we must critically examine not only the international voluntary associations that founded and fostered the movement, but also the actions of involved state officials as well as the relations between the different actors. This examination also requires that we consider the movement in its historical context, as part of a period characterized by economic globalization; by the consolidation of Western European nation-states, their increasing infrastructural development, and the creation of the international state system; by the rise of women's activism as they struggled to define new positions within nation-states; by ongoing but embattled colonialism; and by the rise of ethnonationalism.

Gender, International Politics, and Women's Sexuality

Women's bodies and sexuality are central to the making of nation-states and empires.[4] Women's potential as childbearers and mothers, as well as workers and settlers, positions them in unique relation to state-building projects and as markers of ethnonational boundaries; they are integral to the physical and cultural reproduction of the nation-state and empire.[5] This material and symbolic importance provides a clue as to why trafficking for prostitution became the focus of the first international conventions pertaining to women, and why the problem was addressed by state officials before other issues of importance to feminist social reformers, including women's suffrage. Trafficking was catapulted into the international realm not only because feminists and purity reformers lobbied for change; it was taken up by state officials precisely because of their concern with the regulation of women's sexuality.

Gender, sexuality, and race and ethnicity, in many intertwined configurations, have been important in the discursive delineation of imperial and national boundaries.[6] In constructing the nation, women are evoked as mothers, as symbols of "the national hearth and home," and as wives and daughters who are the bearers of masculine honor.[7] The sexuality of women in any of these roles can become central preoccupations of state officials, who have often sought to ensure women's sexual respectability, that is, their availability to men of their own nation and not of others. Sexual relationships that transgress this boundary have been understood as endangering the very bounds of the nation, whether the women involved had voluntary or involuntary sexual relations with ethnic or national "others" or, in the case of this study, were involved in prostitution across racial, ethnic, or national boundaries. Unbounded female sexual activities have been seen as dangerous and unpatriotic, a threat to the strength of the nation and the honor of men.[8]

Such preoccupation with women's bodies and sexual relationships is strongly tied to the masculinity of nationalism and imperialism.[9] Nation-state and imperial projects have been masculine endeavors and have both constructed and reflected male interests, assumptions, and anxieties.[10] It is not just that men have historically dominated state institutions, but also that nationalism, as a source of identity and action, has been intertwined with a certain type of masculinity, one that has dominated other, alternative forms.[11] If women are the mothers of empire and nation, then men have been cast as their leaders and protectors, ensuring their defense. Thus militarization has been central to the masculinization of nationalism and imperialism.[12]

Racial and ethnic dynamics have also been at work in the protection of national and imperial boundaries, and they have often been sexualized.[13] As Ann Stoler has argued, sexual contracts—whether through cohabitation, marriage, or prostitution—have shaped the boundaries of European membership and the interior frontiers of the colonial state.[14] Colonial "politics of exclusion" constructed who was subject or citizen, using sex, race, and class as central markers.[15] Not only was colonial authority bolstered in this manner, but so too was European sexuality, which was constituted partly by sexual arrangements in particular colonial formations.[16] Non-Europeans in colonial areas took part in this process as well as in their own constructions of sexuality, a point to which we will return in the case studies in Chapters Five through Seven.

Although women's sexual relations have been of central symbolic importance in constructing the boundaries of nation and empire, this book also reminds us about the need to understand and analyze women's sexual labor as an important part of modern state-building. The physical reproduction of the nation-state or empire, after all, depends on women's reproductive labor, and the health of the state has long been linked to the reproduction of its inhabitants.[17] More than that, women's paid and unpaid sexual relations with men have been important for the business of nation and empire. Colonization schemes have been organized around sexual arrangements.[18] In many parts of the world, single men or married men apart from their families were the officers, administrators, laborers, and military men on imperial projects.[19] Given the masculinity of nation and empire, the sexual and domestic needs of such men were presumed, and authorities did their best to regulate those needs using women's sexual labor.

Their efforts involved particular patterns of organizing women's sexual labor in plantation and settler colonies, and in militarized areas. The trajectory of colonialism was also important. For example, in the early stages of colonialism, concubinage was often the preferred arrangement for the use of women's sexual labor; later, prostitution was often put into place, especially in areas with large numbers of migrant laborers or military men. Militarization, in particular, led state officials to attempt to control and regulate women's sexual relations in colonial and metropolitan areas through the use of prostitution.[20] Still later, European women were encouraged to emigrate from the metropole in order to settle and "civilize" colonial areas as wives to European men.[21]

Women's bodies and sexuality, then, have long been put to use in service of the nation-state and empire. The need to specify which women should be paired with different groups of men—what Philippa Levine calls the "taxonomic urge" to control who "bed and wed"—was an ongoing project for state officials and for businesses operating in European imperial states and in colonial areas.[22] It occurred directly in nation-state and imperial projects as population and its control became central concerns of state officials and the state's infrastructure and administration increasingly took on the task of policing and regulating subjects and citizens. Yet just as the politics of women's sexuality led state officials to attempt to channel and regulate women in colonial and metropolitan settings, so too it shaped the international movement to combat trafficking. In its central preoccupation with the protection of women from sexual exploitation, the movement ended up replicating not only national and imperial boundaries, but also gendered ones.

The First International Anti-Trafficking Movement

International humanitarianism was a newly emerging phenomenon in the 1800s. It arose out of Christian missionary and charitable work, the antislavery movement, and the efforts of Henri Dunant, founder of the International Red Cross, who helped to develop the Geneva Convention of 1864. International humanitarian networks were a product of emerging globalization and imperialism, and a challenge to them, even as they constructed empire and nation.[23] These networks began to form international nongovernmental organizations specifically to alleviate the suffering of "distant others" around the world.[24] Using common tactics such as petition drives and protests to achieve change, they began to target the state as a locus of change.[25]

Voluntary associations concerned about the exploitation of women in prostitution were among the first organizations to develop and internationalize, and they took some terminology and tactics directly from the earlier international movement to abolish slavery. Beginning in 1875, reformers in Great Britain founded what would eventually become the liberal feminist International Abolitionist Federation, which worked to abolish the state regulation of prostitution around the world. Later, in 1899, purity reformers founded the International Bureau for the Suppression of the White Slave Traffic, which eventually changed the latter part of its name to the Traffic in Women and Children, and then to Traffic in Persons. I hereafter refer to it as the International Bureau. Both of these international voluntary associations sought to address what was originally called the "white slave trade," a term meant to evoke sympathy toward and similarities with the earlier abolitionist movement against black slavery by alluding to what were understood to be the coercive and exploitive aspects of commercial sex in European brothels of the time.[26] The movement would come to include a focus on women of color in prostitution, and later on boys as well, and the language used would eventually be changed to "the traffic in women and children," and later to "the traffic in persons."

Scholars have written about the movement and these reformers as an undifferentiated group and thus have failed to distinguish between them or their approaches to trafficking and prostitution.[27] The first anti-trafficking movement has sometimes even been conceptualized as an example of the successful development of a transnational moral framework against the sexual exploitation of women, a framework that some have lauded as a step toward a global norm of women's equality and that many others have seen as sexually repressive and culturally imperialist.[28] The postcolonial critique of reformers is warranted, but humanitarianism was not monolithic.[29] Our task is to distinguish who put forward humanitarian ideas, explore how they framed them, and determine why they did so and with what effects. We can then see, for example, that humanitarianism not only bolstered nationalism and imperialism but also sometimes challenged aspects of colonialist discourse or worked against what were perceived to be national interests.

Such was the case with the anti-trafficking movement. There were important differences in the ways the two main international voluntary associations constructed the problem of trafficking, including their views about gender and individual rights, their relations to state officials, and their beliefs about the role of the state in controlling sexual activity and contributing to trafficking. One key difference was in their positions on state-regulated prostitution systems, which many governments around the world had adopted throughout the 1800s.

Officials engaged in the state and nation-building projects that surged in Europe from the late nineteenth century on saw prostitution as both a necessity and a potential danger for nation and empire.[30] They believed that prostitution was needed to provide sexual outlets for military men and laborers in metropolitan and colonial areas. They also believed that prostitution had to be controlled in order to prevent the spread of venereal disease and the potentially negative consequences of uncontrolled sexual activity. By registering brothels and women who engaged in prostitution, placing requirements on them (such as compulsory health checks), and ensuring police oversight of brothel areas, state officials and their supporters believed they could provide for men's presumed sexual needs, maintain public health and social order, and control unwanted sexual activity, including interracial sexual relations and miscegenation, as well as the potential for homosexuality. Because male heterosexuality and men's need for sexual access to women were taken for granted, state officials concentrated their efforts on controlling female sexual activity.

This system of state regulation, which many countries at the time maintained in metropolitan areas, colonies, mandates, and protectorates, raised numerous questions for those involved in the anti-trafficking movement.[31] Did state regulation encourage trafficking in women and girls to and from brothels in different countries? Would the abolition of state regulation help to eliminate trafficking or would it simply go underground? How old should a woman or girl be in order to register as a prostitute in a foreign territory? Did the police oversight of brothels encourage corruption and further abuse of immigrant women or help to prevent it? The relationship between trafficking across borders and state-regulated prostitution within borders was an ongoing dilemma that plagued all anti-trafficking efforts.

The two international voluntary associations that initiated the movement took very different positions on state regulation. The International Abolitionist Federation believed that the abolition of state-regulated prostitution would help to eliminate the traffic in women and consistently worked toward this goal. Its members attempted to frame the issue in universal terms, by championing the protection of all women from state-regulated prostitution and challenging the right of states to organize prostitution in their territories even as they insisted on the civil rights of women in prostitution. The International Bureau, seeking to increase the state's ability to control various sexual activities that they believed were immoral, chose to sidestep the issue of regulation in favor of working with state officials. They framed the issue of prostitution in national terms, with each national committee concerned about protecting "their women" from foreign men, and they proposed measures to suppress foreign prostitution by criminalizing the women involved. The movement was thus divided from the beginning between a universal agenda for protecting women and an internationalism that served only to reinforce national differences.

European women often failed to interrogate their own racial, ethnic, national, and class privileges while they sought to help women across these categories.[32] Yet when we contrast the efforts of International Abolitionist Federation-affiliated abolitionists to the activities of those associated with the International Bureau, we also see an ongoing effort, imperfect though it was, to mobilize women on the basis of a common gender identity, to combat an issue of gender inequality, and to help all women, including those in the colonies. Women in Europe often supported nationalism, but feminists often did not.[33] At the start of the international anti-trafficking movement, the internationalism that feminists were developing held the potential for truly transnational endeavors—one that would use networks across borders to challenge the policies of individual states and international governmental organizations. As the International Bureau put forward its anti-trafficking agenda, however, efforts toward a universal humanitarian response to trafficking and prostitution were challenged by a more nationalist view.

For their part, state officials often preferred working with the International Bureau rather than with the International Abolitionist Federation as a means of maintaining state sovereignty over the organization of prostitution in their territories. They saw the possibility of using international anti-trafficking accords to legitimate their authority to import voluntary (as opposed to coerced or forced) prostitutes for state-regulated brothels, to deport foreign women in prostitution as desired, and to criminalize those engaging in unregulated prostitution. Indeed, discussion at international congresses and at the League of Nations sometimes reflected more concern with protecting the state from "undesirable" women than with preventing the exploitation of women in prostitution.

The International Anti-Trafficking Accords

State officials began to institutionalize the anti-trafficking movement soon after its start by developing a variety of international anti-trafficking accords.[34] These were not binding, but they did outline agreed-upon practices for states to follow. The first international agreement, developed in 1904, established central bureaus for the exchange of information on the traffic, set up aid in ports and railway stations for women and girls, and provided for the government repatriation of foreign women in prostitution and the regulation of employment offices that linked emigrants to situations abroad.[35] A 1910 convention made the prostitution of minors with or without their consent a punishable offense, as well as the prostitution of adult women by means of force or fraud.[36]

An additional convention, held in 1921, was developed under the auspices of the League of Nations, which helped to further legitimize anti-trafficking efforts. This convention extended protection to minors of either sex, raised the age of consent to twenty-one, provided for the extradition of traffickers, and required state legislation or administrative measures to control employment agencies.[37] The League went on to administer all of the international accords, with anti-trafficking efforts constituting a major component of its social and humanitarian work.[38] The League's Traffic in Women and Children Committee, a special working group consisting of nine delegates and five international voluntary associations, collected reports on trafficking and prostitution from participating states, commissioned two research studies of the international traffic, drafted additional conventions in 1933 and 1937, and worked on all matters pertaining to the accords.

Table 1.1 shows the states that signed the first three accords, including those that were appointed to participate in the committee.[39] All of the chief imperial powers—Great Britain, France, Spain, Belgium, the Netherlands, and Japan—were represented and indeed were the main actors in the movement both prior to and in the League of Nations. In the years between World Wars I and II, the

Table 1.1 Adherence to international anti-trafficking accords by country

Country[1]	1904	1910	1921	Date of Adherence to 1921 Accord	On LON TWC[2]
Albania			✓	10/13/1924	
Austria	✓	✓	✓	8/9/1922	
Belgium	✓	✓	✓	6/15/1922	✓
Brazil	✓	✓	✓	8/18/1933	
Bulgaria	✓	✓	✓	4/29/1925	
China	✓	✓	✓	2/24/1926	
Czechoslovakia	✓	✓	✓	9/29/1923	
Denmark	✓	✓	✓	4/23/1931	✓
France	✓	✓	✓	3/1/1926	✓
Germany	✓	✓	✓	7/8/1924	✓
Great Britain	✓	✓	✓	6/28/1922	✓
Greece			✓	4/9/1923	
Hungary	✓	✓	✓	4/25/1925	
Italy	✓	✓	✓	6/30/1924	✓
Japan	✓	✓	✓	12/15/1925	✓
Netherlands	✓	✓	✓	9/19/1923	
Norway	✓	✓	✓	8/16/1922	
Poland	✓	✓	✓	10/8/1924	✓
Portugal	✓	✓	✓	12/1/1923	
Romania			✓	9/5/1923	✓
Russia	✓	✓	✓	12/18/1947	
Siam/Thailand	✓	✓	✓	7/13/1922	
Spain	✓	✓	✓	5/12/1924	✓
Sweden	✓	✓	✓	6/9/1925	
Switzerland	✓	✓	✓	1/20/1926	
Turkey		✓	✓	4/15/1937	
United States	✓			n/a	✓
Uruguay	✓	✓	✓	10/21/1924	✓

SOURCES: League of Nations 1922; 1928a; http://treaties.un.org/Pages/ViewDetails. aspx?src=TREATY&mtdsg_no=VII-3&chapter=7&lang=en (accessed September 13, 2009).

1. This list is not exhaustive in that it does not separate out colonial areas or list countries that adhered after 1950. For a complete list of countries, see the sources cited here.

2. The LON TWC refers to the League of Nations Traffic in Women and Children Committee.

new kingdom of Yugoslavia and the new independent republics of Hungary, Czechoslovakia, and Poland joined the list. Even a cursory glance at the list shows that trafficking proved to be of particular interest to those states that were attempting to affirm their territorial boundaries—states seeking to bolster their rule over colonial holdings, new nation-states, and established states with shifting boundaries engendered by World War I. The potential to use anti-trafficking measures as a means of controlling migration, population, and sexual relations appealed to officials in democratic and authoritarian states alike.[40]

Postcolonial states had their turn as well. After World War II, many of the original imperial European countries who had been most involved in the anti-trafficking movement were no longer interested in the issue. The United Nations picked up anti-trafficking efforts, surveying countries on trafficking activities and developing a 1949 convention that went into force in 1951. This convention made all procurement for prostitution a punishable offense, regardless of the age or consent of the victims. It did not distinguish between internal and international traffic, and it made brothel keeping punishable.[41] Few European countries signed it. Rather, the list of adherents included many postcolonial states in their own processes of state- and nation-building, such as Algeria, India, Pakistan, Morocco, and Myanmar. Socialist states were another group of supporters; most of them took the opportunity to proclaim their superiority over Western countries in stock declaration statements that accompanied their accession. For example, the Soviet Union's statement read, "In the Soviet Union the social conditions which give rise to the offences covered by the Convention have been eliminated," and Bulgaria's read, "The offences referred to in the Convention are unknown under the socialist regime of the People's Republic of Bulgaria, for the conditions favouring them have been eliminated."[42] Socialist states claimed to have made trafficking obsolete.

Comparing Imperial States:
Different Applications of the International Accords

Although many governments signed the international accords, the implementation of anti-trafficking measures varied from country to country, primarily in their applications to colonial areas. Modern European imperialism had dominated the globe by the early twentieth century.[43] By 1900, European states had partitioned all of Africa, most of Asia, and the part of the Pacific that had not been claimed by the United States.[44] The British Empire was the largest colonizer in terms of both land and population, followed by France; the Dutch ruled a long-standing empire that included the Dutch East Indies. Italy, a late colonizer, was engaged in active expansionism in the interwar period.

In this book I use case studies of three imperial states to examine the trajectory of anti-trafficking efforts and their consequences. Examining these processes in particular cases provides an opportunity to analyze gender and sexuality comparatively. The cases exemplify the importance of gender and sexuality in defining the parameters of state responsibilities to subject and citizen, creating national boundaries, and ensuring the moral legitimacy of state rule.[45]

The first case is the Netherlands, where women's influence, in part, helped to build a relatively autonomous anti-trafficking movement that succeeded in persuading the state to apply anti-trafficking measures in all Dutch territories, including the colonies. The second case is France, where purity reformers dominated the movement and the government did not apply either the 1904 agreement or the 1910 convention to its protectorates or the 1921 convention to any of its colonies or protectorates. The last case is Italy, where neither international voluntary association made much progress but state officials instituted a top-down movement. The government signed all three accords and applied the 1921 convention to the colonies, but with a reservation lowering the age of consent for indigenous women and children from twenty-one to sixteen. Regardless, Italians did not follow through in applying anti-trafficking measures in colonial areas.

All of these countries had some similar characteristics of colonial rule. All had tolerated interracial sexual relations, particularly in the form of concubinage and prostitution in the colonies to support military men, colonial administrators, and laborers.[46] All had moved away from concubinage in the interwar period and sought other alternatives to provide for men's domestic and sexual needs. All were increasingly concerned with race in the interwar period, both at home and in the colonies, and rising anticolonial nationalism at that time exacerbated tensions about interracial sexual activity and miscegenation.

There were other similarities as well. Each country had implemented state-regulated prostitution in both its home territories and in colonial areas, and both the International Bureau and the International Abolitionist Federation actively organized in all three countries. State officials from each country took part in the anti-trafficking movement both before and after the movement's institutionalization in the League of Nations, and each country had signed the first international anti-trafficking accords.

Yet the responses of state officials to trafficking and prostitution varied: authorities in only one of these countries actually implemented anti-trafficking measures universally in both metropolitan and colonial areas. The relative influence of feminists affiliated with the International Abolitionist Federation or of conservative reformers associated with the International Bureau along with the perceived importance of prostitution to each state's unique imperial trajectory help to explain the willingness of these countries to abolish the state regulation of prostitution and extend anti-trafficking measures to all of their territories. Given certain conditions, abolitionist goals could be successfully realized, albeit with unintended consequences for the women they were trying to help.

The comparison of the actions of state officials in different empires is meant not to imply that one version of imperialism was more humane or less racially prejudiced than another but to examine how different states addressed trafficking and prostitution in practice, and why. The choice of cases here reflects not only the desire to examine the role of the competing international voluntary associations in each country, but also the wish to contribute to the literature on colonial areas that have been less often studied and presented in English. Great Britain dominates colonial studies, but rather than focus on the country in which the international anti-trafficking movement started, I have chosen to look instead at cases that could demonstrate the effects of the movement as it diffused elsewhere and allow comparison between the countries.

Such comparisons of imperial state policies and practice, particularly policies pertaining to women, are not common.[47] One group of scholars who might do such work, comparative-historical sociologists, have often overlooked gender or focused specifically on gender and modern welfare states; there are also relatively few sociologists who work on imperialism and colonialism.[48] Another group, historians, is only now beginning to look at such policies and practices internationally. As Cooper and Stoler have noted, colonial historiography has been nationally bound, ignoring cross-imperial linkages such as international congresses, and questions about whether such connections provided sites for shared notions of "Europeanness" or perhaps heightened nationalism.[49]

Looking at networks of power comparatively, both within and around the colonial state, can further our understanding of how gender, nation, and empire functioned. It can help us to understand the intent of state officials and the ways in which women's bodies and sexual activity were part and parcel of attempts to delineate boundaries of nation and empire and bolster state-building. It can shed light on international and national linkages, on the ability of international nongovernmental organizations to challenge state power, on the motivations for state involvement in humanitarian issues pertaining to

women, and on the importance of gender and sexual relationships to state officials engaged in nation-state and imperial projects as they negotiated relations
with each other in the international realm.

Sources

Primary sources for this project were located in the archives of the two main international voluntary associations involved in the movement, the International
Abolitionist Federation and the International Bureau, as well as the League of
Nations.[50] The materials include petitions and pamphlets; international voluntary association and League of Nations and United Nations publications;
country-specific reports; correspondence within and between the International
Abolitionist Federation, the International Bureau, and the League of Nations;
notes from the organizations' meetings and conferences; newsletters; and minutes of meetings. Secondary sources, most often country-specific historical
narratives of prostitution, provided corroboration and additional details. Such
narratives were particularly important for the case studies in fleshing out and
verifying information found in the international archives. Because only a few
historical scholars have studied prostitution in modern Europe and the colonies, I relied on their work often, especially in the chapters on the Netherlands,
France, and Italy.

Data on actual incidences of trafficking are very hard to find, in part because trafficking has been and continues to be an underground process, which
makes its documentation difficult.[51] A lack of reliable documentation, dis-
agreement on how to define trafficking, and the difficulties of studying hidden
populations, the size and boundaries of which are not known, all contribute to
the dearth of knowledge.[52] Furthermore, historians and social science scholars
have neglected the subject of prostitution until recently, therefore much work
remains to be done before we are able to document the organization of sexual
labor historically.[53] There is also a particular need to document the voices of the
women who themselves are in prostitution, because they are nearly absent from
the historical record.[54]

The participants in the early anti-trafficking movement did little to help
clarify the definition of trafficking because those involved in the movement
had diverse political agendas that caused them to use the term in very different
ways. At times, feminists included discussion of arranged marriage, child marriage, child prostitution, voluntary migratory adult prostitution, involuntary
adult prostitution within rather than between countries, and child adoption

and other placement arrangements that left girls in the care of men who could take advantage of them. The term trafficking was often shorthand for any situation in which women and girls did not have assurance that they would be protected from men's unwanted sexual advances. Purity reformers usually defined trafficking more carefully, as forced or coerced adult prostitution, or as child prostitution, in which case consent was not a necessary criterion. However, they also often expanded their concerns to include various forms of sexual relations outside of marriage as part of the "immorality" they were fighting.

Given the lack of specificity in most historical records, I use the term trafficking to refer to the general movement of women across territorial borders for prostitution. The percentage of women voluntarily involved in such movement has been and remains open to debate, but it is important to note that women had very limited rights within most countries in the period examined here, and that there is evidence in the historical literature and from the League of Nations that trafficking agents were active and that women were bought, sold, and contracted to brothels for specified periods.[55] There is also evidence that those who organized prostitution—the pimps, procurers, brothel keepers, and police involved in regulation—used coercive and deceptive practices to exploit women and girls, including those who had already been active in prostitution in their countries of origin.[56] The movement of women across borders for prostitution involved both voluntary and coercive aspects, and these were not necessarily mutually exclusive.

Layout of Book

In the following chapters I examine the politics of trafficking both internationally and locally. I show that, as a whole, the first international anti-trafficking movement shifted toward a nationalist framework that appealed to state officials and began to focus particularly on the control of women and their sexual activity. Further, the actions of reformers and the importance of prostitution to particular state and nation-building efforts led to unique anti-trafficking movement dynamics and outcomes in various countries. This analysis allows us to understand the rise of the movement internationally as well as variances in state efforts to address it, because both fit within the purview of states attempting to control the boundaries of empire and nation through gendered and racialized sexual relations.

Chapter Two provides background on the modernization and internationalization of prostitution, paying particular attention to the role of the state. In the late 1800s, prostitution was modernized and bureaucratized, and became migratory in a way that it had not been previously. This was not only a response to labor needs in migrant communities, but also a result of military demand and of state and local officials' desires to manage the sex lives of large groups of men at home and in the colonies through systems of regulated prostitution. I outline particular patterns of migratory prostitution that developed as women were moved between state-regulated brothels to service military men, laborers, and administrators in metropolitan and colonial areas. Ethnonationalism and anticolonial nationalism played a role as officials sought to move women between states and within empires in order to ensure that sexual relations were maintained within particular racial/ethnic groups.

Chapter Three examines the role of the two main international voluntary associations in fostering the movement, paying particular attention to how they framed prostitution and sexual exploitation, to the ways in which they internationalized their agendas, and to their relations to state officials. I show that feminists attempted to organize and frame the issue of exploitative prostitution as a universal social problem that was exacerbated by state regulation. This challenge to the state was countered by an international organization of purity reformers that defined trafficking in nationalist terms and whose members formed close relationships with state officials. State officials in most countries embraced the association formed by purity reformers, incorporating their views as they appropriated the movement. As this process shows, international voluntary associations may sometimes work to increase, rather than oppose, state power.

Chapter Four explores the efforts of state officials in the League of Nations when they institutionalized the movement, working on issues of prohibiting foreign prostitutes from working in state-regulated brothels and repatriating foreign women working as prostitutes. It is here that one can see state officials increasingly speaking of the need to protect themselves from women rather than protecting women from men or corrupt state officials who were part of prostitution regulation systems. Some state officials and purity reformers took steps to prevent foreign women from registering in state-regulated brothels, or worked to require the compulsory repatriation of foreign women in prostitution, which in effect nationalized it. At the same time, many states did little in practice to address this issue, because officials sometimes preferred to have foreign women rather than nationals in their brothels.

Chapter Five addresses the Netherlands, which developed an anti-trafficking movement influenced initially by women and relatively autonomous from the state. As such, it worked toward the abolition of state-regulated prostitution as well as the application of anti-trafficking agreements and conventions to all of the country's territories, including the Dutch East Indies. The movement was particularly successful in these goals; the Dutch government signed every anti-trafficking accord from 1904 to 1921 and applied them universally to metropole and colony. I argue that prostitution was less important to the nation-state and empire-building projects of the Netherlands than to the countries in the other cases I detail. Coupled with the strength and autonomy of the Dutch movement, this difference meant that reformers in the Netherlands were more easily able to achieve some feminist-inspired anti-trafficking protections compared to reformers in France or Italy. Even in the Netherlands, however, ethnonational and imperial tensions partly explain the response of the Dutch state, because Indonesian nationalists there also pressured state officials to take action on trafficking.

Chapter Six shows that the French movement was influenced initially by the International Bureau rather than by feminist abolitionists. Although the country started off with prestige as a leader of the anti-trafficking movement, it increasingly withdrew from international efforts when both French and international feminists began to have success in challenging state sovereignty over prostitution policy. Although state officials signed the 1904 agreement and 1910 convention, they did not apply either to French protectorates, and when the French government signed the 1924 convention, it did not apply it to any colonies, protectorates, or mandates. Influenced by Catholic reformers and regulationist supporters affiliated with the International Bureau and tied to the state, anti-trafficking efforts focused mainly on increasing legislative measures to enforce morality and to control individual women in prostitution. Officials not only failed to address the traffic in women throughout the French empire, but also fought to preserve the state's right to maintain foreign women in state-regulated brothels.

Chapter Seven, on Italy, traces the institutionalization of anti-trafficking efforts by the state. The grassroots anti-trafficking movement in the country was weak despite repeated attempts by both international voluntary associations to organize there. In the interwar period, the committees affiliated with international purity reformers were usurped by Mussolini's administration, and anti-trafficking efforts were thereafter a top-down effort. State officials used the anti-trafficking accords to control women's emigration and to justify the repatriation of Italian women within Italy's borders as part of Fascist population policy.

Although Italy signed the first three conventions, state officials did little to combat the traffic in women in colonial areas and were actually involved in trafficking (non-Italian) European and Ethiopian women under fascism. Prostitution was heavily involved in bolstering the colonial administration as well as public order in the metropole. It was also one area in which state officials sought to enforce new racial policies during Fascist rule by attempting to enforce a hierarchy in state-regulated brothels in colonial areas, with white, but not Italian, women as the preferred providers of sexual services for Italian military men.

Chapter Eight analyzes the similarities and differences between the three empirical cases, which suggest that different types or stages of nation-state formation and imperialism are associated with different concerns about organizing women's sexual activity. It concludes by showing that several factors were key to explaining the different responses of state officials to trafficking and prostitution. In addition to being influenced by the international voluntary associations, officials' responses varied according to whether or not the countries were actively engaged in colonial expansion, which affected the importance of militarization in colonial and metropolitan areas, and according to whether or not territories were intended as settler colonies. I then turn to the implications of the analysis and suggest some considerations for contemporary anti-trafficking efforts.

Today, scholars and activists around the world have again become concerned about the international traffic in women. As they try to understand its causes and dynamics, and to determine the best way to combat it, the trajectory and outcomes of the earlier movement can provide some cautions. The analysis of the first anti-trafficking movement calls attention to the potential interests of state officials in maintaining prostitution and in controlling rather than eliminating trafficking, and to the possibility of anti-trafficking measures being used to control women's movement and sexual activity rather than to protect women from abuse. Contemporary scholars and activists can learn much from the history of the earlier anti-trafficking movement and glean many lessons from the past.

2   The Internationalization of Prostitution and Emergence of the Traffic

PROSTITUTION IS POPULARLY REFERRED TO AS THE "WORLD'S OLDEST PROFESSION," a moniker that belies several important assumptions that should be analyzed rather than taken for granted by scholars. The belief that prostitution is an inevitable form of labor, that it is essentially timeless and truly global, suggests that its organization and meaning have varied little over centuries and across cultures.[1] Like other forms of social organization pertaining to gender and sexual relations, however, prostitution should be considered in historical perspective so that its continuities and differences in various contexts may be better understood.[2] To avoid reifying prostitution, we must consider its social construction and place it within a historical context.

Such an analysis provides the necessary background for understanding the first international anti-trafficking movement, which was in part a reaction to the shift in the organization of prostitution from premodern, small-scale forms to a modernized, bureaucratized, and international industry in the 1800s. This shift not only happened as a by-product of increased globalization involving colonial expansion, economic interconnectedness, and international migration, but also was due to the institutionalization of prostitution by state officials around the world. Globalization created possibilities for the expansion and internationalization of prostitution markets in the 1800s, but their growth was not simply the result of spontaneous entrepreneurship across the world. Rather, state officials routinely set up regulated systems of prostitution and sought to control the type of women (indigenous and foreign) who were in the brothels.[3] They both promoted and sought to control migratory prostitution in service of men, nation, and empire, spurring a nascent infrastructure for the

19

growth of the international sex trade, one that reinforced gender, racial/ethnic, and national boundaries.

Modernization, State Formation, and Women's Paid Sexual Labor

Military and colonial authorities had long been occupied with the domestic and sexual needs of military men and of men in the colonies. This interest prompted their involvement in the organization of sexual relations throughout the nineteenth and early twentieth centuries. The heterosexual and masculinized gender ideology of European countries held that abstinence was not an option for single men or for men who were married but away from their wives for extended periods. Alternative sexual outlets, from masturbation to homosexuality, were widely thought to be physically and morally deleterious. Many state officials therefore believed it was necessary to allow, or at times to provide, what they perceived to be safe and appropriate heterosexual outlets, especially for European men.

Such outlets typically took the form of concubinage in the early stages of colonialism, because it was cheaper than importing European women and it permitted permanent settlement and quick growth.[4] Indigenous women—referred to as *nyai* in Java and Sumatra, *madama* in Eritrea, *congai* in Indochina, and *petite epouse* throughout the French empire—lived with and cared for European men, and such situations were the most prevalent domestic arrangements in colonial areas by the nineteenth century.[5] Nearly half of the European male population in the Indies in the 1880s, for example, was unmarried and living with Asian women. Concubinage had its complications, however, namely the growth in numbers of mixed-race offspring, who transgressed boundaries between subject and citizen and challenged the neat racial hierarchies on which colonial authority rested.

In the later stages of colonialism, other arrangements for women's sexual labor were provided by allowing marriage and the migration of European women, including wives, and families. The perceived danger with this solution was that an increased number of white women in colonial areas could lead to an expanding number of poor Europeans as men tried to support their families.[6] In addition, the presence of European women whose sexual activities officials could not control meant that relationships between white women and men of color could possibly ensue. As Philippa Levine, who has written extensively on state regulation in the British Empire, has argued:

> White women choosing relationships with colonial men implied danger to the colonial state and to white men's supremacy. . . . Such liaisons had to be signalled

as deviant and disorderly, while white men sleeping with women of colour was seen merely as a natural extension of their residence in the colonies, and certainly as greatly preferable to the prospect of male-male sexual encounters.[7]

Given the complications of having white women in the colonies, officials often opted for prostitution, even advocating it as an acceptable form of labor and arguing that it was a normal part of traditional indigenous cultures as well.

Over time, concubinage was replaced by prostitution, and even in late colonialism, when authorities hoped to encourage the settlement of certain groups of people through women's migration and marriage, prostitution was often maintained. Prostitution and marriage replaced concubinage in colonial Sumatra and Java from 1900 through the 1920s, for example, and in British Malaya and other British colonial holdings, marriage and prostitution co-existed as strategies to meet the presumed sexual needs of men.[8] Marriage *was* sometimes touted as a means of ending prostitution. For example, part of the process of saving and reforming Chinese women involved in prostitution in colonial areas—an effort often supported by local Chinese merchants—was to marry them off to Chinese laborers.[9] The Po Leung Kuk Society (Office for the Preservation of Virtue), an organization set up in 1878 to provide refuge for Chinese women and girls rescued from forced prostitution, endorsed this strategy.[10] With branches in Singapore, Hong Kong, and other areas that had Chinese communities, it became a marriage agency of sorts, with former prostitutes (who were particularly desirable as wives because men did not have to pay a bride-price for them) kept in homes run more like prisons. Prior to or concomitant with efforts to promote marriage, then, regulated prostitution enjoyed a long tenure in many metropolitan and colonial areas, protectorates, and mandates.

Historians have pointed to the existence of different forms of prostitution, often tied to systems of slavery, in many countries prior to the 1800s. Ancient Greece had in place a graded prostitution system, from the lowest streetwalkers to courtesans (*hetairas*) in upper-class brothels; India had well-known systems of temple prostitution; and China had state-licensed brothels in the T'ang Dynasty (618–906 AD), to cite just a few examples.[11] To say that prostitution was modernized and bureaucratized in the 1800s is not to suggest that organized systems did not exist prior to this time. Municipal brothels existed in ancient times, as noted here, and they were found in medieval Europe prior to prostitution being targeted for repression by ecclesiastical laws. Systems of prostitution specific to particular locales were also found in areas that were later colonized, such as Asia and Africa.[12] In all of these areas, prostitution was typically organized on a small scale prior to the 1800s and often involved in-kind exchanges; a more expansive relationship in which women might also provide food, bathing, and conversation in addition to a sex act; or both.[13]

With regulation, these small-scale, culturally varied, indigenous forms of prostitution were overlaid by a modern, Western approach to its organization. As state officials and colonial men involved themselves in the organization of women's sexual labor, and increasingly implemented regulated prostitution systems, they tended to expand and commercialize women's sexual labor in new ways. Historians of Africa, for example, have noted that indigenous women ran brew houses and provided ongoing sexual services to small groups of men, but this practice was usurped by colonial state regulation, which turned prostitution into a commercial enterprise devoid of other aspects of domestic labor.[14] The Nailiyat women of Algeria, who combined dance and sexual service, and Chinese courtesans in Shanghai met similar fates. Rather than being exempt from state regulation, they were reduced to "common prostitutes" and subject to the same rules.[15] In Lucknow, India, courtesans were pulled into the military brothels for regulation under the English Contagious Diseases Acts.[16]

It is important to understand the role of the state in the expansion and internationalization of prostitution, on both the demand and supply sides. State-mediated political and economic projects contributed to the demand for women's sexual labor in the 1800s. The building of nation-states and empires required large groups of men to serve as military troops, laborers, and administrators. In both metropolitan and colonial areas, brothels were first set up by military officials in port cities and garrison towns to service military men, and then extended to the civilian population in order to service laborers. Trafficking emerged as women were moved to meet the demand of large groups of laborers in colonial and frontier areas.[17]

Moreover, prostitution was a fundamental form of female labor that state officials employed to support imperial ambitions. For example, state-regulated prostitution was part of an economic advancement strategy that Japanese officials supported prior to their political and military advancement into Southeast Asia.[18] Government officials allowed women in prostitution to migrate because businesses could be set up around brothel districts. Kimono shops, pharmacies, restaurants, and laundries thrived in such areas and helped to secure economic bases in new territories, at least until the interwar period. Such development not only fostered prostitution but also provided new customers. In India, for example, colonialism helped to produce a class of newly rich men who provided a client base for the growing prostitution market that the British regulated.[19]

The state was also involved in exacerbating the supply of women in prostitution in both colonial and metropolitan areas.[20] Political upheaval, pogroms, and war created conditions for mass migrations of women throughout Western Europe and overseas.[21] Women fleeing such conditions were especially vulnerable and often ended up in prostitution; for example, Russian and Polish Jewish women were disproportionately likely to be found in foreign brothels from the late 1800s through the interwar period.[22] Women were also in vulnerable positions in colonial areas. The uprooting and pauperization of the Algerian people through the late 1800s, for example, left many women with no material support and made them susceptible to coercion and induction into prostitution.[23] In French North Africa, poverty led to the sale of daughters, to more frequent repudiation in marriage, and to more widows, who became involved in prostitution as a survival strategy.[24] State officials were therefore implicated both in organizing and institutionalizing prostitution and in fostering the conditions that led to the mass movement of women into regulated prostitution markets around the world.

The Global Spread of Regulated Prostitution

How did state-regulated prostitution come to be a governing mechanism of choice for controlling women's sexual behavior in metropolitan and colonial areas? Initiated originally by Napoleon, who was concerned about the health of his military during the height of the empire, the "French model" of regulation began in Paris in 1802 and expanded from a focus on military prostitution to prostitution in the general population. Table 2.1 shows the array of countries around the world that have adopted such a system and the approximate dates of regulation. Russia, for example, began regulating prostitution in 1843; the Netherlands did so in 1852; Sweden, in 1859; Italy, in 1860; England, in 1864; Japan, in 1871; and Argentina, in 1875. Imperial states sometimes instituted regulation in the colonies before they did so in metropolitan areas, and more extensively. Regulated brothels were set up by, among others, the British in India and Palestine; the French in Syria and Lebanon, Indochina, and Algeria, Tunisia, and Morocco; the Dutch in the East Indies; and the Italians in Ethiopia and Eritrea.[25]

Table 2.1 The international spread of state-regulated prostitution

Country	Approximate Dates of Regulation
Argentina	1875–1934; reinstated 1954
Austria/Hungary	Abolished 1921 in Vienna, 1926 in Graz
Belgium	1844–1947
Brazil	Regulation through at least 1950
Czechoslovakia	1918–1922
Denmark	Abolished 1906
France	1802–1946
Germany	1830–1871, 1891–1927, reinstated 1933
Great Britain	1864–1888
Greece	1922–1955
Hungary	Abolished 1950
Italy	1860–1958
Japan	1871–1946
Mexico	Abolished 1942–1943
Netherlands	1852–1913
Poland	Abolished brothels 1922 and registration in 1956
Portugal	Regulation through at least 1950
Romania	Abolished (partially) 1929
Russia	1843–1917
Spain	Abolished 1956
Sweden	1859–1919
Switzerland (Geneva)	1896–1925
Turkey	Regulation through at least 1950
Colonial Holdings/ Mandates/Protectorates	
Algeria	1830–1962
Cape Colony	1868–1919
Dutch East Indies	1852–1910
Egypt	Implemented 1882–1885 through 1949–1951
Hong Kong	1857–1932
India	Implemented 1864–1888 (unofficially continued thereafter)
Indochina	1886–WWII
Lebanon	1920–post-WWII
Manchuria (Kwantung)	Regulation under Japan
Palestine	WWI–1927
Shanghai	1869–1919 in the International Settlement Ongoing regulation in the French settlement
Singapore	1870–1930
Tientsin (Tianjin)	Regulation in the Japanese settlement

Regulation entailed the licensing or toleration of brothels, compulsory registration of women in prostitution, obligatory examination of women for venereal disease, and enforced treatment in confinement. Prison infirmaries, or "lock hospitals," as they were known, were intended to prevent infected women from continuing to work in prostitution, thus safeguarding potential clients and public health. Administrative oversight was usually taken care of by "morals police" who ensured the registration of women, the collection of fees, compliance with physical exams, and adherence to brothel regulations, such as where the buildings could be geographically located, when and how they could advertise, how many women could be working in each brothel, and when the women could be seen outside of them. They also controlled the ability to remove a woman from the registry, requiring that certain conditions be met before they would take a name off of the list. A woman might have to provide proof that she had married, that she had a steady source of income, that she had remained "honest" for a specified period, or some combination of these requirements.

Countries with varying state structures, such as absolute monarchies (for example, Russia), unifying states (such as Italy), countries with weak central governments (for instance, Switzerland), and those with comparatively stronger ones (such as France), adopted and maintained regulation systems. In some cases, such as in France and the Netherlands, there was no national law or imperial decree that governed regulation. Rather, regulation was based on interpretations of a variety of local laws, which benefited its supporters, because a local administrative status allowed considerable flexibility as well as an ambiguity that could obscure its operations. In France, the system was widespread but decentralized, although the Ministry of the Interior did encourage municipalities to carry out regulation rigorously.[26] In other cases, such as in Italy and Great Britain, regulation was by national law or imperial decree, but local police were in charge of enforcing it. In all of these countries, police and doctors worked in conjunction to enforce the system at the local level.

In most areas (such as France, Italy, the Netherlands, and Russia), both brothel prostitutes and "independent" prostitutes working on the streets or in other venues were registered. In a few cases (such as in Great Britain and in Germany between 1871 and 1891), brothels themselves were not licensed, but the registration and medical regulation of women in prostitution were in force. The latter system was termed *neo-regulationism* and was a kind of "reformed" system of regulation that purported to address some abuses of women by allowing them to work outside of brothels. In Japan, regulation of brothel prostitutes only was allowed and independent women in prostitution were criminalized if they were found soliciting or practicing outside of the brothel.

The regulation system was promoted both within and across countries by coalitions of military administrators, medical doctors, and conservative politicians, often with the tacit approval of the dominant religious organizations. In Europe, the Anglican Church was generally silent on the issue of regulation, as was the Catholic Church in Europe and Latin America.[27] Internationally, medical men concerned about venereal disease organized to diffuse the regulationist model to other countries.[28] At the International Medical Congress of 1867 in Brussels, for example, there was a vote to form a commission to share Belgium's model of regulation with all other governments in order to combat disease on an international basis.[29]

Regulation was part of the increased infrastructural power of states during this period and was implemented by numerous government officials who saw it as a secular, rational, and progressive way to deal with prostitution in metropolitan and colonial areas.[30] Regulation functioned as a system, a political and medical paradigm that, although not hegemonic, informed practices across nations and throughout the empire.[31] There was also an undeniable economic component in that governments could benefit financially from the fees and taxes generated under regulation. In France, for example, prostitutes paid monthly taxes (or madams paid, at a lower group rate) to support the police operation, doctors' fees, and overhead for the dispensary; these taxes kept the whole operation running in the black "to an almost embarrassing extent," with surpluses of between nine and ten thousand francs in the 1820s.[32] In Japan, prostitution-related taxes and fees generated enormous sums.[33]

The regulation of prostitution, intertwined as it was with processes of state-building and with claims for states' moral legitimacy on the basis of this "improved" system, was a prime example of the way that gender and sexuality "make politics."[34] Regulation of prostitution was part of the overall growth of state intervention in matters of sexuality; it moved prostitution from the realm of religious oversight to a secular domain, but its claims of progressiveness were not born out in practice. In fact, the administration of regulation was similar to that of the nineteenth-century prisons—complete with Foucault's concepts of enclosure, surveillance, and the disciplining of bodies.[35] These methods were not gender neutral either, but were aimed at the control of women's bodies rather than men's. Women in prostitution were registered, segregated into brothels, medically examined, and forcibly confined to lock hospitals, but male customers were not. Women could be and were registered against their will when brothel "supplies" were short, or kept on a registry long after they had asked for their names to be removed.

The experiences, in their own words, of the masses of women under regulation systems are absent from most historiography and from the archives of the organizations that addressed trafficking, which is not surprising given the oppressed status of women in most countries of the time. Many middle-class women were just finding their voices and beginning to organize themselves in various countries around the world, but others were not yet in a position to do so. Literacy, although it was increasing rapidly with industrialization, was likely the exception rather than the rule for many women, especially working-class and poor women involved in state-regulated prostitution. Most of what we know or assume about women in prostitution historically, therefore, has been written by others and filtered through their perceptions, although surveys and other documents recorded some aspects of their experiences, especially as science and scientific methods began to permeate state bureaucracies and the efforts of social reformers alike.

At times, both regulationists and abolitionists gathered statements from women in prostitution in order to bolster their claims about the benefits or harms of regulation. Regulationist doctors, such as those in interwar France, might show letters authored by women in prostitution as evidence of their satisfaction with life in state-regulated brothels.[36] Some women no doubt felt safer in brothels than on the streets, and brothels did provide a community in which women could form bonds with one another.[37] Some may even have welcomed compulsory health checks as a means of obtaining cards that showed a clean bill of health in order to better market themselves and increase business. Such was the case of at least one woman whom reformers met in India who "considered her business perfectly legitimate because she was in a 'Government position.'"[38]

Abolitionists contended that such cases were exceptions rather than the rule, and they countered regulationists with the words and actions of women who had suffered under regulation systems as evidence of these women's dissatisfaction.[39] For example, Indian women in British cantonment areas who were interviewed by social reformers affiliated with the International Abolitionist Federation and the Women's Christian Temperance Union in the late 1800s expressed their hatred of the compulsory medical exams.[40] Clearly this was the case in many countries over time, because regulationist doctors were continually seeking ways to ensure that women could not evade the exams, which they frequently did. Women also sometimes protested confinement in lock hospitals, by rioting, smashing windows and furniture, prying open windowpanes, or breaking down doors in order to escape. Such rebellions were common in France, with some of the most violent occurring in 1908, including at the Sainte-Lazare infirmary, which International Abolitionist Federation founder Josephine Butler had visited at the start of the abolitionist movement; but uprisings have also been documented in other countries, such as Russia, and in colonial areas.[41] Most historians agree that regulation created conditions that were oppressive for women.[42]

The Emergence of the International Traffic and Its Patterns

The institutionalization of prostitution solved some problems for state officials, but it created new dilemmas as well, particularly along racial/ethnic and national lines. The question of which women should be housed in state-regulated brothels dogged state officials, potentially bringing state- and nation-building projects into conflict where interracial mixing was a concern. When prostitution was thought to be a requirement for European military men and laborers, and when containing sexual relations within racial categories was also a concern, European women were necessary for brothels. Yet European women were held to be the bearers of the imperial and national morality. This contradiction created difficulties for state officials, particularly those in colonial areas, who worried about imperial prestige. They sometimes opted for indigenous women, as in the case of the British in India, and at other times oversaw brothels in which European women serviced European men.[43] At home, they preferred European women from neighboring European countries to stock their brothels.

Such dilemmas "reveal dramatically and vividly the importance of sexual politics in colonial rule" and the gendered and racialized aspects of power.[44] Although cross-sexual relationships could be tolerated, or even be preferred, between European men and non-European women in colonial areas, the converse was particularly threatening.[45] The British, for example, went to some lengths to ensure that the few European women in prostitution in India would not service Asian men, because they assumed such service would undermine the basis of colonial rule.[46]

Imperial state-building and colonialism increased both the demand for prostitution and the supply of women for it, and the "ethnosexual" politics of nation-states and empires facilitated trafficking as one component of the overall growth of prostitution.[47] European states, their colonies, some South American countries, China, and Japan were all involved in the movement of women across borders for the purposes of prostitution. The main European supply states were Italy, Poland, Russia, and to a lesser extent France and Germany. China and Japan were also sending countries. The primary destinations, aside from neighboring European countries, were Argentina, Brazil, Singapore, Shanghai, Indochina, and to a lesser extent countries of the Middle East and the United States.

International voluntary association documents and League of Nations reports outline what reformers and officials saw as the common methods of trafficking from the turn of the century through the early interwar period.[48] Some information on trafficking in the immediate aftermath of World War II is also available, though it is sparse. These data suggest that the main methods of trafficking involved using fake (that is, legally invalid) marriages, promises of marriage, and recruitment via employment agencies for domestic or other types of service work abroad. Women who accompanied procurers abroad under such circumstances were subsequently sold to brothels. There was also acknowledgement that women who were already prostitutes were procured for brothels abroad and that some moved to and from brothels in different countries, for example, from France to the colonies and back, from Europe to Argentina, or from some colonial areas to the Middle East. For the most part, traffickers were thought to be individual men and women, including husband and wife teams, or part of small networks of traffickers who tended to procure women of their own race/ethnicity/nationality.[49]

Journalists often exaggerated the "white slave traffic" with sensational stories of young women and girls being drugged, kidnapped, and sold by nefarious foreign procurers, pimps or madams, which thoroughly racialized the issue and focused on the corruption of innocent European girls. Newspaper accounts, plays, and "penny dreadfuls" based on such scenarios were churned out for voracious public consumption. These stories, while appealing to the public, belied the more mundane aspects of trafficking, which both reformers and the League of Nations understood to involve the exploitation of "professional" women and girls migrating to new countries to work in the sex trade, women and girls migrating for other kinds of work, and women and children being made vulnerable by political and economic conditions in their countries of origin. As we will see, feminists hoped for protection for all of these women and children regardless of whether they had been involved in prostitution, whereas state officials and those associated with the International Bureau tended to distinguish between "innocent" victims of trafficking who were in prostitution involuntarily and "guilty" migrant prostitutes in need of control.[50]

Traffic patterns reflected four main trends:

1. There was *the movement of European women between European states.* This trend can be thought of as *regional trafficking* and often entailed the movement of women to neighboring countries. For example, Belgium had French women in prostitution, while in France there were Italian and Spanish women in prostitution and a smaller number of German, Swiss, Belgian, and Algerian women.[51] Switzerland had French, German, and Italian women in prostitution; Italy had Austrian, French, Yugoslavian, Hungarian, German, and Czech women; Holland had German, French, Belgian, Polish, and Austrian women; Germany had Polish and Hungarian women; and so on.

The overall proportion of women in prostitution from other European countries is difficult to ascertain given that it was only at the turn of the century that many countries had begun to categorize immigrants and attempt to control migration, but the registers of regulated brothels show that up to 25 percent of women in prostitution in some areas of France and Italy were foreign.[52] In Portugal, in 1924 about 20 percent of women in prostitution were foreign, mostly from Spain and France.[53] These were small percentages compared to other receiving countries that were overseas, such as Argentina.

2. There was *a pattern of European women moving to the Americas, particularly Argentina and Brazil.* Russian, Polish, French, and Italian women at times constituted the majority of women in prostitution in these two South American countries. Foreign women in prostitution in Argentina increased from a reported 25 percent in 1913 to a high of 75 percent in the interwar period.[54] By the late interwar period, the traffic to South America began to slow.[55]

3. There was *a small movement of European women to colonial holdings, protectorates, and mandated areas.* Some colonial territories boasted a large array of women, including some from Europe. Shanghai had an estimated two thousand non-Chinese women, mostly Russian, Eastern European, and Japanese, in prostitution in the early 1900s.[56] Russian, Polish, and Austrian women were present in Bombay prior to World War I.[57] What we would now call sex tourism in Algeria was a thriving business in the interwar period, with French as well as German, Italian, Spanish, Lebanese, Armenian, and Turkish women in prostitution. Egypt, a winter sex tourist destination for Europeans, had

about 40 percent foreign women in prostitution in 1924.[58] They were mainly French, Italian, and Greek, with a smaller number of Syrian, Turkish, and Russian women.

Other colonial areas sported a smaller selection of European women in prostitution in the interwar period. Indochina, for example, had some French and Russian women in prostitution. They were expelled in 1923, but some French women in Saigon continued to service European men.[59] Likewise, in Syria and Lebanon, foreign women in prostitution were mainly Greek, Italian, and French, but their number was not large; the secretary of the International Abolitionist Federation noted during her visit to Beirut in 1931 that 14 percent of registered women in prostitution were foreign.[60]

Russian women were a particular concern in the interwar period.[61] They were moved to Northern China, especially to Manchuria, in response to the revolution and to service Russian laborers and elite exiles. Russian traffickers helped to move women to Harbin (Russian headquarters in the Russo-Japanese War and later for anti-Bolshevists), Tientsin (Tianjin), and Shanghai, and to the villages and cities along the Chinese Eastern Railway, in order to better service British, French, and American men, among others.

4. There was *the movement of women of color regionally and/or to colonial holdings, protectorates, and mandated areas.* This trend largely involved the movement of Chinese women to the Malay States, British Hong Kong, Singapore, the Dutch East Indies, and Indochina. Japanese women and women of Korean ethnicity were also moved, to Manchuria, Singapore, the Dutch East Indies, and even India, until the Japanese government began repatriating Japanese women in prostitution in the interwar period. Hong Kong, the Straits Settlement, the Federated Malay States, and Shanghai all had regulated prostitution systems with women of color from other areas. Some of Singapore's licensed brothels, for example, included both Chinese women and Chinese clients; some offered Japanese women for both European and Asian men; and some were Thai houses that provided Thai women to service European men. Mixed Eurasian women serviced European men in brothels in that colony as well.[62]

There is much less documentation of the post–World War II traffic than of traffic from the late-1800s through the interwar years. In the earlier period, international voluntary associations had the resources and participation of numerous reformers to help them investigate and document the traffic, and the League of Nations, in addition to its other anti-trafficking work, commissioned reports to study the traffic. After World War II, the voluntary associations were struggling to survive and they accomplished less in the way of information gathering. On the basis of journalistic accounts, a report by an author affiliated with the Anti-Slavery Society, and self-reports from the United Nations, however, we can glean some information on post–World War II traffic patterns.

First, traffic patterns changed during this period, becoming mostly regional, and the traffic to colonial holdings was moving to North Africa and the Middle East, primarily, rather than to Asia. French women were moved to brothels in North Africa—for example, in Algeria—and continued to be found in Egypt along with other European women.[63] A representative of the Paris police reported in 1958 that French women were being shipped to Spain, South Africa, North Africa, South America (especially Caracas), and Belgium, where half of the women in prostitution in Antwerp were reportedly French.[64] European women were also apparently moved to West Africa and South America.[65] In West Africa, the traffic was controlled by an Italian who moved French, Belgian, and Italian women to and through the Congo.[66] There was also some trafficking of women from Africa to France.

Traffickers in Morocco and Algeria, who left when those countries became independent, allegedly moved to the Middle East, particularly Lebanon, and continued to procure Lebanese, Danish, Armenian, German, French, Spanish, Italian, and Turkish women for the trade there. Lebanon admitted to having foreign women in prostitution after World War II; state officials reported to the United Nations that 43 percent of the women in their brothels were foreign, mainly from Syria and Israel.[67]

Overall, however, United Nations reports suggested that most countries had few foreign women in prostitution in the 1950s and that the overall incidence of trafficking was low. Government officials from many countries, including Austria, Egypt, France, Greece, India, Iraq, Italy, Malaya, the Philippines, Portugal, South Africa, Turkey, and the United Kingdom, reported that almost all women in prostitution were nationals.[68] Trafficking had lost its importance in international politics and would not resurface until decades later.

Race, Class, Nationality, and the Traffic

In the trends just described we can see that race/ethnicity, class, and nationality intersected in myriad ways to determine which women were moved in the prostitution markets, sometimes fostering the traffic in women and at other times hindering it. In occupied colonial areas there were typically a few European authorities; a large group of indigenous peoples categorized hierarchically depending on religion, language, social custom, and so on; and often a third group of non-Europeans who were brought in to perform intermediate economic functions, such as the Indians in East Africa, Burma, and Malaya; the Chinese in Indochina and the Dutch East Indies; and the Lebanese in French West Africa.[69] Prostitution was organized to service each group separately, because interracial sexual relations were increasingly seen as problematic by European authorities and local groups alike.

A rigid sexual code was part of an increasingly dominant ideology that asserted white superiority and insisted that "'pure' white descent lines [must] be maintained," but local groups also objected to mixing across racial/ethnic lines.[70] Thus, women were often moved from one territory to another—European women to Egypt to service British troops and European tourists, Italian women to Ethiopia for Italian troops, and Chinese women to the Dutch East Indies for Chinese men, for example. For most officials, the importation of foreign women into colonial areas for prostitution was acceptable, provided that they were servicing their "own."[71]

Most locales physically separated their brothels according to the race/ethnicity and/or religion of the women and clients to ensure sexual endogamy and contain sexual encounters within racial/ethnic, religious, and national groups. In interwar Hong Kong, for example, Chinese and European brothels were separated physically from one another. The governor of Hong Kong reported that in 1923 there were 296 brothels in the colony, seven of which were for European men. The proscription against racial mixing was strong. In the governor's words:

> The circumstances make it practically impossible to imagine a common brothel and almost as impossible to imagine brothels for the same classes for the different nationalities within reach of each other. It is stated that no such cases exist."[72]

Interwar British Malaya also had racial and class segregation of brothels, as did many other areas, and these trends continued even after World War II.[73] In post-World War II Casablanca, for example, there were separate brothels in the Jewish and Arab quarters, and these were also geographically separated from European brothels. Even within the European brothels, care was taken to ensure separate rotations of troops from different countries so as to avoid conflict between the men.[74]

When ethnic similarity between women and their clients was not possible, as when state officials were reluctant to move their "own" women for prostitution, racial similarity was still preferred. For example, in 1936 the British branch of the International Abolitionist Federation cited the Fascist paper *L'Azione Coloniale*, which had quoted the governor of Somaliland (and then its minister of state) as saying:

> It will be necessary to regulate in all centres of the Italian African colonies a sufficiently large and often renewed supply of white women of another quality than honest women. They must be white women but not Italian—Italian women of that class should never be allowed to pass the frontiers of our Empire: it is an elementary question of prestige in relation to the natives.[75]

Tensions occurred in many cases where this proscription was violated or where there was even a possibility of mixing.

Concerns about the potential for sexual activity across racial, ethnic, and/or national lines were often raised by both state officials and reformers in the context of war and its aftermath. As mentioned, Russian women were of particular concern at the League of Nations because they were trafficked in the aftermath of the 1917 revolutions, but also because they were involved in prostitution across racial/ethnic lines:

> These unfortunate victims fall into two different categories. One is composed of women refugees who in their flight were stranded, without means of subsistence, in remote parts of Manchuria, where in exchange for the expense of their maintenance they were made use of as prostitutes by local Chinese. The other consists of destitute Russian women of the Railway Zone of Northern Manchuria, both refugees and impoverished residents in that part of the country who to-day form the source of supply of almost the entire occidental prostitution in the great international commercial centres of China.[76]

There were class concerns as well, because Russian refugees and migrants included upper-class women in addition to Russian peasants.[77] Elite Russian women often fled to Harbin, where, some reformers believed, they would find local conditions of labor "entirely strange" and should not be expected to work in domestic service, laundry work, or needlework but rather be given office jobs or simply housed by well-to-do English-speaking families when possible. This solution was suggested in particular by the International Bureau, whose interwar Secretary-General was concerned about "massage establishments; and establishments where unfortunate Russian white women are exposed to the view of coolies who pay a few cents for the sight."[78]

In another example, German as well as international activists complained bitterly about the "Horror on the Rhine," by which they meant the presence of French troops, about half of whom were from Algeria, Tunisia, Morocco, Madagascar, and West Africa, in occupied territory in the interwar period.[79] They were concerned about the troops' presumed sexual aggressiveness, including allegations that they were forcibly abducting, raping, and murdering German women. Feminists were among those initially sympathetic to the Germans, but upon investigating and finding no evidence of atrocities, the International Abolitionist Federation and the International Council of Women decided that the concerns were overblown.[80] Reformers affiliated with the German National Committee of the International Bureau, on the other hand, pressed the issue within the Bureau and at the League of Nations, and they received quite a bit of international support.

The French regulation of prostitution exacerbated and prolonged the issue. A pamphlet penned by E. D. Morel, a British politician, former journalist, member of the British pacifist movement, and campaigner against the continuation of slavery in the Belgian Congo, recounted the offenses:[81]

> Many a small German town which never boasted a brothel has been compelled to set one up. . . . At Wiesbaden, where two brothels for French troops have existed for some time at a cost of 41,000 marks, the French Command has now requisitioned another for African troops in a public-house which has had to be set aside by the Municipality. . . . Last month a brothel for African troops was demanded at Dietz—in this case the order is for the establishment of an "Arabic brothel" . . . At Kostheim, where there is a large camp of African troops, the brothel (into which some coloured women have been imported) costs the Municipality 130,000 marks.[82]

The members of the German National Committee of the International Bureau, who were staunch regulationists, were not upset at the prospect of state-regulated brothels per se, though they did complain that Germans were bearing the costs of setting up the brothels, paying for the medical inspection and treatment of the women in them, and paying the salaries of the soldiers who were using the brothels. It was the prospect of interracial sexual relations that fueled the most protest.

Rather than simply arguing for the end of regulation, the German National Committee objected to the nationality of the women who were working in the brothels. In a 1923 letter to the International Bureau headquarters in

London, the German National Committee argued that if the French believed it was necessary to have brothels for the troops, "they should take care to provide them with girls and women of their own nations." In 1924, the president of the German National Committee again complained, "But what I strongly object to is, that we shall be compelled to put our German women at the disposal to satisfy the physical demands of foreign subjects, while women of their own countries shall not be admitted as inmates."[83] A year later there were still seventy-six brothels in French-occupied territory with German women in them; nineteen of these brothels were apparently established after the occupation began, and the women in them serviced Germans as well as French troops of all colors.[84]

Although racial, ethnic, and national endogamy was the preferred set up in systems of state-regulated prostitution, there were many places where men were serviced specifically by women outside of their racial and ethnic or national background. In Saigon, it was reportedly Vietnamese women dressed in Chinese clothing who serviced Chinese men, because "Chinese sentiment" would not allow Chinese women there.[85] Likewise, although British government and military officials ensured that few British women in prostitution would be found abroad, they also regulated mainly non-European women for colonial use. The racial hierarchy of prostitution in India ranked Burmese and Indian women at the bottom, with Japanese above them, and a few European (but not English) women at the top, all for the service of European men.[86] Class privileges sometimes undermined this racial hierarchy, however, because some rich Indian men did go to the European brothels. British officials tolerated this, believing it was better to overlook this limited and class-specific mixing than to risk widescale interracial sexual relations between Indian men and white women among the "domiciled British."[87]

If sexual relations across racial and ethnic lines rarely involved European women and non-European men, the converse was much more commonplace. The use of indigenous women by foreign, including European, men was a concern for European feminists, who critiqued it from a gender point of view, and for some purity reformers concerned about racial purity. Yet indigenous men also often opposed the practice; for example, Indian women in brothels reserved for British men were ostracized in their communities.[88] Chinese men in Hong Kong were against regulation and lobbied for officials to spare Chinese women medical examinations, which they did, as long as the women were servicing only non-Europeans.[89]

Indigenous elites often found purchase in the issues of concubinage and prostitution, raising them as part of anticolonial nationalisms in India and Indonesia, among other places.[90] Indigenous women in prostitution could be called on for their nationalist support, such as when African women refused white patrons in celebration of Sudan's independence, and foreign women in prostitution could become targets of anticolonial nationalists, as reportedly happened in Ethiopia, where Italian prostitutes were killed as the Italians were driven out.[91] Indigenous women in prostitution could also find themselves in mortal danger if they had been servicing European men, which could be used to brand them "collaborators."

Gender, race and ethnicity, and nationality were at the heart of regulatory practices, but so too was class. Class boundaries were often reinforced via regulation, which was clearly intended to police the working class and poor rather than elites. At times class concerns were even transmuted into racial ones, with poor whites, such as the Russian and Polish women in prostitution in the British Empire, "orientalized" in much the same manner as were colonial subjects, who were considered to be "not quite white" and treated accordingly.[92]

Most often, upper-class prostitution was left outside of regulatory boundaries. There was a brief movement to regulate courtesans in Paris in 1817, for example, but after a few attempts so many complaints and problems arose that all efforts were dropped by 1830.[93] Such efforts, and their failures, were duplicated in other countries as well, and they were not limited to metropolitan areas. A double standard that left local upper-class women in prostitution outside of government interference was put into force in some colonial areas as well, particularly if local elites or the merchant class objected to such regulation. The Nailiyat of Algeria and the Courtesans of Shanghai and Lucknow may not have escaped regulation, but the Devadasis of Madras did. They were not subject to the Contagious Diseases Acts that sought to control prostitution in Great Britain, in part because of the objections of Indian nationalists.[94]

One the other hand, class interests sometimes led indigenous elites to support the regulation of indigenous women. Some Indian elites, for example, argued that regulation actually protected "respectable" Indian women by providing an outlet for the masses of men who might otherwise look for sexual relations across class lines.[95] The implementation of regulation could and did vary, with local and imperial politics as well as racial, ethnic, and class concerns among Europeans, indigenous peoples, and other local groups leading to differences in the way regulation played out in particular locations.[96] What is constant across cases is the presumption of male heterosexual need for prostitution and a concern to protect women in instances when their sexual activity might transgress racial and ethnic, national, and imperial boundaries.

State-Regulated Prostitution and Trafficking

In regulating prostitution, states not only "captured" more of social life and secularized the means for dealing with prostitution,[97] but also, as feminist abolitionists contended at the time, legitimated prostitution as a profession and provided institutional mechanisms for the traffic in women. This relationship between state-regulated prostitution systems and trafficking posed a problem for states from the start. Almost as soon as state-regulated prostitution systems were adopted around the world, international protest against regulation surfaced. Shortly after, because the growth in migratory prostitution occurred at the same time as the spread of regulation, a major point of question arose for all who were involved in anti-trafficking work: Did regulation contribute to trafficking or did it help to combat it?[98]

On one side of the debate, some abolitionist reformers contended that state-regulated systems were a major contributor to increasing the traffic in women. In contacting the League of Nations to plead for action in addition to the development of anti-trafficking conventions, the British branch of the International Abolitionist Federation wrote:

> We desire to point out that these agreements cannot destroy the traffic though they may increase its risks and difficulties. The traffickers would not undertake the expense and risk of conveying their victims to foreign countries unless they were assured of a market in which to dispose of the merchandise. That market exists wherever houses of debauchery are licensed and protected by Government.[99]

They argued that the traffic supplied inmates for legal or tolerated brothels, providing fresh women so that customers would not become bored, and replacing women who were sent to lock hospitals due to venereal disease.

They also blurred the lines between state-regulated prostitution and trafficking, suggesting that where brothels were institutionalized, women in prostitution were not exercising free choice. They argued that the third-party organization of prostitution set up a system of brothel keepers, police, procurers, and pimps who denied civil rights to women in prostitution who were literally sold to brothels, restricted to particular working and living spaces, prevented from being on the streets without being subject to morals police, and kept in debt bondage. Police corruption certainly occurred in numerous countries that had regulation. Local authorities in France in the early 1800s began to donate their excess income to rescue homes for women in prostitution after being caught pocketing immense sums of money. Their ill-gotten gains were obtained by various methods, the simplest being the collection of fees from women they did not report, which allowed them to keep the money for themselves.[100] Some police even owned brothels, as did a police chief in Belgium in the 1880s, a fact that the International Abolitionist Federation and founder Josephine Butler used to bolster their campaign against regulation there.[101] In another example, the Italian Gherardo Della Porta, director of the governorship of Addis Ababa in the 1930s, had financial interests in brothels.[102]

These are hardly isolated examples. Corruption was found in regulation systems around the world. In 1800s Algeria under French colonization, police were bribed by men to keep women in prostitution from leaving regulated areas, and by the women themselves so they could get out.[103] In Bombay, a police inspector who had been decorated with the King's Police Medal in 1916 had to return the medal and resign from his post a year later when he was found to be receiving illegal gratifications from prostitutes, pimps, and mistresses.[104] In Japan in the early 1900s, British, American, and Japanese Salvation Army workers reported that police, siding with brothel keepers, routinely forced girls who ran away from local brothels to return to them.[105] Rather than allowing the girls to stay with the reformers, police set up "consultations" between the girls and the brothel keepers to "persuade" them to go back to the brothels.

On the other side of the debate, supporters of regulation argued that regulated brothels were not the source of the traffic. Rather, they suggested, women were trafficked to clandestine houses. State-regulation therefore had little to do with the increased traffic in women and instead actually provided conditions to safeguard women. An interwar memo by the governor of Hong Kong defending state regulation summarized the matter as follows:

> Such control [of prostitution] takes the line of prevention of actual crime: of enforcing responsibilities (on those in charge of prostitutes): of securing freedom of action to those who are allowed to practice prostitution: and of seeing that those who are for any reason considered unfit (e.g., too young) shall not practise. There is the smallest possible interference with those who are supposed

to know their own minds and whose prostitution does not involve others; and Government "regulation" becomes merely a broad supervision against abuse. . . . the Hong Kong "customs are good" is a phrase constantly heard, not from the prostitutes only (when it means that their freedom is assured and that they are accorded consideration in any trouble) but also from responsible Chinese, who speak with a knowledge of the conditions elsewhere and a realisation of the necessity for keeping up the standard of Chinese family life.[106]

Information on the history of clandestine prostitution in Europe and its colonies is lacking, but regulationists were very likely correct that women were trafficked to clandestine brothels.

As we can see from the earlier outline of trafficking patterns and from the dates of state regulation in Table 2.1, however, women were also moving from and especially to state-regulated prostitution markets in places such as Algeria, Argentina, Brazil, Egypt, Hong Kong, and Shanghai. It appears that even within Europe, countries with state-regulated systems have had a broader array of foreign women in prostitution. For example, regulationist France and Italy had higher rates of foreign women in prostitution compared to the abolitionist Netherlands in the interwar period—a finding that would not necessarily be expected given the fact that at the time Italy was primarily an emigration country, and that the Netherlands had its share of women immigrants from Germany.[107]

Summary

This chapter has shown that European officials sought to regulate sexual relations within and between nation-states and empires along gender, racial and ethnic, and class lines. They did so not only by encouraging particular domestic arrangements, but also by regulating prostitution, particularly in areas with large numbers of laborers and military men. The presumed sexual needs of these men made women's sexual labor a direct concern of state officials and an assumed necessity for the success of nation and empire.

The regulation of prostitution that spread throughout the world in the 1800s helped to modernize and institutionalize women's paid sexual labor in ways that previously had not been the case. It also provided conditions that helped to foster the internationalization of prostitution that was occurring with colonialism, international migration, and the growth of modern nation-states. A traffic in women emerged that involved the movement of European women between European states and to the Americas and to some colonial areas, and the movement of women of color to and between colonial holdings. Abuses of indigenous women in colonial areas and of European women in metropolitan areas also occurred in state-regulated brothels.

Regulation was intended to help ensure racial, ethnic, national, and class endogamy wherever possible, thus appealing to European, indigenous, and other local groups in metropolitan and colonial areas who typically sought to safeguard the sexual activity of their "own" women as part of imperial, national, and anticolonial nationalist projects. Therein was the dilemma for European regulationists, for to keep prostitution within racial and ethnic lines required the movement of European women to service their "own," yet imperial and national prestige demanded that they spare their "own" women from prostitution. The solution was to import women of other nationalities or ethnicities, or to make use of indigenous groups, thus risking the ire of anticolonial groups.

Such scenarios played out in various ways in different metropolitan and colonial areas, leaving regulation in a precarious position. The international abolitionist movement seized on regulation as a cause of trafficking, while purity reformers argued that regulation actually allowed states to control prostitution further and in fact helped to decrease the traffic. Contention over the relation between state regulation and trafficking led to fierce battles between reformers affiliated with the International Abolitionist Federation and the International Bureau and various state officials, who sought to define the anti-trafficking movement in their own interests. The anti-trafficking agenda was shaped by regulationist countries trying to preserve their control over the organization of prostitution in their territories and by international voluntary associations seeking to define the scope of their reforms. It is to these battles, and to the construction of trafficking as an international social problem, that we turn in the next chapter.

3 Constructing the Traffic as an International Social Problem

THE RESPONSE TO THE INTERNATIONALIZATION OF PROSTITUTION and the increase in trafficking in the late nineteenth century emerged out of the work of the two main international voluntary associations that fostered the movement and struggled over its agenda and direction: the International Abolitionist Federation and the International Bureau. Abolitionists and their supporters worked to pressure state officials to change their policies in the name of broad, universal beliefs about gender and individual human rights, while purity reformers worked explicitly with state officials to control sexual activity in the nation and empire. The movement was thus characterized from the start by conflict between the effort to construct a transnational movement—one that would use networks of reformers across countries to challenge state policies in domestic and international settings—and an internationalism that would serve only to reinforce state interests.[1] It was the latter influence that eventually won out, accounting for the success of the movement in attracting state officials and becoming part of the formal work of the League of Nations.

Academics often conflate the many and varied actors in the anti-trafficking movement and condemn it rather sweepingly for a variety of faults: promoting Victorian prudery; focusing on the "white slave trade" while ignoring the traffic in women of color or, conversely, calling for an end to the exploitation of non-European women in the colonies because of fears about race mixing; and being elitist and paternalistic by failing to include prostitutes in the movement and portraying them as "victims" rather than as voluntary agents who were migrating of their own free will.[2] To understand the development and dynamics of the movement fully, however, it is important not to gloss over the distinctions between the specific international voluntary associations involved and their divergent views on trafficking and prostitution.

The International Abolitionist Federation and the International Bureau were quite independent and autonomous, and in fact rivaled each other for control over the direction of the movement. Judging from these organizations' meeting minutes, subscriber donation lists, and congress and conference attendance lists, only a handful of reformers took part in both organizations' activities or provided funding to both. For example, of the 390 people who attended the 1898 International Abolitionist Federation congress and the 1899 International Bureau congress, only seventeen attended both.[3] Distinguishing between the various participants in the movement provides a clearer understanding of the international voluntary associations, their relationships to the state, the possible implications for state power, and the consequences for the women they were trying to help. Such distinctions can also help to illuminate the racial, ethnic, national, and class components of the movement, which comprised networks that included not only European men and women but also local men and women of color, both indigenous and migrant, as well as colonial authorities.[4]

International Voluntary Associations and the Start of the Movement

The International Abolitionist Federation and the International Bureau were both London-based international voluntary associations that organized throughout Europe and in many other parts of the world. They each had central offices that guided the association's work, though the organizations were not monolithic in any sense, and there could be differences within the associations when national chapters or local committees had conflicts over the policies and goals of the organization. For example, by the interwar period some committees of the International Abolitionist Federation had moved away from individual rights arguments and toward the state repression of women, and the Netherlands International Bureau committee continually pressed for abolition despite the wishes of International Bureau secretaries. Such internal divisions, as well as interactions between domestic activists associated with the two international voluntary associations, sometimes affected the organizations' ability to achieve goals in particular national and colonial contexts. Still, each international voluntary association developed its own approach to prostitution and worked diligently to develop national chapters in line with its philosophy.

In their efforts to combat the sexual exploitation of women, these two associations were joined by other international voluntary associations that sought
to assist emigrating women, and by state officials who expanded and institutionalized the movement. Three such associations assisted female emigrants by
providing aid to traveling girls and women: the International Union of Friends
of Young Women, a Protestant organization founded in Switzerland in 1877
at the first Geneva congress of the International Abolitionist Federation; the
Travelers' Aid Society, started in 1885 under the auspices of the YWCA and
founded by Lady Frances Balfour (an ally of the English suffragist Dame Milli-
cent Fawcett, who was herself a suffragist); and the Catholic Association for the
Protection of Girls, formed just before the turn of the twentieth century, with
headquarters in Fribourg, Switzerland. In addition, the Jewish Association for
the Protection of Girls and Women assisted emigrating Jewish girls and specifically fought the traffic in Jewish women around the world.[5]

Of these organizations, the International Bureau and the International Abolitionist Federation were most active in defining the parameters of state intervention in prostitution, and they both sought to influence the issue in international
settings. They both developed into international associations quite quickly, and
each organized committees in Europe, in the Americas, and in colonial areas in
Asia, Africa, and the Middle East, as Table 3.1 shows. The similarities between
these organizations were limited, however, by some very important differences
between them. Their relations with state officials and their involvement in state
institutions, and their framings of prostitution and trafficking in more or less
transnational terms, led to their having different perspectives on the role of the
state in protecting women and dealing with prostitution.

Early Feminist Abolitionists and the
International Abolitionist Federation

Women and men associated with the International Abolitionist Federation were
the first to work internationally on the issue of women and girls in prostitution.
Prompted by the implementation of state regulation in the British Empire, they
organized in the 1870s to abolish all such regulation, consciously adopting the
abolitionist terminology used by the earlier international movement to combat
slavery. Christian feminist Josephine Butler helped form the Ladies National
Association for the Repeal of the Contagious Diseases Acts, by which regulation had been extended from military areas to the civilian population in Great
Britain. Butler had personally been active since the 1860s in helping women in

Table 3.1 International voluntary association committees by country

Country	International Abolitionist Federation Committees			International Bureau Committees		
	1890–WWI	Interwar	Post-WWII	1890–WWI	Interwar	Post-WWII
Argentina		✓		✓	✓	
Australia	✓	✓				
Austria		✓		✓	✓	
Belgium		✓	✓	✓	✓	✓
Canada			✓	✓		✓
Czechoslovakia					✓	
Denmark		✓		✓	✓	✓
Egypt		✓		✓	✓	✓
France	✓	✓	✓	✓	✓	✓
Germany	✓	✓	✓	✓	✓	✓
Great Britain	✓	✓	✓	✓	✓	✓
Greece					✓	
Hungary		✓		✓	✓	
India	✓	✓	✓		✓	✓
Indonesia	✓					✓
Italy	✓	✓	✓	✓	✓	✓
Japan	✓				✓	
Lithuania		✓				
The Netherlands	✓	✓	✓	✓	✓	✓
Norway	✓	✓		✓	✓	✓
Pakistan						✓
Peru		✓				
Poland	✓				✓	✓
Portugal		✓	✓	✓		
Romania		✓				
Russia				✓		
South Africa	✓			✓		
Spain	✓	✓		✓	✓	
Sweden	✓	✓	✓	✓	✓	✓
Switzerland	✓	✓	✓	✓	✓	✓
United States		✓	✓	✓	✓	
Uruguay		✓			✓	
Yugoslavia					✓	

prostitution by bringing sick and dying women into her home to care for them and establishing shelters for them.

The Ladies National Association was formed to fight regulation, which had been implemented in colonial areas even before metropolitan ones, and the group soon branched out into an international organization. The British, Continental and General Federation for the Abolition of the Government Regulation of Vice was formed in 1875; it later changed its name slightly, using the term *state regulation* rather than *government regulation*, and in 1898 it changed its name to the International Abolitionist Federation. It was this organization that, as early as 1877, first raised the issue of the trafficking of women for prostitution.[6]

Butler was aware of the allegation that English girls, especially young ones, were being moved to brothels in Brussels because the age of consent was lower in England than in Belgium.[7] Some were already involved in prostitution before emigrating, but Belgian brothels were exploitive, locking in the women and practicing debt bondage, and Belgian police were corrupt.[8] The issue of the traffic in English girls was picked up and confirmed by British government officials in 1881 at the behest of Quaker reformers in contact with Butler. Later, an 1885 yellow journalism exposé written by *Pall Mall Gazette* editor W. T. Stead about the traffic in girls and the ease with which one could be purchased thoroughly sensationalized the issue.[9]

In 1887, at their annual congress, the British, Continental, and General Federation for the Abolition of State Regulation of Vice called for international measures to combat the traffic; at their congress two years later they passed resolutions calling for penalties in the legislation of all countries for those making a direct profit through the prostitution of another person, and for international treaties both for the repatriation of women or girls in prostitution and for suppressing the white slave traffic.[10]

Abolitionists and their supporters helped to foster an interest in the traffic early on, but it was really of secondary concern to them. They saw this effort as a way to gather public interest and support for dealing with the larger issue of state-regulated prostitution, which they wanted to abolish. From early on the abolitionists blurred the distinction between trafficking and state-regulated prostitution. They argued that trafficking was merely a way to supply women for regulated brothel systems, and because trafficking could involve force, deception, or the voluntary movement of women and girls into what were understood to be abusive brothel systems, it made state regulation more difficult to defend. Addressing the traffic was a valuable entry point into the issue of state-regulated prostitution, and it allowed feminist abolitionists to gain sympathy rather than scorn for women in prostitution, bolster public support for abolition, and criticize those who gained from the prostitution industry.

International Abolitionist Federation participants therefore often used the term *traffic* to refer to any movement of women and girls into brothel prostitution, and they fought for expansion of the definition of trafficking. They wanted it to be defined as the procuring of *any* woman or girl for prostitution, with *or* without her consent, within *or* across territorial borders. Any procuration, then—any third-party profit from prostitution—would be included in the definition sought by abolitionists.

The International Abolitionist Federation came to this definition not purely from an ideological stance about prostitution but also out of pragmatic recognition that limiting the definition of trafficking to only underage girls or women involuntarily forced into prostitution would leave the traffic in many countries unscathed. For example, ages of consent for sexual relations varied tremendously across countries and in colonies, so traffickers could recruit young girls "legally" in one country and move them to another with a higher age of consent.[11] Additionally, it was accepted practice in some countries, such as Japan, for girls to be contracted or even sold to brothels by family members.[12] This was the case in India and China as well. Such examples not only complicated notions of "voluntary prostitution," because women in most countries did not have individual rights outside of the family system, but it also pointed to an "internal traffic" of rural girls for urban brothels within countries.[13]

Organization

International Abolitionist Federation organizers, most often volunteers but occasionally including paid staff members, traveled to various countries, communicated with supporters and attempted to find new ones, founded local committees, organized international congresses, disseminated pamphlets and petitions on prostitution, held lectures in various countries, and endured verbal and physical abuse by brothel owners, brothel keepers, pimps, and police for interfering with the business of prostitution in many countries. Butler and her supporters were bullied by male mobs in England when she spoke, and similar scenes occurred in France and Italy, where supporters of the International Abolitionist Federation were suppressed by authorities during various periods.[14]

Working initially to repeal regulation in Great Britain, India, Hong Kong, the Cape of Good Hope, Italy, the Netherlands, Switzerland, France, Germany, and Belgium, the abolitionists then spread to other European countries as well as to Japan and to additional colonial holdings, settlements, and mandated areas such as Egypt, the Straits Settlements, the Federated Malay States, and the Dutch East Indies.[15] The committees in some of the colonies, such as India and the Dutch East Indies, had indigenous members, and as early as 1888 Butler reported that Hindu women were signing petitions to British Members of Parliament. She noted the "awakening of the women of India on the subject of this imperially imposed degradation of their race and to kindred questions vitally concerning womanhood."[16]

The British influence on this international voluntary association remained strong from its inception through the interwar period, even after its central office was moved from London to Geneva in 1898. The British branch continued to be one of the Federation's most active committees, and over the years of its activities it provided the majority of the Federation's funding as well as the direction of its agenda. Yet, as shown in Table 3.1, the International Abolitionist Federation was geographically widespread and increasingly built networks and ties to other international organizations, particularly feminist ones.

What groups did the International Abolitionist Federation attract? Women affiliated with the International Council of Women and the International Women's Suffrage Alliance were regularly involved in prostitution reform, and the latter group, in particular, consistently supported the abolitionists' positions.[17] International Abolitionist Federation organizers in many countries also linked up with socialist politicians and supporters. They typically attracted emerging feminist groups, doctors and lawyers, liberal politicians, academics, working-class men's groups, and religious moral reformers such as Quakers and Unitarians as members. In Germany, for example, it was social democrats who helped initiate the movement; and in France, as we will see, it was liberal politicians. In the Netherlands, women affiliated with a religious reform movement supported the abolitionists and some later associated themselves with the International Women's Suffrage Alliance.

When the International Abolitionist Federation visited a new country in the hopes of developing a committee, women were not always the initial supporters. In most countries, women were just beginning to develop feminist movements and demand rights in public settings. They had not yet received even the right to vote in any European country when the abolitionists began their work, yet participation in the movement required them to speak publicly on a topic that was considered shameful for women to acknowledge.[18] Because of gender relations in many countries at the time, some women, such as those in the Netherlands, took part in gender-segregated abolitionist committees.

Politically conservative women tended to have rocky relationships with the International Abolitionist Federation. Although they were included at the outset, they sometimes favored reform measures for regulation, a position that purity reformers tended to support. Abolitionists firmly resisted any suggestions for the reform of regulation and from early on it was clear that those affiliated with the Federation would need to adhere to a feminist philosophy that rejected regulation entirely. In 1887, for example, Belgium women at the annual conference of the British, Continental and General Federation for the Abolition of State Regulation of Vice supported the compulsory examination of women under certain circumstances, which caused heated discussion with Butler. Finally, a participant asked for all of the women who agreed with Butler to stand up, and they did, thus affirming the fundamental principles of the organization, along with its insistence on personal rights. One Belgian member left, another reaffirmed abolition.[19]

This struggle was repeated in many countries where the International Abolitionist Federation organized and it often resulted in the attrition of women supporters whose philosophies were more in keeping with that of the International Bureau.[20] Butler continually affirmed the abolitionist stance, denouncing, for example, the Women's Liberal League of New Zealand, which called for the extension of the British Contagious Diseases Acts to men as well as women in prostitution in order to protect wives from venereal disease. She did the same with German women who wanted prostitution to be made an offence punishable by the states, and with other English women, such as Lady Henry Somerset, the first vice president of the World Women's Christian Temperance Union, who advocated regulation in India in the name of protecting British soldiers and English women there.[21]

Although abolitionists alienated some politically conservative and aristocratic women, they did attempt to operate across traditional divides; they incorporated into the organization's statutes an article specifying that it was independent of any political party, philosophical school, or religious creed.[22] They also worked with indigenous men. As Butler explained:

> We accept also the aid and fellowship of Hindus, Mohammedans, and men of different non-Christian lands, *just* men, who come to us to plead the cause of their own women (as in the case of the downtrodden and outraged native

women of India, brought under the yoke of legalised vice). These men were, and are so far as we know, men of pure lives. Should I have refused the co-operation of a dark-skinned man, pleading for justice for his dark-skinned sister, because he worshipped Buddha or Vishnu, and not Christ? But this fact, that we accept the co-operation of unbelievers both of heathen lands and among Christian people, has staggered many—notably some rigidly orthodox German clergy-men, who have expressed themselves shocked to see a Parsee or a Chinaman on our platform at Exeter Hall, and we have lost a few valuable fellow-workers from this cause.[23]

As early as 1874, Sri Keshab Chandra Sen, renowned reformer and founder of the Brahmo Samaj in Bengal, contacted Butler for help regarding the "regular system of procuring Indian or Japanese women for British troops stationed in India."[24] She agreed to help, and both English and Indian reformers challenged the system in various cities there.

Gender, Nationality, and Class in International Abolitionist Federation Rhetoric

The International Abolitionist Federation reflected a distinctly feminist narrative that opposed the gender-based assumptions of regulation and the negative consequences for women as a group. Federation reformers worked from a perspective that emphasized both gender exploitation and the denial of individual rights. Regarding gender, they argued that the sexual double standard for men and women led to state-sanctioned sexual access to women's bodies by men:

> We cannot successfully elevate the standard of public opinion in the matter of justice to women, and of equality of all in its truest sense, if we are content that a practical, hideous, calculated, manufactured and legally maintained degradation of a portion of womanhood is allowed to go on before the eyes of all.[25]

Regarding individual rights, Butler and the International Abolitionist Federation pointed out that prostitutes' civil liberties were being denied by regulation laws pertaining to women rather than men.

International Abolitionist Federation reformers worked to stop the medical regulation and registration of women in prostitution, and to criminalize brothel keeping, procuring, and third-party profit from prostitution. They did not, however, believe they could stop individual cases of prostitution, nor did they believe that women in prostitution should be punished for engaging in acts of prostitution. They firmly resisted any special laws pertaining to prostitutes as a group and sought to lift public morality through education rather than legislation.[26] They also resisted efforts to regulate the men who were customers of prostitutes, opposing such regulation not only because of their liberal philosophy but also because of the class implications of such a policy. In a letter dated 1887, for example, Butler stated that regulationists would not pacify her by saying they would also attempt to regulate men, because certainly only *poor* men would end up being regulated, she argued; "two wrongs do not make a right."[27] She attracted the support of British philosopher and sociologist Herbert Spencer, who commended abolitionists for "opposing coercive methods for achieving moral ends" and for their defense of individual rights; he saw their work as a means of resisting "the present alarming drift toward Socialism which the yearly increase of meddling legislation shows."[28]

Later feminist abolitionists affiliated with the International Abolitionist Federation argued that "the voluntary illicit relations of adult persons provided that there is no public indecency or exploitation of third parties" should be "ignored" by criminal law. "Such relations concern morals and ethics, but do not come within the scope of the law."[29] Late in the interwar period, the British branch of the Federation summarized their continued resistance to moral legislation at the forty-seventh international congress of the International Abolitionist Federation:

> Abolitionists are well aware that, however desirable it may be to abolish prostitution, such a result cannot be achieved by legislation. . . . What really shocks us is the disregard of justice, of human right, of the liberty of the individual. We Abolitionists stand for the essential of true democracy; we believe that every man and woman should have equal justice regardless of race, class, creed or sex. . . . And it was because Abolitionist work was based on this fundamental demand for Justice that it gained the personal support of Victor Hugo, de Laveleye, Yves Guyot, Mazzini, and John Stuart Mill—all men whose lives were dedicated to the defence of the rights of man. And when these leaders spoke of the "rights of man" they fought for the inalienable rights of women, as well as men, to liberty, equality and justice. True democracy means the rights of *all* not of *half* the human race.[30]

International Abolitionist Federation documents remained remarkably consistent on this point throughout the period under study, reflecting the Federation's liberal feminist underpinnings.

The Federation's staff considered liberalism a central point of the Federation's principles, often reiterating that it was "not the duty of the law to say 'Purity,' 'Purity,' to the people, but to secure that within its jurisdiction, there shall not be one single victim sacrificed to others. It must guarantee and protect the liberty of each person."[31] This point was included in two of the first six articles of the statutes of the International Abolitionist Federation. One of these articles reiterated the autonomy of the human person and condemned all laws or regulations affecting particular groups or classes of people; another asserted that "personal and private prostitution is a matter which concerns the conscience, but which does not constitute a legal offence."[32]

International Abolitionist Federation reformers worked against increased state control over women's lives, calling attention to corrupt police who took advantage of the regulation system in various ways, from taking payoffs to allow underage girls into brothels, to using police powers to detain women in public and register them even against their wills, to helping return women who had escaped brothels to the brothel keepers. Long before academics began to grapple with issues of representation and power, feminists affiliated with the International Abolitionist Federation deconstructed the label *prostitute.* They argued that through the regulation of prostitution, state officials were themselves creating the category *prostitute,* normalizing it, and trapping working-class women who might periodically engage in prostitution into becoming prostitutes for life. They cited the example of morals police requiring proof that a woman had married or could provide for herself via other work before her name could be removed from the prostitution registers.[33] They also called attention to the organization of the brothel system itself, with its well-known system of debt bondage, and argued that it was analogous to slavery or indentured servitude.

In contemporary language, the abolitionists were fighting what they understood to be the commercialization of (primarily poor) women's bodies, the state's legitimation of this process, the gendered sexual mores of the time (that is, that men could not be chaste and that a group of women, differentiated from the rest, should be maintained to service them), and the imposition of state interests over women's individual rights. Although they and their detractors understood their quest as a challenge to state authority, they were not calling for a complete halt to state intervention in prostitution. Rather, they wanted the state to eliminate the police control of prostitution, but also to support female social workers who could assist women and girls in prostitution and help provide resources and services for them; and they wanted to criminalize the third-party organizers of prostitution.[34]

It is true that feminist abolitionists did not combine their gender criticism with an overt challenge to imperialism, but they were attempting to work from a universal notion of gender and sexual exploitation that led them to critique imperial practices.[35] This meant that abolitionists were frequently accused of being on the same side as anticolonial nationalists in colonized areas, and because of their heated rhetoric it is easy to understand how they left themselves open to such charges. As one abolitionist wrote,

> People talked of the massacre of Cawnpore. They shuddered over its atrocities. We all did. We all do, when we think of it. But of what atrocities could not Indians tell, perpetrated on Indian women in the name of a Christian Government, atrocities that have gone on for long years, and in comparison with which the atrocities of Cawnpore sink into insignificance.[36]

It is surprising even now to see the juxtaposition of the regulation of Indian women with the 1857 uprising in Kanpur, where as many as three hundred English women and children were purportedly killed by Indian mutineers.[37]

That the founders and supporters of the International Abolitionist Federation had personal racial prejudices and often failed to transcend the imperialist and nationalist currents of the period is without dispute.[38] Yet in their rhetoric and policy positions on prostitution it is also clear that the abolitionists viewed themselves as transnational, as fighting against increased nationalism in the world:

> The Federation was founded when there was a great movement towards international action . . . since then there have been many changes and developments in public opinion, and no doubt at the present moment there is a great feeling of nationality. . . . We aim at creating a common sentiment by meetings such as this, and by intercommunication among ourselves, and there is nothing so likely to change the face of the world, which we aim at doing, as having certain great common principles which run through all the nations, and which are capable of application throughout all of their varied circumstances, while at the same time we are perfectly confident of the righteousness of our cause.[39]

It was a goal from which they never waivered.

As a result, from early on abolitionists were concerned about crossing racial and ethnic lines to protect women from male sexual exploitation.[40] They focused not only on the few European women in prostitution in the colonies, for example, but also on the majority of Indian women, who were subject to British regulation. As Butler wrote:

> I can say with truth—and hundreds of English women can say the same—that I feel as deep a pity and indignation on behalf of the Indian women submitted to this system, as I should do if they were Anglo-Saxon women. They are our fellow-citizens, our sisters, the women of a gentle and a conquered people, even less able to resist, or protest, or to call in, in any way, the aid of justice on their own behalf, than are the women of the West. I believe that their greater helplessness in their subordination to a conquering race increases, in the eyes of our just and merciful God, the guilt of those who have plunged them into this slavery. Anglo-Indian upholders of the vice Regulations speak of these women as already so degraded—being heathen—and so wanting in the moral sense, that they cannot be much further degraded by being made to officially minister to the vice of our Army.[41]

It is true that the abolitionists emphasized the modesty and helplessness of the Indian and other Asian women under colonial regulations, thus fostering the feminist orientalism that has been well-critiqued in academic literature.[42] It is also important to note, however, that this rhetoric was developed as a specific way to counter regulationist state and military officials who used racist stereotypes to justify the procurement of Indian women and their detainment in military brothels (*chaklas*).

Colonial authorities and supporters of regulation, including military administrators and conservative politicians, often portrayed Indian women as "naturally" sexually impure compared to "virtuous" European women, and they defended regulation on the grounds that indigenous cultures supported prostitution, which, the authorities and supporters reasoned, was an acceptable way to lower rates of venereal disease and protect "innocent" European women in both the metropole and the colonies. For example, they argued that British men required sexual intercourse with women, and if no prostitution outlet was available, these men would rape British women in the colonies. They also argued that regulation protected European wives from getting venereal diseases from their husbands, because men would have ready access to "clean" women in prostitution rather than resort to unregulated prostitutes, who could be sick. Here, then, was an early precursor to the cultural relativist arguments used to justify local practices in the face of an emerging global ethic, arguments not unlike those used to dispute and excuse human rights violations today.

Abolitionists countered the cultural relativism argument with a universal, gendered one.[43] They emphasized the understanding that all women are degraded by the assumption that men cannot control their sexual impulses and that a group of women should be maintained specifically for their sexual service. They discounted popular racist notions that saw European prostitution as a moral problem and as exploitative of women while excusing the regulation of indigenous women in the colonies. They emphasized that prostitution exploited all women, and called attention to the implicit assumptions about male sexuality that justified regulation.

They addressed the issue directly in their fight against regulation in colonial areas. Elizabeth Andrews and Kate Bushnell, two American Women's Christian Temperance Union reformers, were funded by the International Abolitionist Federation to go undercover to India, China, and Hong Kong to investigate regulation. In response to justifications for regulation based on the perceived protection it afforded to women and children, they wrote the following:

> Again, we ask, Which wives and which children—the British or Indian? There are hundreds of such wives and children who have been forsaken by husbands and fathers. . . . The chaklas hold many such unwilling prisoners, left there by treacherous husbands and fathers. Some day this wife of the officer or soldier will be turned out to perish of the disease her system could no longer throw off, and the children will either be retained as soldiers' prostitutes or sent out to share the fate of the diseased mother. The women of England are being besought to turn their eyes on the future wives of British officers and soldiers; it would be for England's lasting good would they but persistently keep their eyes on the British officers' and soldiers' *present* wives and children in the far-off East.[44]

It is clear that abolitionists saw a link between imperialism and the abuse of women in prostitution, though they did not often extend the analysis to call for the end of empire; instead, they sought reform.[45]

The class aspects of prostitution were less evident in abolitionist writings, but they did frequently point out that it was poor women and girls who were involved in regulated prostitution:

> for it is upon the daughters of such (those from the humblest ranks of life) that the oppressive laws for the licensing of prostitution fall; and in large part the supposed advantages of licensed prostitution accrue to the upper social

classes, which are, in fact, the lower moral classes. The crusade against licensed fornication is a war between respectable daughters of the poor and rich and powerful men and women.[46]

This acknowledgement resonated with socialist and working-class men's groups that viewed regulated prostitution as a system in which poor and working-class women were exploited by the bourgeoisie with the help of the state. They sometimes joined abolitionist efforts as a result.

Purity Reformers and the International Bureau

After the formation of the International Abolitionist Federation, British religious purity reformers formed an organization of their own, the National Vigilance Association. Founded in 1886, this association eventually became the International Bureau for the Suppression of the White Slave Traffic and was later renamed the International Bureau for the Suppression of Traffic in Women and Children. The National Vigilance Association came into being as a means of enforcing Britain's Criminal Law Amendment Act of 1885, which raised the age of consent to sixteen; criminalized the procurement of girls for prostitution by administering drugs, intimidation, or fraud; criminalized the abduction of girls under eighteen for sexual purposes; allowed magistrates to issue search warrants to find missing girls; provided for summary proceedings to be taken against brothels; and provided language under which homosexuality could be prosecuted.[47] The National Vigilance Association thus had a close relationship with the state from the beginning of its existence, and this connection grew with time.

In practice, the association worked on a variety of issues related to the protection of girls. Cases involved everything from helping to place girls in legitimate (that is, morally acceptable) work situations; placing "incorrigible" girls in training homes; helping girls who had become pregnant; placing girls who were neglected or abandoned; trying to prevent relationships between domestic servants and their employers; trying to convince girls not to "go bad," that is, to have sex or become prostitutes; and helping girls who wanted to leave "disorderly houses."[48] It acted as a kind of child welfare and social service organization, one that sought to enforce moral standards through casework to identify, prevent, and prosecute offensive sexual behavior.

Aside from casework, the National Vigilance Association actively sought to create and enforce legal standards for sexuality. They prosecuted cases of obscene literature.[49] They busied themselves with cases of rape and involved themselves in allegations of indecent assault, sometimes between domestic servants and their employers but also involving children, including those who were very young. They also intervened when employers or "keepers of disorderly houses" kept domestic servants' or prostitutes' belongings after they left the situation, and they attempted to ensure that men paid child support to women.

The National Vigilance Association's interest in the traffic in women evolved in part because its secretary, William Alexander Coote, while looking for missing girls, found some of them suffering from diseases in lock hospitals in other countries. These girls had taken offers of employment abroad and ended up in brothels, a problem that the association found difficult to address due to an absence of international legal guidelines.[50] After a year of travels to European countries in 1899, Coote formed a number of committees and then held the international congress that created the International Bureau.[51]

Coote went first to Germany and gained the interest of the empress; he met with governmental department representatives, including the police and members of the Foreign Office. He then went to the Netherlands, Denmark, and Sweden, where he received the support of a member of the Upper Chamber, as well as the approval of Louise of the Netherlands, who was queen of both Sweden and Norway. In Russia, Coote met with the Russian foreign minister, who set up a meeting that included the ministers of education and the interior, the chief of police, and a baron who was minister of the Imperial Court. The czar commanded the formation of a committee. In Belgium, the minister of state formed a committee and became its president. In France, as we will see in Chapter Six, Coote found Catholic supporters, including politicians. In Spain, a committee was formed by the king's decree in 1902.

While abolitionists focused on prostitution in general and sought to blur the distinction between the state regulation of prostitution and trafficking, purity reformers took the opposite approach. The International Bureau sought to address trafficking specifically, and it trod carefully around the issue of domestic prostitution. Like the abolitionists, participants in the International Bureau organized volunteers to patrol ports and railway stations to assist traveling girls, but they also worked to establish international agreements against the traffic in women, called for greater mechanisms for governmental control of immigration, worked for the prohibition of foreign women in prostitution in regulated brothels, and called for the compulsory repatriation of foreign prostitutes. They also supported new laws for policing morality, including criminalizing prostitution and forms of entertainment that contributed to the moral downfall of men, women, and children.

The International Bureau was clearly concerned with protecting young girls from sexual exploitation, albeit with a tendency to discriminate along ethno-national lines. Because of their ties to conservative state officials in most countries, International Bureau reformers did not challenge the state-regulation of prostitution but instead sought to control the traffic in women through two other strategies: working with regulationist state officials to ensure that brothels were filled only with voluntary, local, adult women; and increasing state power to control the traffic by developing governmental structures to address it and enhanced legal powers to control sexual activity.

Organization

International Bureau reformers organized throughout Europe and in some colonial holdings to build committees including male and female religious reformers, elites, and conservative state officials in various countries: counts, ministers of state, senators, princesses, even the chaplain to a king were made leaders and members of committees. Coote first organized in Germany, the Netherlands, Denmark, Sweden, Russia, Belgium, France, Austria, Hungary, Italy, and Spain (see Table 3.1).

From its beginnings, then, the International Bureau was closely tied to state officials. From 1908 to 1910, for example, many of its national committees were quasi-governmental, with state officials as leaders. Germany, Spain, Portugal, and Hungary fell into this category.[52] Even committees that were not official could count on support from state officials. Table 3.2 shows governmental attendance at the International Bureau's seven major international congresses and conferences between 1899 and 1913, and at the 1921 conference co-organized by the League of Nations and the International Bureau. The table shows that many states sent representatives to the meetings from 1899 through the interwar period.

In addition, International Bureau committees received financial assistance from states. The International Bureau, like the International Abolitionist Federation, received much of its funding from British subscribers, but governmental support helped many of the Bureau's national chapters. For example, the national committees in the Netherlands, Denmark, and Austria received funding in 1908, and Hungary received a government grant in 1910.

Table 3.2 Governmental delegates at selected international bureau congresses and conferences

Country	1899 London	1904 Paris	1906 Paris	1910 Madrid	1913 London	1921 Geneva[1]
Austria	✓	✓	✓	✓	✓	✓
Belgium	✓	✓	✓	✓	✓	✓
Brazil			✓		✓	✓
Bulgaria				✓		✓
China					✓	✓
Czechoslovakia						✓
Denmark	✓	✓	✓		✓	✓
France	✓	✓	✓	✓	✓	✓
Germany	✓	✓	✓	✓	✓	✓
Great Britain	✓	✓	✓	✓	· ✓	✓
Greece			✓			✓
Hungary			✓			✓
Italy		✓	✓	✓	✓	✓
Japan						✓
The Netherlands	✓	✓	✓	✓		✓
Norway	✓	✓	✓		✓	✓
Poland						✓
Portugal					✓	✓
Romania						✓
Russia	✓	✓	✓		✓	
Spain		✓	✓	✓	✓	✓
Sweden	✓	✓	✓		✓	✓
Switzerland	✓	✓	✓	✓	✓	✓
United States	✓				✓	
Uruguay			✓			✓

PRIMARY SOURCES: National Vigilance Association, The White Slave Trade: Transactions of the International Congress on the White Slave Trade (London: National Vigilance Association, 1899), GL, FAI Brochures, 300(6), 343.545.NVA(758); National Vigilance Association, "International Conference on the Suppression of the White Slave Traffic Held at Zurich, September 15th and 16th, 1904," Vigilance Record, 1904, October, no. 10, pp. 1–6 (London: National Vigilance Association),WL; National Vigilance Association, "Third International Congress for the Suppression of the White Slave Traffic Held at the Hotel Continental, Paris, from the 22nd to the 25th October, 1906," Vigilance Record, 1906, November, No. 11, pp. 85–92 (London: National Vigilance Association), WL; National Vigilance Association, "Fourth International Congress for the Suppression of the White Slave Traffic Held at Madrid from October 24th to 28th, 1910," Vigilance Record, 1910, 82–88 (London: National Vigilance Association), WL.

SECONDARY SOURCES: League of Nations 1921b; National Vigilance Association 1913.

1. This refers to the 1921 League of Nations conference on trafficking that was organized with the assistance of the International Bureau.

Also from its beginning, and reflecting some state officials' interests in controlling increased migration, the International Bureau's focus was on preventing the exploitation of girls in foreign brothel systems while sidestepping the issue of state regulation. It did not call for the abolition of state-regulated prostitution in countries where state officials supported its continuation. In France, for example, the International Bureau committee developed under the leadership of Catholic Senator René Bérenger, known as Father Prude because of his work on obscenity laws. Despite his moral misgivings about obscene literature and art, Senator Bérenger was proregulation, and he actively barred abolitionists from membership on the committee. He also, with the help of Secretary Coote, thwarted attempts to discuss abolition in early International Bureau congresses (see Chapter Six).

Gender, Nationality, and Class in International Bureau Rhetoric

International Bureau rhetoric often appealed to much more explicitly nationalist sentiments compared to those of the International Abolitionist Federation and the Bureau's supporters sometimes blatantly called for exclusionary and suppressive measures for dealing with trafficking and prostitution. As its London-based members explained:

> In the course of our work we have for a long time been convinced that the foreign criminals, both men and women, are a dangerous menace to our social, moral, and national life. The terrible condition of the streets of London was almost exclusively due to their presence. So strongly did we feel on the matter, that the committee drafted a Bill and submitted it to the Home Office. It was not accepted, but we are glad to be able to record that the clause referring to the Aliens who offend under the Criminal Law Amendment Act and the Vagrancy Act were incorporated in the Government Bill and have become law.[53]

Many International Bureau committees expressed similar xenophobic concerns. The French International Bureau committee, for example, claimed that "foreigners carry on the trade, generally bringing from other countries the unhappy ones whom they have succeeded in leading astray."[54] The Swedish committee, meanwhile, saw corrupt Danish and German immigration agents as the problem and they approved of an 1884 law that allowed only Swedes to act as agents for Swedish women emigrating to Denmark and other countries for work.[55]

The emphasis, in practice, was on controlling the movement—and sexual activity—of girls along racial, ethnic, and national lines, and on promoting measures that would help to achieve this. For example, the German national committee of the International Bureau expressed a desire to send a person to Buenos Aires to watch for German girls arriving there in 1913. The following year it showed a keen interest in the International Bureau's repatriation efforts, suggesting that the German committee send representatives to visit prisons and return German women to Germany.

International Bureau reformers, although they often used rhetoric that emphasized the victimization of women, tended to make distinctions between women on the basis of ethnicity and nationality. As one International Bureau supporter explained, "I have seen them in the Eastern ports—one of the greatest tragedies, there are our Western women in the licensed houses. Nothing but an International Convention [on repatriation] will stop the traffic."[56] Note the language of "our" women versus "their" women. Another example states this even more clearly: "it will certainly be a safeguard to our native girls if foreign girls are prohibited from being employed in those houses. . . . You have to teach the ordinary mother in those countries (with tolerated houses) that it is not right for her to have foreign women in those houses in order that she might save her own daughter."[57] Reformers stressed the need to protect "their" girls while bypassing the issue of state-regulated prostitution. Foreign prostitution, not prostitution in general, was seen as the problem.

This concern with "their" women meant that European International Bureau representatives resisted efforts to universalize the association's name, and presumably, therefore, its agenda. In 1910, for example, Coote disagreed with and dismissed a proposal to change the name of the International Bureau for the Suppression of the White Slave Traffic to the International Bureau for the Suppression of the Slavery of Women, "so as to include women of all races and colours."[58] He stated, "the time had not yet arrived for any suggested alteration to be recommended."[59] Again, in 1913, a call to change the name to the International Bureau for the Suppression of the Traffic in Women and Children was opposed. Such resistance was in direct opposition to feminist thought of the time; around 1909 to 1910, the International Council of Women, which had a white slavery committee, changed its terminology from the "white slave trade" to the "traffic in women," emphasizing the need to combat the trafficking and prostitution of non-European women.[60]

From the distinction between "our women" and "their women," it was only a short step to International Bureau rhetoric that denounced foreign women in prostitution as an underlying threat to moral order. As Coote himself argued:

> It becomes obvious that if foreign women of this class were not allowed to prac-
> tise prostitution outside their own country we should be grappling with the
> White Slave Traffic at the very roots. And while we could not say that prohibi-
> tion [of foreign women in tolerated brothels] would abolish the traffic, yet it
> would so nationalise it that each country would be able to deal with it within its
> own borders, and perhaps entirely suppress it.[61]

This argument is notable because the secretary-general of the International Bureau focused on the women themselves as the problem rather than on others involved in the organization of prostitution.

Other International Bureau representatives would follow suit. For exam-ple, the Belgian representative, also a governmental employee, announced at an International Bureau congress, "In six months—that is, from January 1st– July 31st 1924—we expelled 98 [prostitutes] on the strength of police regu-lation, 22 by Royal Decree. . . . And here I must add that it is not enough to expel them, we must see that they are not allowed to return. They often come back, and then we are forced to resort to more severe measures, such as impris-onment."[62] This issue would play itself out at the League of Nations, with the International Bureau maintaining its stance against foreign women in prostitu-tion despite considerable objection from abolitionists.

Underlying the concern with foreign women in prostitution were vary-ing levels of racism and xenophobia. The growth of eugenics across Europe contributed to concerns about the health of nations, and International Bureau members were often sympathetic to racialized eugenics arguments. British International Bureau reformer Sybil Neville Rolfe, for example, wrote to the League of Nations asking to establish a subsection on eugenics in its Health Section.[63] She and an American associate pressed for the subsection to "deal with racial, hereditary eugenical differences and with the consequences which flow from such differences" in order to advance the "progress of the world."[64] The under-secretary-general of the League of Nations, Inazo Nitobe, disagreed. He wrote, "In view of the historical fact that races of all colors and grades have freely mingled all through the ages, I cannot share Dr. Davenport's view that the progress of the world would be advanced by accentuating race differences."[65]

The International Bureau's defense of state sovereignty in matters pertain-ing to sexual morality, trafficking, and prostitution did lead it to one central difficulty: how to address the issue of regulation. From a purity perspective, it could not logically say that it supported regulated prostitution, and in fact many purity reformers wanted all prostitution suppressed. Yet to call for the abolition of state regulation would be to call for a reduction in state control over sexual activity. Worse, it could lead to problems with the state officials who supported the international voluntary association. Coote himself resisted any efforts to include a vote on the issue of regulation in any International Bureau congress. As he explained,

> It was strongly felt by several members, myself included, that such a vote would be disastrous to the future action of the [International Bureau] National Committees, especially in their relationship to their respective governments. . . . Certain it is that had such a vote been taken and carried certain governments would have been constrained to break their official connection with us.[66]

This pragmatism, and the bureau's support for increased state control over morality, characterized the association well into the interwar period, even after Coote died in 1919. It also paid off in the international realm. The International Bureau was the first association to which staff at the League of Nations turned when they wanted to address the issue of trafficking, and the association was called on immediately to help organize the first League of Nations anti-trafficking conference.

Because of its concern for maintaining and increasing state power, and its supportive stance toward the state legislation of morality, the International Bureau saw the liberal and feminist underpinnings of the International Abolitionist Federation as dangerous. It called the approach of International Abolitionist Federation reformers to prostitution "laissez faire" and juxtaposed it to the bureau's own strategy of increased state control. If that meant increased control over women themselves, so much the better. For example, the International Bureau's secretary, F. Sempkins, approved of police tactics to reform prostitutes in Egypt in the interwar period. In describing a refuge in Cairo that had been underutilized, he wrote, "The principal factor in the success of the Refuge in recent years has been the unfailing support of Bimbashi Major Tegg, a police officer who has 'provided' many of the inmates. His methods are perhaps unorthodox, but decidedly helpful."[67] Sempkins did not specify what these methods were, but it is likely that the inmates were forcibly detained.

In addition to lacking a gender perspective, which led the International Bureau to support repressive tactics for dealing with women in prostitution, the association, in contrast to feminists, also failed to develop a class analysis of trafficking. From the beginning, the International Abolitionist Federation sought the support of socialists in many countries by emphasizing connections between economic conditions, lack of equal pay for women, poverty, and prostitution. For the International Abolitionist Federation, prostitution was a moral problem as well as a gendered, political, and economic one. To members of the International Bureau, however, prostitution was primarily a problem of moral failing. They at first blamed the low moral standards of men who abandoned pregnant women and left them vulnerable to prostitution; they later stressed the moral failings of the women and girls themselves.

Contestation Within the Movement

The tensions between the liberal, gendered philosophy of the International Abolitionist Federation and the more conservative state-focused morality of the International Bureau were thus built into the movement from the start, and they worsened in the interwar period. Both trafficking and prostitution were contested issues from the earliest days of these two international voluntary associations and they were increasingly at odds as to how to define trafficking and how to proceed in relation to prostitution.

Butler and other International Abolitionist Federation reformers had doubts from the outset about working on the traffic with regulationist governments. The month prior to the first International Bureau congress, Butler wrote in her association's monthly publication about her belief that regulationist governments, France in particular, were involving themselves in the movement only to weaken it and disrupt unity. She characterized such governments as hypocritical and criminal, as upholding a system that commodifies and uses up young women while purporting to repress and punish those men who provide the system with its fodder.[68] The British committee later summarized the International Abolitionist Federation's position:

> What are we to understand by the expression "The White Slave Traffic"? ... The honoured President of the Federation has just pointed out that the White Slave Traffic has two principal aspects, viz., firstly the traffic in innocent young girls, who are forced by fraud or violence into an immoral life; and secondly, the sale and purchase of persons who are already in tolerated houses, and their subjection to different forms of slavery. But there are many people of importance among the opponents of the traffic who refuse to consider the second of these

aspects as an integral part of it. It will be easy to show that they are wrong, and that every operation which makes merchandise of women must be considered as part of the traffic. . . . The Federation bases all its action on the principle that woman is not a *thing*, but a human person, who ought to enjoy all the rights of the human person.[69]

Therefore, the committee reasoned, the traffic in women could be understood only in relation to prostitution in general, and could be dealt a blow only if regulated prostitution systems were abolished: "the only practical method of abolishing, or at least reducing, the traffic in women and girls, is to strike hard at those who, for their own profit, exploit the prostitution of others. This profit out of the prostitution of others (even where there is no question of immaturity or definite force or fraud) is the real 'traffic' we have to combat. . . ."[70] Blurring the lines between trafficking and prostitution was not difficult given the low social status of women, even through the interwar years; the abusive conditions in many brothels at the time; and the health consequences for women in prostitution, such as continued suffering from sexually transmitted diseases.

International Bureau reformers saw things differently. In his recounting of the formation of the International Bureau, Coote reflected:

One thing is certain, had I listened to the demands of the Abolitionists at the beginning of the crusade, and asked the different countries to take up the question of Abolition of State Regulation of Vice, as well as that of the Suppression of the White Slave Traffic, I should not have been received, or even listened to, by many of the European governments; and the work, as now constituted, would never have been started.[71]

In part what was going on was the negotiation of state sovereignty in the international realm, but also the degree to which the state should be penetrating the "private" realm of sexuality.

The International Bureau often took pains to clarify its differences from, and opposition to, the International Abolitionist Federation. In trying to set up a national committee in Lithuania in the early 1930s, for example, Secretary Sempkins wrote to a prospective contact, "the distinction between the work of the [International Bureau] National Committees and that of abolitionist committees lies in the fact that the work of suppression goes farther than that of abolition per se."[72] Things eventually became so tense that in the interwar period the International Bureau put out an informational flyer clarifying "what it is and is not." The flyer explicitly stated that the International Bureau was not "an extremist body" and not "a feminist body."[73]

The difficulties between abolitionists and the International Bureau were particularly visible in Egypt in the interwar period. When a newly recruited secretary of the Egyptian International Bureau committee suggested joint meetings with International Abolitionist Federation reformers, Sempkins dismissed the idea, explaining:

> The doubts about the joint meeting were based on political as well as personal grounds. The Abolitionists are not too tactful in their references to nationalities; they have been very offensive at past meetings and there is a strong distrust of them amongst some [International Bureau] National Committees. You will readily appreciate what I mean.[74]

He did not explain further but it is likely that he was referring to ongoing tensions between the International Abolitionist Federation and the International Bureau in Egypt on the issue of state regulation. As he had written over a year earlier, he objected to abolitionist involvement in Egypt because abolitionists had a "one-sided" view of social work and were of one opinion: "feminist and anti-brothel."[75]

One abolitionist reformer in particular had given public talks promoting the end of state regulation in Egypt. The Bureau found this particularly threatening, for a number of reasons. First, the Bureau believed that it upset accepted gender norms in Egypt for a woman to speak publicly about prostitution. Second, if abolition was successful, it would mean less British control over prostitution in the area and, if capitulations were challenged, the possibility that Egypt would simply close state-regulated brothels altogether. Third, abolitionists previously had little compunction about publicly naming European countries, such as Italy, that they held responsible for the trafficking of European women to parts of Egypt.

In Egypt, as elsewhere, while International Bureau reformers attempted to keep the movement strictly focused on the issue of trafficking, International Abolitionist Federation reformers sought to obtain international agreement that regulation should be abolished by all states and thereby deal a blow to the traffic as well as to domestic prostitution. Initially, International Bureau reformers and regulationist state officials were successful in keeping the focus on trafficking. The first international agreement and convention, in 1904 and

1910 respectively, focused only on the traffic and were specific in calling for central authorities in each country to deal with the traffic, punish traffickers, and exchange information with other countries on trafficking cases; they also established twenty as the age of consent for women who wished to work as prostitutes in foreign countries.

At a minimum, all parties could agree, at least for the purposes of the first international accords, that trafficking involved the forced movement of adult women and the movement of underage girls whether voluntary or not. The methods of force were not specified in the first agreements but were generally understood to mean that women and girls were drugged, kidnapped, or fraudulently enticed into purposely crossing borders for marriage or for various types of employment, only to find out that upon their arrival in the new territory they would be involved in prostitution.

This definition suited International Bureau reformers particularly because of their interest in the safety of young girls and because the agreement gave states improved abilities to control migratory prostitution. Regulationist state officials approved because through the agreements they could defend their regulation systems and show that brothels were humane because no women were forced to work in them and no children were procured for them. Feminists, dissatisfied that regulation was not explicitly addressed, nonetheless approved because the agreement did denounce the exploitation of women by third parties, and it opened the way for increasing challenges to state regulation by continuing to highlight the connections between regulation and trafficking.

Regulation was finally dealt a big blow in the late 1920s when the League of Nations Special Body of Experts published its report on the traffic in women and children. The conclusions were straightforward: immigrant women in prostitution came from countries with great poverty combined with low marriage age, where war or other disasters disrupted families, where wages were so low that women supplemented them with prostitution, where prostitution paid comparatively well, and where demand for foreign women in prostitution was stimulated.[76] The report connected such demand to systems of "licensed houses," thereby linking trafficking and regulated prostitution.[77] After the report came out the International Bureau began using more abolitionist language, although it never altered its view that state involvement was necessary for enforcing morality. It increasingly called for police suppression of prostitution in general and for control of women themselves.

Summary

This chapter has shown that the anti-trafficking movement was characterized from its start by debates about the causes of trafficking, the role of the state in organizing prostitution, and the best strategies to combat the problem. Neither of the two main international voluntary associations, nor any of the other participants in the movement, achieved lasting agreement on the definition of trafficking or on the scope of the trafficking movement. In fact, the movement to combat the traffic was a continual struggle among international voluntary associations and state officials to define what constituted the sexual exploitation of women, what goals should be set, and what policies could be agreed on internationally. Trafficking was the umbrella term for a variety of concerns pertaining to gender, sexuality, race, ethnicity, and nationality.

The International Abolitionist Federation worked across countries and as a relative outsider to the state institutions it sought to change. It targeted the traffic in order to highlight the connections between trafficking and state-regulated prostitution, and it worked to force states to repeal regulation in their territories. Moreover, it developed an internationalism that sought to challenge state interest in prostitution, working to gain support from local and international groups and developing universal discourses based on gender and individual rights. The solutions proposed by the Federation were therefore also universal: a worldwide minimum age of consent, the abolition of state-regulated prostitution in all countries, the prohibition of any and all procuring of women for prostitution within or across borders, and the elimination of all legal standards that reinforced the sexual double standard for women and targeted women (including those in prostitution) as a group.

The efforts of the International Abolitionist Federation had limited success in that the organization sometimes linked with the working classes in metropolitan areas and with indigenous groups in colonial areas. However, in its gendered, universal approach, the Federation only implicitly challenged the racial, ethnic, class, national, and imperial dynamics that contributed to the traffic in women. Its members also tended to be divided by class themselves, with elite and politically conservative women finding the International Bureau more in keeping with their interests.

The International Bureau, on the other hand, took up the issue of trafficking in national terms. It organized in alliance with state officials, and its national committees were often institutionalized as part of state institutions. By explicitly positioning themselves against abolitionists and declaring themselves to be for state involvement in sexual morality and for the protection of "their women" from foreigners, purity reformers ignored the fact that much trafficking involved ethnic and national groups moving their "own" women from one country to another, including to and from those with regulated systems. Loathe to challenge states' authority to control prostitution within their territories as they saw fit, the Bureau's national committees often became quasi-governmental organizations helping to police it.

The purity reformers affiliated with the International Bureau sought not to transcend national interests but to reinforce them. Even the solutions they proposed emphasized national interests. They saw the movement against trafficking as a means of increasing state administration over sexual activity within their territories and as a way to defend state-regulated prostitution as a national rather than an international concern. The focus on trafficking placed only *migratory* prostitution and *foreign* prostitutes in the international realm, leaving states with continued sovereignty over domestic prostitution.

Ultimately, the abolitionists won some battles to deregulate prostitution in particular countries and helped to sway the League of Nations and United Nations to incorporate universal, gender-based abolitionist language in their trafficking conventions and in their stance toward prostitution.[78] The purity reformers, however, won the war: many countries followed the abolition of regulated brothel systems with national legal efforts to suppress prostitution and increase state control over sexual activity.[79] Despairing of the trend toward suppression and of attacks on women in prostitution, the secretary of the British Committee of the International Abolitionist Federation lamented in 1935:

> I am feeling really anxious about the whole question of genuine abolition in Europe. . . . M. Reelfs [Secretary of the International Abolitionist Federation] tells me that even in Switzerland and, he thinks, all over Europe there is a rising force of public opinion demanding the abolition of licensed houses but the rigid regulation of prostitutes. It is of course part of the Totalitarian State idea that the State is of more importance than the individual and that small items like the constitutional justice and respect for the rights of human personality cannot be bothered about when the interests of the State are at stake. I have always believed that if you believe in liberty you will see to it that your weakest link in the chain is secure. The weakest link is the prostitute since few people care whether she is justly treated or not.[80]

Her concerns were well-founded. The next chapter shows the development of this suppressionist trend in the League of Nations as state officials incorporated the movement in the international realm. Through efforts to prohibit foreign prostitutes in regulated prostitution systems and the forcible repatriation of women, state officials moved toward the understanding of foreign prostitution as a problem in and of itself. Even as abolitionists won some success in condemning state regulation at the League of Nations, state officials were moving toward the nationalization of official brothel systems and toward measures that targeted migrant women in prostitution.

4 Reforming Regulation and Nationalizing Prostitution

THE LEAGUE OF NATIONS, the precursor to the United Nations, was an intergovernmental organization founded in 1919 with the aim of achieving international peace and security. Established by the Treaty of Versailles after the horrors of World War I, the League was composed of a secretariat with a general secretary, an assembly with representation from all member states, and a council or executive body. It had fifty-seven member countries at its largest, although some key powers of the time failed to support or eventually withdrew from the League. The United States never joined, Japan and Italy withdrew in the 1930s, and Germany was initially precluded from membership and then joined only from 1926 to 1933.

The League worked to resolve international disputes through arbitration and conciliation, and if necessary, sanctions, but it relied on the cooperation of member states, and it had no military power or agency to enforce its resolutions. Although the League had some early successes, the aggressions of Axis powers and the eventual outbreak of World War II sealed the League's fate as a failed peacekeeping organization. It remained in existence but nonfunctional until 1945, when the United Nations formally took over its duties.

The League is remembered for its peacekeeping failures, but it did have much more success in fostering international cooperation in social, economic, and humanitarian affairs. Under the League's auspices, conferences and committees met, developed, and implemented conventions on a variety of issues, such as health, labor, slavery, finance, transportation and communication, intellectual cooperation, and the traffic in women. When the League formed, state officials took over anti-trafficking work and the administration of earlier agreements and conventions, and they continued their anti-trafficking agenda throughout the interwar period.

In the Traffic in Women and Children Committee, League of Nations state delegates, counseled by representatives of international voluntary associations whom they appointed as members, oversaw the League's anti-trafficking work. The committee, and League of Nations members in general, addressed the traffic in as rational and objective a manner as possible. As they set about holding meetings, collecting reports, and overseeing empirical investigations, League of Nations participants worked to gather facts about the traffic in both European and non-European women. Trafficking and prostitution were treated as humanitarian concerns and incorporated into the League of Nations Section for Humanitarian and Social Questions, along with child welfare, the repatriation of prisoners of war, and refugee issues.[1]

Trafficking proved to be a contentious issue at the League of Nations as the schism between feminists and purity reformers played out in the Traffic in Women and Children Committee. Officials' ties to feminist international voluntary associations or to purity reformers, their own policies on regulated prostitution, and their political conflicts with other states all created tensions. Great Britain, strongly influenced by the International Abolitionist Federation and international feminist groups, was the key abolitionist country whose delegates worked to address regulation at the League of Nations. These delegates argued that all women, domestic as well as foreign, should be safeguarded from abuse in regulated prostitution systems around the world.

State officials from regulationist countries such as France, Italy, Spain, and Japan, all of which were appointed to the Traffic in Women and Children Committee, tended to regard prostitution as a domestic issue and sought to limit the scope of the committee to matters pertaining to foreign women in prostitution. Even then many states had qualifications: they did not necessarily want to prohibit foreign women from registering as prostitutes, as long as they did so voluntarily. As noted in Chapter Two, state officials sometimes preferred to have immigrant women in their brothel systems. This was true even of Great Britain, which abolished regulation comparatively early in metropolitan areas but moved more slowly in colonial areas because colonial administrators and military doctors were reluctant to relinquish control of prostitution.[2] Military and geopolitical interests could prompt contradictory responses from state officials within countries.

The international politics of women's sexual activity meant that prostitution was bound to create disagreements among international voluntary associations and state delegates at the League of Nations.[3] This chapter examines such dynamics in the cases of two resolutions put forward in the League's trafficking committee: an eventually successful agreement to prohibit foreign prostitutes from registering in licensed houses, and an ultimately unsuccessful bid to mandate the repatriation of foreign prostitutes. These proposals shifted the focus of the movement from the universal protection of women and girls in prostitution to the protection of states from foreign women in prostitution as officials took measures that in effect nationalized prostitution. The irony for feminists who were looking to the international realm as the arena in which to force change across nation-states and throughout empires is that the League of Nations tended to reinforce state sovereignty in the regulation of prostitution even as it addressed what state officials considered to be the more appropriately international issue of trafficking.[4]

The Incorporation of Anti-Trafficking Work in the League of Nations

The influence of women's groups was important in placing gender-specific issues on the agenda of the League of Nations, and from the League's beginnings, feminist international voluntary associations lobbied for the inclusion of anti-trafficking and prostitution work.[5] The International Council of Women, the International Women's Suffrage Alliance, and the British chapter of the International Abolitionist Federation drafted resolutions and sent letters to that effect. The International Women's Suffrage Alliance also sent a deputation to the League's secretary-general, Sir Eric Drummond, to ask, among other things, for the League of Nations to address trafficking, venereal disease, and prostitution, but Drummond's reply was that the latter two were domestic matters.[6] This response was a standard one; for example, feminists at the League of Nations worked long and hard to convince the League's member states that the equality of women was a legitimate problem for international attention rather than a purely domestic concern.[7] Early internal correspondence among League of Nations staff shows that they believed that the majority of countries in the League of Nations were regulationist and would not have sympathy for abolitionist resolutions.[8] They, like the International Bureau, saw trafficking rather than regulation as the appropriate issue for the League to address.

The League of Nations subsequently took on trafficking primarily because officials wanted to ensure coordinated policy for overseeing existing international conventions already signed by member states, including the 1904 and

1910 accords dealing with the white slave traffic.[9] The trafficking of women for prostitution was therefore included in Article 23 of the League of Nations final covenant, along with trafficking in opium:

> Subject to and in accordance with the provisions of international conventions existing or hereafter to be agreed upon, the Members of the League will entrust the League with the general supervision over the execution of agreements with regard to the traffic in women and children and the traffic in opium and other dangerous drugs.[10]

Bureaucratic logic rather than humanitarian concern seems to have led the League to its anti-trafficking work.

As the League's staff set about their initial anti-trafficking efforts, they coordinated first with the International Bureau. They met with Bureau Secretary William Coote and his secretary, as well as with a Jewish reformer who was active with the Bureau and a leader of the Jewish Association for the Protection of Women and Girls. Secretary-General Drummond asked the British Home Office to convene a trafficking conference comprising International Bureau committees and the state officials from countries that had signed the 1904 and 1910 accords.[11] Geopolitical tensions delayed the conference for a time: postwar grievances led the French International Bureau committee to refuse to attend if Germany was present, after which the Swiss and Dutch committees warned that they would not participate if Germany was *not* invited. Feminists with the International Council of Women inquired about sending a delegate to the conference after learning that the International Bureau was going to have representatives there, and although this request was initially turned down, the conference was eventually opened up for general attendance.[12]

The conference was held in 1921 and attended by thirty-four states.[13] For six days participants gave speeches, held committee meetings, and developed recommendations and resolutions. By the end of the conference they had adopted a list of fifteen documents, including recommendations for countries to ratify the 1904 agreement and 1910 convention whether or not they were League of Nations members, and to adhere to them on behalf of colonies and dependencies; to consider twenty-one the minimum age of consent if they had adhered or would adhere to the agreements; to agree to extradite traffickers; to help women who had been expelled by the authorities of another country to return to their own country; to license and supervise employment agencies; and to provide regular reports of their work on combating the traffic.[14]

It was at this conference that an additional anti-trafficking convention was established, over the objections of the French delegation that the process was too rushed. This convention specified that a standing League of Nations committee be created to deal with the traffic.[15] France was directed to be a member of the committee because it had previously volunteered to assume certain obligations of the 1904 and 1910 accords and could furnish the League of Nations with all the information it had collected in relation to them. The other countries chosen for membership were Great Britain, Denmark, France, Italy, Japan, Poland, Romania, Spain, and Uruguay. Almost all of these countries were regulationist. Great Britain and Denmark were the only abolitionist countries; and Poland, a newly independent country, was in the process of abolishing regulated brothels, but not the registration of individual women in prostitution. The Netherlands, which was staunchly abolitionist and historically active as a leader in the international anti-trafficking movement, and which had a strong International Bureau committee, was not among the countries with delegates on the Traffic in Women and Children Committee.

Voluntary associations were appointed to provide information and reports as well as to participate in the committee's meetings, although they could not vote. These included the International Bureau, the International Catholic Association for the Protection of Girls, the Federation of National Unions for the Protection of Girls, and the Jewish Association for the Protection of Girls and Women, as well as various international women's organizations.[16] The latter group was represented by the International Council of Women and comprised a variety of international organizations, such as the International Women's Suffrage Alliance, the Women's International League for Peace and Freedom, the World's Young Women's Christian Association, the Women's Indian Association, the Association of Hindu Women, and St. Joan's Social and Political Alliance. Many of these groups supported or had members involved with the International Abolitionist Federation.

The diversity of reformers on the Traffic in Women and Children Committee often led to tensions during meetings, when different positions on trafficking, prostitution, and gender were put forward. For example, the organizations on the committee had varying perspectives on the equality of women, with the Catholic Association for the Protection of Girls, the Jewish Association for the Protection of Girls and Women, and the International Bureau preferring to emphasize gender difference and the protection of women, while the international women's organizations remained interested in discussing trafficking from the standpoint of women's equal rights.[17] Thus divisions among reformers on the Traffic in Women and Children Committee were sometimes as pronounced as those among state delegates.

State delegates and the voluntary associations also disagreed about regulation as a practice, and state delegates argued among themselves as well. Disputes sometimes arose when the state delegate of one country accused the delegate from another country of allowing trafficking and prostitution activities. In the early 1920s, for example, the Polish delegate claimed that the French were recruiting Polish women for agricultural work, but moving them into French brothels instead. This the French delegate denied. Later, the Romanian delegate defended his country against the accusation that officials paraded Russian women in prostitution through the streets to present them to doctors for medical exams. There were too few doctors and too many women, he explained, so the circumstances were special.[18] He later criticized the representative of the international women's organizations for not reporting that Romania had taken steps to deal with the problem.[19]

Shaming by the international voluntary associations often prompted such responses from state officials, who felt compelled to answer for their country's action, or lack thereof, when it came to trafficking. Even feminist delegates were not immune to such challenges. In one case, the Uruguay delegate on the committee, departing from her typical transnational gender arguments, defended her country against the Jewish Association's charge that too much trafficking was occurring there. Argentina, she insisted, was much worse.[20]

Overall, the Traffic in Women and Children Committee and the League of Nations in general proved quite dedicated in their anti-trafficking activities. They worked to have the 1904, 1910, and new 1921 accords signed by all League of Nations member states. The latter accord had extended its scope to include boys as well as girls, and the language had shifted from the "white slave traffic" to the "traffic in women" so as to include women of color. The committee also developed two further conventions: the 1933 Convention for the Suppression of Traffic in Women of Full Age, which made procurement of adult women, even with consent, an offense (making it incompatible with regulation); and a 1937 draft convention made all procurement illegal, even when women consented and when it occurred within a country rather than between countries. The latter convention addressed the issue of internal trafficking, which previously had been overlooked. Progress on the convention was interrupted by World War II, but was later picked up at the newly formed United Nations.

In addition to drafting conventions, the Traffic in Women and Children Committee met regularly in the interwar period to address a variety of matters pertaining to trafficking and prostitution. For eighteen years, from 1922 to 1939, the committee collected annual reports on trafficking and prostitution from states, heard reports from the voluntary associations, and grappled with questions about state regulation, women police, emigration, the age of consent, and particular instances of trafficking raised by delegates. The committee also commissioned two extensive and widely read expert studies of the traffic to "secure the facts and to refute sensational exaggerations or general denials as to the traffic and—what would seem to be for the Committee of supreme importance—an intelligent basis for a sound program for international co-operation for the suppression of the traffic, if it is found to exist."[21]

The first study, published in 1927, focused on Europe and North and South America, and it was not accomplished without some political maneuvering.[22] Behind the scenes, a representative of Great Britain, S. W. Harris, and the staff person to the Traffic in Women and Children Committee, Dame Rachel Crowdy, worked to balance the members of the first Special Body of Experts. Harris was concerned that France would try to pack the committee with regulationists, and thus interfere with an objective inquiry into the situation of foreign women in regulated brothels and the means by which they came to be in them.[23] The committee was eventually chaired by William F. Snow, former director of public health in California and leader of the American Social Hygiene Association, which also provided the funding for the study. Representatives of Belgium, France, Great Britain, Italy, Japan, Switzerland, and Uruguay were included.

The study covered 112 cities in twenty-eight countries where a staff of investigators spent a minimum of 5 and up to 187 days investigating trafficking conditions. They interviewed six hundred officials, including those in the central authority that had been established in each country by the 1904 International Agreement for the Suppression of the White Slave Traffic, as well as chiefs of police and migration and health care officials.[24] They also interviewed 5,000 people involved in prostitution and 250 people working in voluntary societies, and they collected questionnaires and information on trafficking and prostitution from governments.[25] The result was an in-depth report that confirmed the existence of trafficking, identified its geographical trends, and tied it to the state regulation of prostitution.[26]

The League of Nations later extended its inquiry to China, Japan, and other Asian countries, including colonial areas. The American Social Hygiene Association again provided funding and a traveling commission of three members from the United States, Sweden, and Poland overtook the work. They met with police, migration, public health, and other officials, and with members of voluntary associations in seventeen countries, an endeavor that lasted from late 1930 to early 1932.[27] Again, the League of Nations confirmed the presence of trafficking routes, this time between various Asian countries, and the majority of women were Chinese. It subsequently held a conference in Bandoeng (Indonesia) in 1937 to try to set up a coordinated system to deal with trafficking in Asia, but little progress was made.[28] China, the main focus of the second League of Nations inquiry, remained largely removed from the League's anti-trafficking efforts and concealed Chinese involvement in trafficking.[29] Japan had earlier repatriated Japanese women in prostitution but maintained regulation systems in its territories, and as the country became involved in war, the authorities trafficked ethnic Koreans to be "comfort women" in military brothels, a practice that came to include Chinese and other Asian women as well.[30]

Prohibition of Foreign Women in Prostitution

Even at the first League of Nations anti-trafficking conference in 1921, in which the need for a convention was discussed, the trafficking/regulated prostitution schism was apparent. The Dutch delegate, an abolitionist, linked trafficking and regulated prostitution; he proposed to extend the definition of trafficking to include punishment of those who procure women who are of legal age, *even with their consent*. The convention thus would have made all procurement, even for regulated brothels, illegal. This proposal was strenuously objected to by the French delegate, who asserted the necessity of regulation. The Dutch proposal was voted down because it did not have a three-quarter majority, although it did have wide support—seventeen of twenty-nine countries.[31] The issue would come up again in the draft of the 1933 convention.

The relationship between trafficking and regulated prostitution continued to be a contentious issue in League of Nations work. Feminist abolitionists had their supporters, mainly in the international women's organizations' representative to the Traffic in Women and Children Committee, Avril de St. Croix, and the Union for the Protection of Girls, which usually allied itself with their positions. In addition, Great Britain's League of Nations representative, S. W. Harris, and the Netherlands and Uruguay delegates regularly supported the abolition of regulation.[32] Regulationist countries, especially France, along with the International Bureau, the Jewish Association, and the Catholic Association, consistently attempted to restrict discussions to involuntary trafficking and to legal remedies for miscreant sexual behavior and other moral issues, such as alcohol consumption and pornography, rather than include the regulation of prostitution.

Soon after its formation, at its second session, in 1923, the Traffic in Women and Children Committee was faced with a proposal that would again renew the debate about regulation, as well as about women's equal rights. The resolution, which called for the prohibition of foreign prostitutes in brothels pending the abolition of regulation, was put forward by the Polish delegate to the League of Nations Assembly. It was unanimously supported, although France and Spain, both regulationist countries, abstained.[33] The prohibition proposal clearly indicates that League of Nations state representatives were more interested in controlling the movement—and sexual activity—of women than in protecting them from exploitation in prostitution. A shift in focus to prostitutes themselves rather than to traffickers was already in process despite feminist attempts to fight this trend.

In the committee, regulationist France vigorously disputed the Polish proposal, on the basis of two premises. The first premise was state autonomy. France objected to prostitution being the subject of international agreements and argued that prostitution and its regulation were domestic concerns. The second premise had to do with the relation between trafficking and regulation. The French delegate, Léon Bourgeois, argued that trafficking was actually associated with clandestine prostitution, therefore the resolution would have the effect of increasing rather than decreasing the traffic. In an attempt to frame his concern as a women's rights issue, Bourgeois additionally argued that the resolution would restrict women's liberties, keeping adult women who wished to enter brothels from doing so.

There was what might seem like an unlikely show of support for French officials in opposing the prohibition resolution: feminists also objected to it. Avril de Sainte-Croix reported that only three of the thirty-six International Council of Women national councils that she had consulted were in favor of the proposal, and none of the other five international women's organizations that she represented were in favor of it.[34] Feminists strongly opposed the resolution as inadvertently condoning brothels, as impossible to implement because the nationality of women in prostitution was often not clear, and as unfair because women should not be expelled from countries simply for being prostitutes, especially when prostitution itself was not considered a crime. As de Sainte-Croix protested, "the proposal, which was so contrary to feminine dignity, had so many practical objections that it was worthless.[35]

Feminists also opposed the resolution because it left authority in the hands of morals police, which, they argued, would lead to further bribery and corruption, and to the greater vulnerability of immigrant women to exploitation. They asked, "Does it not rather give the police a fresh means of tyranising over the hapless foreign women?"[36] The International Abolitionist Federation's British committee strongly objected to the proposal, sending letters to the League of Nations and publishing pamphlets that suggested that it was unable to support the prohibition proposal because "as abolitionists, we cannot do anything to improve a system or an institution which we declare to be abominable, nor can we agree to a proposal which implicitly recognises the brothel slavery of women, foreign or otherwise.[37] They argued that the measure supported the reform of regulation rather than its abolition.

The Uruguay state representative to the Traffic in Women and Children Committee, Paulina Luisi, also objected to the resolution. A feminist and a doctor, she consistently supported the positions of the international women's organizations and opposed any gender-specific legislation. Luisi warned the committee to be careful about their policies pertaining to women migrants lest they impinge on women's freedom to travel, and she cited examples in Greece, Portugal, and Spain where regulations prevented women over twenty-one from traveling alone without the permission of a husband or relative.[38] Against the French delegate's objections, she later put forward a proposal that government laws on the traffic should not impede the personal freedom of women of full legal age and that emigration laws should be applicable to persons of either sex.

She opposed the prohibition proposal not only at the League of Nations but also at an International Bureau conference that voted to support it. She pointed out that brothel keepers could not be trusted to abide by the rule of not registering foreign prostitutes, and she disputed the legal basis for expelling foreign women in prostitution:

> I would like to know how my Government could expel a woman merely on the grounds that she is a foreign prostitute? Is prostitution a crime? In my country only people who are guilty of offences against the law can be deported. The foreign women are to be expelled because they commit a crime in leading a life

of prostitution? In that case prostitution is a crime; then why should we allow our nationals to commit crimes?[39]

She pointed out both the gender and the national biases of the proposal.

Feminists also asked state officials and purity reformers to consider carefully the implications of the prohibition proposal. Predicting the possible outcome, Luisi argued at one International Bureau conference:

> Do you realise what would be the result of M. Sokal's [the Polish League of Nations delegate's] motion? I am speaking in my own name and in the name of the women who have sent me here. It looks to me very like protection of home industry against the foreigner! We should be nationalising prostitution and not admitting foreign competition. That would be too base a principle to accept. Do not let us deal in anything that is bad![40]

Finally she offered an additional reason that the resolution would not be useful, suggesting that many immigrant women in prostitution were in clandestine brothels.

International Bureau reformers and most state officials were not convinced. For example, regulationist Belgium's International Bureau committee supported the proposal, and its representative reported that the country expelled foreign prostitutes. It was the delegates of this country that asked for the proposal not only to prohibit the registration of foreign prostitutes, but also to mandate the expulsion of all foreign prostitutes, whether in regulated brothels or found to be working clandestinely.

Even purity reformers in abolitionist countries supported the proposal, such as the aforementioned Sybil Neville Rolfe, who was a member of the British International Bureau committee and the Secretary-General of the British Social Hygiene Council, a rival to the British chapter of the International Abolitionist Federation. In arguing in favor of the prohibition proposal, Rolfe asked:

> We have a united ideal that we want clean family life, that we want sex conduct to be straight, and that we want to recognise the principles of Christian teaching. . . . What are we in the abolitionist countries going to do if there is nothing to prevent our women being taken and made slaves of in regulationist countries?[41]

The Jewish Association, another member of the Traffic in Women and Children Committee, likewise backed the proposal.

With strong support from the International Bureau, the Catholic and Jewish international voluntary associations, and many governments, the resolution went forward in the Traffic in Women and Children Committee, over the objections of League of Nations delegates from France and Uruguay, and of feminist reformers.[42] It was seen by some abolitionist state officials as a first step in expanding anti-trafficking work to include state-regulated brothels and challenging the understanding of regulation as a domestic issue. They supported the proposal to prohibit the registration of foreign prostitutes on the basis that it was a temporary measure to be put into place *pending the abolition of brothels.*

Regulationist governments that supported the proposal believed it would strengthen the right of governments, if they wished, to prevent foreign prostitutes from entering their territories, and provide a first step toward measures that would allow such women to be expelled by governments as well. In this they were correct, because the compulsory repatriation of prostitutes was soon placed on the agenda of the League of Nations. They also believed that the measure would ensure the continuation of regulation within their territories, in effect helping to nationalize brothels and therefore take them off the League of Nations' agenda. Because the League of Nations was to include within its scope only matters pertaining to foreign prostitution, nationalizing regulated brothels and ensuring that they were filled with voluntary, local women would assist regulationist governments with the argument that the matter was a domestic rather than an international concern. French officials, believing even this small concession to be a challenge to state sovereignty and to the ability of French officials to regulate brothels as they wished, rejected the strategy.

Repatriation of Foreign Women in Prostitution

Having banned the entry of foreign women into state-regulated brothels, the League of Nations state officials next addressed what to do with foreign prostitutes when they found them in their territories. Repatriation had been taken up by states in the anti-trafficking movement early on. The 1904 international agreement, for example, provided that foreign women who had been trafficked were to be sent home at public expense should they or their relatives desire it and private means were not forthcoming. Repatriation was now to become another arena for debate in the League of Nations as well as among the international voluntary associations on the Traffic in Women and Children Committee. Many countries, regulationist and not, were interested in receiving international cooperation to help them deport "undesirable" women. Understanding that such women often returned to the country from which they had been deported, and that other countries might return "undesirable" women to their own territories, these countries wanted to maintain some discretionary control over the process.

When the issue of repatriation was discussed in 1925, state officials were at first preoccupied with the practical issues associated with it: Who would pay for the travel expenses? Would voluntary associations need to be consulted to accompany a woman back to her country of origin, and if so, which ones? How would they link women of particular nationalities and religions with the appropriate voluntary associations for assistance? There was some extended debate about the latter question, because the Jewish and Catholic Associations wanted to keep jurisdiction over girls of their own religious faith. Although some women's organizations said they would take girls of all religions; others sought to help women on the basis of racial/ethnic, national, or religious identity.

State officials on the Traffic in Women and Children Committee advocated that women should have help in becoming reestablished in their home countries, but this proposition seems to have been less a reflection of humanitarian concern than a fear about the uncontrolled movement of women. Officials were worried that immigrant women would return to their destination countries after having been deported, that "undesirable" women would return "home" to countries that did not want to include them as nationals, and that women would perhaps move to a third country to practice prostitution there. The international voluntary associations were therefore needed to help prevent these possibilities.

The statements of League of Nations delegates provide evidence of such concerns. For example, the Belgian delegate warned:

> The solidarity of nations had been insisted upon again and again, and, in the opinion of the speaker, this expulsion, which was not exactly a manifestation of solidarity, sometimes increased the social danger of prostitution. . . . Governments should agree to distinguish between the undesirables and only expel foreign prostitutes after getting in touch, as far as possible, with the voluntary associations so as to give these women every opportunity of becoming reestablished.[43]

Here it seems that the nations are under attack, that they need to come together in solidarity against the social danger of prostitution. It is unclear whether the Belgian delegate was afraid that undesirable Belgian nationals could be returned to the country or worried about an influx of immigrant women in prostitution from neighboring countries who would set up shop in Belgium when they were deported from other countries rather than returning home. In either case, this state official, as well as others, wished to control which women entered his country's territorial boundaries.

The shift in focus from the control of trafficking to the control of women did not go unnoticed. Paulina Luisi, the Uruguay delegate to the Traffic in Women and Children Committee, commented: "After listening to some of the speakers, she wondered whether the task of this Committee was to defend society against prostitutes. She thought, on the contrary, that it was called upon to find means to contribute to the rescue of these women and to prevent the infamous traffic."[44] She pointed out that the committee's discussions had begun to focus on the women's actions rather than on the actions of the traffickers—all the more ironic because the international conventions combating the traffic had made procuring, not prostitution, a criminal offense.

In fact, many state officials had begun targeting prostitutes and wanted to maintain their ability to deport women within their territories. By 1928, women could be deported simply for being prostitutes in Poland, Germany, the Netherlands, Belgium, England, Hungary, the United States, and Canada. Of these countries, mainly the Netherlands, Belgium, and the United States actively repatriated women in prostitution. Germany, France, and Austria also increasingly did so in the late interwar period.[45] Some of these countries, such as the Netherlands, adhered to the early international anti-trafficking conventions and paid for the voluntary repatriation of women; others simply deported "undesirable" women.

Trafficking and prostitution discourses at the League of Nations reflected this increasing preoccupation with managing the movement of women. The early emphasis on the moral necessity of protecting women gave way to discussions of "national honor" and "undesirable" men and women. The Japanese delegate to the Traffic in Women and Children Committee, for example, speaking in the abstract about repatriation, argued, "It was a question of national honour that, when a national of a country had made himself undesirable in another country, the necessary steps should be taken to repatriate him [sic]."[46] Japan did just this, repatriating Japanese women in prostitution in the interwar period. It was the only country to bring its "own" women in prostitution back from other countries and colonial holdings, and it began to do so even before the repatriation proposal was debated at the League of Nations.

Ethnonational concerns likely prompted this response. Although in the interwar period migrant women in prostitution generally serviced men of their own race/ethnicity/nationality, Japanese women in prostitution did not practice such exclusivity.[47] Those in Hong Kong, Singapore, Bombay, and elsewhere serviced men of all nationalities. Beginning in 1921, Japan began bringing these women back to Japan, leaving them only in enclaves where they were needed to service Japanese men. The country's consuls, along with Japanese residents abroad, "grouped themselves together to bring pressure to bear on Japanese women engaged in the trade of prostitution to return to Japan."[48] This was apparently effective, according to League of Nations experts:

> As an example of the remarkable energy with which the policy of liquidation of Japanese prostitution in those regions has been pursued, it may be cited that more than nine-tenths of the Japanese prostitutes in the district of Singapore left for Japan within a period of two or three years. In the same way, the Japanese prostitutes in Bombay, Calcutta, Bangkok, Saigon, and Hong-Kong were induced to leave.... From Rangoon, 60 Japanese prostitutes were repatriated in 1920.... In China ... now (Japanese prostitutes) are not more numerous than is required to meet an almost exclusive demand by Japanese men in the cities concerned.[49]

The concern of the Japanese government seems to have been the prevention of interracial mixing rather than trafficking or prostitution, because they left enough women in prostitution to service Japanese men in Japanese communities. Women in prostitution who left went to other colonies where regulation continued or returned to Japan.[50]

Aware that many state officials were concerned about controlling the movement of women, International Bureau reformers began to press long and hard for a League of Nations agreement on repatriation. At the Bureau's 1927 conference, as the League of Nations was moving toward an acknowledgement of the connection between trafficking and regulated systems, a delegate put forward a proposal for a convention on repatriation. At issue was whether repatriation should be voluntary or compulsory, who would pay the expenses (that is, the sending or receiving government or voluntary associations), and what to do when women returned to a foreign country to engage in prostitution. International Bureau reformers hoped for a clause that would prevent the return of women in prostitution who had been repatriated. The League of Nations agreed to include the issue of a convention on its agenda, pending a forthcoming International Bureau conference in 1930.

The issue of compulsory repatriation predictably raised the ire of feminist groups, and even a few members of the International Bureau's national committees objected. The former protested yet again on the grounds that the policy singled out and would harm women as a group; the latter did so out of a desire to protect their countries from the return of "undesirable" women. A Polish representative to a 1927 International Bureau conference, for example, argued, "It is undesirable to send such girls back to places where they lived formerly because they would there disseminate moral and physical epidemics."[51] They maintained this stance at a 1930 conference as well:

> The Polish Committee could absolutely not accept the proposal to consider a woman's nationality in cases of doubt, as that of the country where she was born. If the woman had no nationality, such nationality could not be artificially created, and they could see no object in repatriating a woman to a country which was not her own and with which she had nothing in common.[52]

This representative of the nationalizing Polish state may have been referring to Jewish or German-speaking women in prostitution.[53]

In general, however, the International Bureau continued to promote compulsory repatriation and to defend the punishment of women who incurred the cost of repatriation a second time. At their 1930 congress, over the objections of their own Polish committee, they agreed that the International Bureau would propose an international convention on repatriation to the League of Nations Traffic in Women and Children Committee. The proposal included suggestions for (1) prohibiting entry of women into foreign countries for prostitution, "considering that the importance of attainment and preservation of a high standard of morality over-rides any objection to action being taken against any particular class of either sex;" (2) compulsory repatriation of every foreign prostitute guilty of a breach of any law or municipal regulation; (3) repatriation even in situations of doubtful nationality, such as "cases of Jews from Eastern Europe," wherein authorities of the country of birth should not put obstacles in the way of repatriation; and (4) penalties for return, because "a definite problem exists of prostitutes who, having been expelled from a country, make their way back again."[54]

Given that they had tangled with feminist abolitionists many times before, the International Bureau members acknowledged that "any proposal for compulsion invariably encounters strong opposition on the grounds that it is an infringement of the principle of individual liberty, unfairly discriminates against the woman, and is profoundly humiliating for her."[55] They nonetheless defended their proposal by arguing that the traffic in women was largely a voluntary enterprise that needed more rather than fewer restrictions. Positioning themselves against feminist abolitionists, they argued that the

> traffic in women of European races is at present mostly a commercial trade in prostitutes. . . . there are comparatively few victims of force. . . . the work for the suppression of the traffic in women has in general been directed toward freeing such women from restrictions, toward preventing them being forced to live in licensed houses, and toward punishing the third parties who profit from the trade . . . but the success of the work as carried on at present . . . would potentially result in providing a strong additional inducement to the free movement of prostitutes. . . . [56]

Therein lay the most pressing problem, according to the International Bureau. Feminist involvement in the trafficking movement was leading to fewer restrictions on prostitutes while the International Bureau wanted more.

Feminists were quick to respond. They pointed out, among other things, that any special measures to prevent the entry of women in prostitution as such were not necessary and that they would result in hampering the free movement abroad of women in general or in subjecting them to special inquiries into their moral character. Feminists warned that repatriation would give police a free field to abuse, exploit, and blackmail women. They could threaten immigrant women—prostitutes or not—with deportation or force them to register as prostitutes in regulated systems, and they would be open to corruption and bribery to allow immigrant women into brothels. The proposal would also give *souteneurs* (pimps) an additional means of exploiting immigrant women, because they could threaten to denounce them to police, and they could then more easily coerce women working in entertainment to move into prostitution. Feminists pointed out the discriminatory aspects of the proposal, arguing that punishing women who returned to a country after repatriation meant that there was a special penalty for prostitutes as such. They also criticized the assumption that prostitution was an offense committed by women and women posed a threat to society.[57]

The British Committee of the International Abolitionist Federation summarized feminists' objections to the proposal:

> We are opposed to the *whole principle* of these proposals because they are solely concerned with "prostitutes" as such, and therefore constitute "measures of

exception" applied to certain women on account of their morals. These en-
actments against "prostitutes" confuse the public conscience in regard to responsibility for prostitution and the traffic in women. The people responsible
for traffic in women are the men who are willing to pay money for the hire of
women, the procurers and brothel-keepers who sell women, and the Regulationist Governments who provide facilities in licensed houses for the sale of
women and who also, by licensing and registering "prostitutes" label women as
legitimate "articles of commerce."[58]

As they had in the past, they now attempted to shift the focus onto traffickers,
pimps, and procurers as the main agents in prostitution, so as to move blame
away from the women involved in prostitution.

Furthermore, they argued, the proposal entrenched a sexual double standard rather than challenging it, a point that feminists often raised:

It [the repatriation proposal] said that it holds the State entitled to say that adult
women shall "behave themselves" or be punished as "any other class of citizen
would be punished for failure to behave." Yet nowhere in its proposals did it suggest that adult *men* should "behave themselves." The Bureau says "it in no way
condones prostitution by women," but it says no word of censure or reprobation
concerning the men who are women's partners in acts of prostitution. . . . In fact,
it is fair to say that all through these proposals of the International Bureau the
theory is implicit **that prostitution is an offence in women only**, and that it is
only **against women** that society needs protection in regard to prostitution.[59]

Deportation of immigrant women in prostitution was not a humane action,
they insisted: "In any case, expulsion is rarely an act of kindness to the person expelled, and unless proper assistance were given, many of these foreign
women would suffer great injustice and hardship if turned out."[60]

Feminists went directly to League of Nations officials. They privately suggested to the head of the League of Nations Social Questions Section, Dame
Rachel Crowdy, who was also staff person to the Traffic in Women and Children Committee, that in practice certain countries, such as France, would not
deport foreign women in prostitution and that no country wanted to see its
women nationals as prostitutes. The British branch of the International Abolitionist Federation put out a pamphlet in French, German, and English warning
about the proposal.[61] In it they outlined their objections and called instead for
voluntary repatriation, already agreed to under the 1904 trafficking agreement,

and they appealed to national and international organizations to send reso-lutions to the League of Nations. The League received at least forty letters in response, including from Austrian, Danish, Greek, Hungarian, and Portuguese women's groups; the International Women's Suffrage Alliance; the Women's International League; a variety of associations in Great Britain, including the Fabian Society and the National Union of Teachers; and the International Abo-litionist Federation.[62] In the end, these actions, along with divided state interest in the issue of repatriation, quelled the International Bureau's attempts to put the issue forward at the League of Nations.

Dynamics and Consequences of International Anti-Trafficking Work

Feminist abolitionists had some successes at the League of Nations in the interwar period. They helped to stop the compulsory repatriation proposal, even though they had less luck with the prohibition of foreign women in state-regulated brothels. They pressed for the expansion of anti-trafficking conventions to address boys as well as girls, and to cover internal as well as international trafficking. They also succeeded in calling into question the state regulation of prostitution with the backing of the League of Nations expert reports that had confirmed an association between regulated systems and traf-ficking patterns. At the same time, state officials were increasingly concerned with the movement of women and the control of prostitution, and their efforts were moving toward the nationalization of prostitution in order to defend the state's ability to control it.

These tensions were still playing out in the late interwar period when anti-trafficking efforts were interrupted by World War II. Trafficking and regu-lation were set aside as reformers in both the International Bureau and the International Abolitionist Federation worked to document the sexual abuses of women during the war. The International Bureau polled its national com-mittees to gather information about the types and extent of the atrocities, and compiled a digest of the replies.[63] After the war, the United Nations took over the League of Nations' anti-trafficking work, but interest had waned. When it surveyed member countries about trafficking, the response rate was low and the results led staff to the conclusion that trafficking had ended because women in prostitution in most countries were nationals.[64]

Trafficking was no longer an important issue in the international arena. With the understanding that war had nationalized prostitution around the world, prostitutes were considered to be free of foreign threat. As a 1959 United Nations report stated, "there is reason to believe that in many countries today the prostitute is a freer person, less regimented and in general less subject to coercion. . . . the trend appears to be towards a freer prostitute whose relationship with those living on her earning is more or less voluntary."[65] Foreign women, their mobility, and their sexual relations across ethnic and national boundaries were no longer a major concern, but domestic women in prostitution became the next focus. New psychological discourses began to emphasize the deviance of women in prostitution and the need to rehabilitate and "re-educate" prostitutes.[66] For example, a 1959 United Nations research report explained:

> Current research studies into prostitution . . . indicate also that prostitutes have generally slight mental and psychical abnormalities (instability, abnormal lack of emotion, excitability, pronounced nervousness) and that a great number of them suffer from a psycho-sexual immaturity, very often due to arrested development caused by early childhood frustrations. The number of prostitutes who are mentally, psychologically and emotionally normal appears to be very limited.[67]

Although this United Nations report and others sought to emphasize the psychological differences between prostitutes and other women to show that they were not "choosing their calling in all moral and psychic freedom," it had the effect of setting prostitutes apart as a group.

It also reflected an overt concern with the social control of women and girls. Alarmingly, the definition of prostitution expanded at this stage to include "promiscuous" women. Sexually active young women as well as adult women were thought to be "prostitutes" in the making. Because promiscuity was thought to lead to prostitution, the United Nations suggested that facilities were needed to examine promiscuous persons, juveniles as well as adults, to determine "whether a better control of their tendency towards promiscuity could be attainable by means of psychiatric treatment."[68] Welfare and psychiatric centers in the United States were cited as model examples. Early "detection and treatment of promiscuous propensities and mental deficiencies" were recommended, especially for juveniles.

The assumed causes of prostitution had changed from explanations involving the sexual double standard, poverty, women's low status within countries, and the institutionalization of paid sexual labor by the state to the women's own failing. Although many newly independent countries and those hit hard by the war continued to emphasize poverty and economic conditions as important causes of prostitution after World War II, as did many feminists, others suggested a variety of individual psychological, emotional, and moral flaws. Swedish officials blamed overindulgence in alcohol, broken homes, and the desire for luxury and pleasure.[69] Spanish officials attributed prostitution to "the craving for luxuries, the desire to earn easy money."[70] Officials in Burma, India, Indonesia, and the Philippines blamed strong sexual inclinations, love of luxuries, heredity and sexual maladjustment, and nymphomania and psychological insecurity, respectively.[71]

The United Nations did manage to pass one more anti-trafficking convention based on a 1937 draft from the League of Nations after joint action from the International Bureau and the International Abolitionist Federation. The International Bureau had finally yielded on the issue of regulation, after the affirmation of the connection between trafficking and regulation in the 1927 League of Nations expert report and the Bureau's failure to achieve success on the repatriation proposal. The nationalization of prostitution and the dropoff in trafficking had also made the issue less of a concern to International Bureau reformers than it had been previously. By the mid-1930s the Bureau began to use some abolitionist language, and Dame Rachel Crowdy, the former staff person for the Traffic in Women and Children Committee, became active with the Bureau when she left the League of Nations.

Some coordinated action was then possible. As an internal letter from the British branch of the International Abolitionist Federation to its headquarters in January 1944 optimistically explained:

> It is very gratifying to know that the International Bureau now fully accepts the principle that State Regulation and the tolerated houses are the main causes of the traffic in women, and the necessity to abolish Regulation is recognised without qualification. At long last, therefore, the International Bureau and the International Abolitionist Federation will fight the traffic in women on exactly the same terms.[72]

The collaboration proved short-lived. When the United Nations wanted to give the two organizations joint nongovernmental organization status, the British branch of the International Abolitionist Federation objected: "although their relations are very cordial and they work together to a certain extent, the Bureau deals only with the Traffic, while the International Abolitionist Federation is concerned with prostitution in all aspects, and ought to be consulted on several points which the Bureau does not touch."[73] For its part, the International Bureau began to accuse the International Abolitionist Federation of being too "legal" and too "polemical" in its approach to prostitution. The Federation argued that the Bureau took a more "modern approach" to prostitution, studying it psychologically and sociologically, and focusing on the "practical work of our social problems."[74]

Still, the two organizations jointly drafted a successful petition signed by thirty-seven nongovernmental organizations that urged the United Nations to proceed with the 1937 Draft Convention. Eventually, in 1949, the United Nations drafted a new convention and it went into force in 1951. The convention made all procurement, with or without consent and within or between countries, punishable, rendering it incompatible with state-regulation of prostitution. It also included a colonial clause that required states to enforce the convention in all dependent territories. This provision raised objections by France and even Great Britain, which had previously applied anti-trafficking accords to most but not all of its colonies. British delegates also objected to language that moved the convention toward the criminalization of prostitution itself, and thereby of anyone who participated in it.[75] The convention was passed, but neither France nor Great Britain signed it, nor did the Netherlands, Italy, or many of the earlier players in the anti-trafficking movement. The prediction of the International Bureau's founder, William Alexander Coote, was affirmed: the incorporation of abolitionist language and the insistence that the convention explicitly address the way states could organize prostitution in their territories eroded governmental support.

Summary

This chapter has shown how, at the League of Nations, national interests outweighed humanitarian concerns about the sexual exploitation of women. When it came to "their own" women at home or abroad, many officials worried about foreign men and the possibilities of sexual relations across racial and ethnic lines, leading to tensions between countries and the wish to control women involved in prostitution. Officials split according to whether they wanted to maintain foreign women in prostitution in domestic and colonial areas or whether they saw such women as threats to national and imperial order. This divide led to vigorous debates in the League about whether to prohibit foreign women from registering in state-regulated brothels, and whether and how to repatriate foreign women in prostitution.

Although feminists and their supporters at the League of Nations worked simultaneously to challenge state-regulated prostitution and to affirm the rights of women to migrate as they wished, their efforts met with only limited success. Increasingly, states began to target women in prostitution as the problem, rather than trafficking or the exploitation of women by others. Ultimately, the masculinity of nation and empire was not challenged, and nearly all state officials agreed on the continued need for women's sexual labor and the right to control it domestically.

The desire to continue domestic control of prostitution may have even been the reason that Dame Rachel Crowdy's contract with the League was cancelled at the end of the 1920s, after she had been warned several times from 1924 to 1927 not to let programs and policies encroach on national concerns.[76] The League sought policies of international cooperation, but in the matters of trafficking and prostitution, as with its other humanitarian efforts, the League relied on the cooperation of its member states.

What effect did these anti-trafficking efforts have? They did, as sociologists and political scientists who study international politics often suggest, create an agreed-upon set of principles for states to follow in dealing with trafficking, and as Table 1.1 shows, more than twenty-five countries signed the first three international accords. This kind of normative framework, promoted by international nongovernmental organizations, can influence state policies and practices, at times even leading officials to go against what they perceive to be the best interests of the state as they concede and eventually implement international standards.[77]

Whether this happened in the case of the international anti-trafficking movement is certainly debatable, because there was never universal agreement about the definition of trafficking or the humanitarian aspects of the conventions, and each successive accord renewed the battle lines. International feminists do seem to have swayed the British government, and this was perhaps one factor leading the delegates from Great Britain to press repeatedly for abolitionist measures against the French and other regulationist delegates. Great Britain did abolish regulation in metropolitan and colonial areas, though they were slower to do the latter, and they clearly had some impact on the language of draft conventions at the League of Nations. Yet regulationist governments generally continued as before, with some small concessions, such as the prohibition of foreign women in state-regulated brothels, which actually went against the intent of feminist abolitionists. They also increased state capacities to deal with trafficking, through the establishment of central authorities that were often under the minister of the interior, but with no guarantee that women themselves would not be targeted for state control.

Adhering to the international accords did not typically result in substantial changes to state practices, although many countries did adopt national laws dealing with trafficking and prostitution, and they also began to monitor employment recruitment and emigration processes more closely. In reinforcing the need to protect young, innocent girls involuntarily involved in prostitution, the international accords actually left open the possibility for states to control the bodies and movements of women and girls within their territories. Did this occur?

To assess the adoption and implementation of the anti-trafficking accords, we need to take a closer look at the way anti-trafficking efforts played out in local settings. As we will see, similar battles between feminists affiliated with the International Abolitionist Federation and more purity-oriented International Bureau reformers occurred at the local level just as they had in the international arena, and each group struggled to direct the scope and direction of anti-trafficking work. Analyzing the organization of prostitution, the trajectories of the anti-trafficking movements, and the responses of state officials in each case will show us how gender, race, ethnicity, class, and nationality played out in the politics of anti-trafficking work in the Netherlands, France, and Italy.

5 International Abolitionist Federation Reformers and the Dutch Movement

THE MOVEMENT OF DUTCH WOMEN FOR PROSTITUTION was not a particularly salient issue for officials in the Netherlands compared to other countries of the time. It was an emigration country in the late nineteenth century, though small compared to other European countries such as Italy. Dutch emigrants went to neighboring European countries, such as Germany, and then moved increasingly to the United States and later to the Dutch East Indies, South America, and South Africa after 1895.[1] Single Dutch women were a growing proportion of this migration, which peaked in the first two decades of the twentieth century, and they, like single men, went increasingly to colonial areas.[2] Despite this growth in the numbers of Dutch women emigrants, they were rarely noted as being involved in migratory prostitution. Neither international voluntary associations nor state officials at the League of Nations found a pattern of Dutch women in prostitution abroad or in neighboring countries.

The Netherlands was mainly a transit, and to some extent a destination, country for prostitution. Rotterdam was especially notorious as a transit point. German women were said to be trafficked through the Netherlands to other destinations and to the Netherlands through Poland.[3] The League's 1927 trafficking report also noted the interwar presence of Belgian and German women in prostitution, especially in Rotterdam and the Hague.[4] The latter, Dutch officials claimed, caused problems with Dutch women in prostitution who then alerted authorities to their presence.[5]

As it had been in so many other imperial countries of the time, women's sexual labor had long been a concern of Dutch state officials in metropolitan and colonial areas and they sought to organize it in various ways. The Indies also had a long history of concubinage, including arrangements that involved servants who provided sexual service to and had children with European men.[6] Alongside such arrangements was the growth and regulation of prostitution in the Dutch East Indies (now Indonesia) from the mid-1800s through 1913. Regulation was introduced in the Dutch East Indies in 1852, and in the metropole it had been established in thirty-eight towns by 1877.

Historical anthropologist Ann Stoler argues that concubinage increasingly came under attack from the turn of the twentieth century through the 1920s because it "disturbed the racial sensibilities of the Dutch-born elite" and upset the hierarchical racial boundaries of empire; but prostitution too was increasingly frowned upon after having been previously tolerated and regulated.[7] Prostitution was thought to be a necessary outlet for men in Dutch metropolitan and colonial areas, and it was regulated for more than fifty years before authorities adopted abolition and worked to address the trafficking of all women in the Dutch East Indies, including Chinese and Japanese women. Racial, ethnic, and imperial concerns certainly played a part in the Dutch efforts to reduce trafficking and prostitution, but they were not the only factors contributing to the government's actions, nor were the issues of concern to Europeans only. Dutch authorities responded both to reformers, including women and men affiliated with the International Abolitionist Federation and the International Bureau and to members of the Chinese and Javanese communities in the colony.

Anti-Trafficking and Prostitution Efforts in the Dutch Metropole

It was International Abolitionist Federation reformers who first organized on the issue of prostitution in the Netherlands, in 1875.[8] Josephine Butler was in contact with Protestant reformers in the Dutch Réveil movement who were increasingly concerned about the spread of regulation in Dutch towns from 1852–1877 after a state committee recommended municipal ordinances.[9] These reformers, led mainly by the Reverend Hendrik Pierson, ran asylums for women in prostitution and published translations of Butler's writings.[10]

In 1877 Pierson attended the first International Abolitionist Federation congress in Geneva, where Butler met with and recruited him personally despite his initial concerns about socialist feminists at the congress and about the secular humanitarian approach of the international voluntary association.[11] During the congress, the Dutch branch of the International Association of Friends of Girls (*Union internationale des amies de la jeune fille*) was founded. The association was a travelers' aid society founded in Switzerland and affiliated with the

International Abolitionist Federation.[12] The following year Pierson traveled to various Dutch towns, recruiting men who agreed with International Abolitionist Federation goals and founding the Dutch men's branch of the association. His wife, meanwhile, helped to form the Dutch Association for the Protection of Young Girls, which, in addition to providing aid to travelers, established rescue homes and employment agencies, and disseminated literature aimed at educating girls and their parents about potential dangers in travel.[13]

Josephine Butler's influence had helped to move the male reformers toward a more liberal approach, and she had even persuaded Pierson to collaborate briefly with Ferdinand Domela Nieuwenhuis, a libertarian socialist leader concerned about the traffic, but it did not sway the men to open the committee to women.[14] Butler preferred that they would, but Pierson believed that women should attend to rescue work and men to political work.[15] Knowing that an integrated committee was not possible, during her visit in 1883 to an International Abolitionist Federation congress Butler expressed her desire for a women's organization. Dutch women responded enthusiastically, giving the movement momentum. Anna van Hogendorp and Marianne Klerck-van Hogendorp, two sisters connected with Protestant reformers who had been introduced to Butler by Pierson, quickly held meetings in the spring of 1884 and organized the Dutch Women's Union for the Promotion of Moral Consciousness (*Nederlandsche Vrouwenbond tot Verhooging van het Zedelijk Bewustzijn*).[16]

The Dutch Women's Union was an agglomeration of aristocratic women, middle-class workers in rescue homes, wives of local reverends, correspondents in the East Indies, teachers, and workers for the protection of girls, and it did include politically conservative women.[17] Over time it helped to transform the existing women's movement in the Netherlands into one with explicit feminist goals, including an equal moral standard for both men and women.[18] The president of the Dutch Women's Union, Marianne Klerck-van Hogendorp, became a member of the executive committee of the International Abolitionist Federation and visited London for their meetings.[19]

Members also became involved in other feminist issues in the Netherlands, bringing with them the International Abolitionist Federation's resistance to special legislation targeting women. For example, Anna van Hogendorp went on to help form other committees to oppose employment protection measures for women workers in the Netherlands.[20] The van Hogendorp sisters moved increasingly toward a women's rights perspective and went on to become founding members of the Dutch Association for Women's Suffrage.[21] Marianne also became the first president of the Dutch National Council of Women.[22] Dutch women, like English women, were well organized in pressing for rights. They managed to gain suffrage in 1919, earlier than women in many other European countries such as France and Italy, where women would have to wait another quarter-century.

In 1885, the Dutch Women's Union sent the first petition to the Dutch government asking for the abolition of trade in girls and women. It was signed by fifteen thousand people.[23] The Netherlands then ratified treaties with Belgium, Austria-Hungary, and Germany to collaborate on trafficking cases, precursors, and possible templates for the first international anti-trafficking agreement of 1904.[24] By 1889 there were more than three thousand women in more than 125 cities and towns working toward both abolition of regulation and the prevention of prostitution via traveler's aid to young girls.[25] Nearly a decade later the Dutch Women's Union reported five thousand members and still considered themselves to be an offshoot of the International Abolitionist Federation.[26] The Dutch men's branch of the International Abolitionist Federation also remained active, with Pierson acting as the International Abolitionist Federation's president in 1898.

The abolition movement, in which both male and female reformers were now involved both at the local level and within the International Abolitionist Federation itself, held meetings to recruit doctors, academics, emerging feminist leaders, and even some socialists.[27] The prominent feminist Aletta Jacobs, a leader in the Dutch women's movement, the only female physician in the Netherlands, and soon to be one of the founders of the International Women's Suffrage Alliance, signed on to the abolitionist cause despite her distaste for the religious leanings of the van Hogendorp sisters.[28]

Opposition to the International Abolitionist Federation's framings of prostitution and its stance against regulation was minimal. Pierson did write to Butler that abolitionists sometimes found themselves in "enforced opposition" to some "well-intentioned friends, especially among Christians" who promoted "purer morals" while refusing to address regulation.[29] Once he had rebuked them, he reported, they quieted. By 1900, when William Alexander Coote came to organize an International Bureau committee in the Netherlands, he was forced to form one out of already-existing abolitionist leaders.[30] This situation prevented the potential split, apparent in other countries such as France, between the abolitionist and social purity views of prostitution.

It did not completely quell the conflict, however, which was uniquely gendered in the Netherlands.[31] Dutch women maintained their affiliation with the

International Abolitionist Federation while Dutch men in the movement, never more than two hundred strong, formed an additional separate International Bureau chapter in the Netherlands.[32] Founded in 1900, the National Committee to Combat the Traffic in Women (*Nationaal Comité tot bestrijding van den Handel in Vrouwen*) was part of, but did not follow, the International Bureau's insistence on separating the issues of trafficking and regulation.[33] Headed initially by Pierson and later by the lawyer A. de Graaf, the committee attended International Bureau congresses. It was initially quite autonomous from the state, in comparison to the International Bureau committees in France and Italy, which can be deduced from the lack of governmental titles among the International Bureau committee's members. The name of not a single person listed as a member in 1906 included a title after it.[34] Later, the Dutch government would provide funding to the International Bureau national committee.[35]

With agreement about their agenda, the reformers in the Netherlands targeted regulation and worked on abolition as a component of anti-trafficking work. In late 1902 they began organizing masses of people to support a ban on brothel keeping, holding large protest meetings in fifty municipalities and towns, paving the way for the inclusion of the ban in a set of new morality laws addressing, among other things, homosexuality, abortion, and pornography.[36] They were successful in gaining the abolition of licensed brothels in Amsterdam in 1906, and after working to pass a national law, they succeeded in winning the abolition of all brothels in the Netherlands by 1911.[37] In 1913 the continued registration of individual women in prostitution, which was the only remaining vestige of regulation, was also prohibited.

State officials were also sympathetic to international anti-trafficking efforts, signing both the 1904 and 1910 anti-trafficking accords. In keeping with the 1904 agreement, in 1908 the Dutch created a governmental bureau or "central authority" on the traffic—the Royal Office for the Suppression of the Traffic in Women—with the prefect of police at Amsterdam as its director, working under the supervision of the minister of justice.[38] It regularly provided reports to the League of Nations.

The Dutch International Bureau committee, with de Graaf at the lead, remained active throughout the interwar period. It took part in both International Bureau and International Abolitionist Federation congresses and conferences, and de Graaf even acted as the International Abolitionist Federation's president during this period.[39] Much to the chagrin of regulationists and Coote, de Graaf emerged as a vocal proponent of abolition at International Bureau meetings, and Dutch leaders consistently tied the issue of regulated prostitution to the traffic in women. When the League of Nations held its first congress on the traffic in 1921, for example, it was de Graaf who raised the issue of regulation via a proposal to extend the definition of trafficking to include those who procure women who are of age, even with their consent. When he was countered by the French delegate, who sought to table any discussion that would raise questions about the legitimacy of state regulation, de Graaf complained:

> But now you ask me not to speak of this chief cause [of trafficking, which is regulated prostitution]. This is impossible. It is as though you said: we have a cholera Congress but you must not speak of bacilli. It would be better to have no meeting at all, if we cannot speak of the causes against which we are pretending to fight.[40]

He would prove to be persistent, pressing for abolition as well as for the universal application of the anti-trafficking conventions within the International Bureau and at the League of Nations, despite the fact that the Netherlands was not appointed to the Traffic in Women and Children Committee.[41] The Dutch committee had good relations with its governmental bureau and felt well-represented by the government delegate to the League of Nations.[42]

Dutch state officials took their anti-trafficking work seriously, taking steps to suppress the traffic between Belgium and Holland prior to World War I. They also reported actively repatriating women in the interwar period, for example, 420 women in 1922, 228 in 1924, 114 in 1929, and more than 115 from 1932 to 1933.[43] These were mostly German women, which is in keeping with the general character of immigration to the Netherlands at the time.[44] Most immigrant women in Dutch metropolitan areas were from German areas, though a smaller number were from Belgium, and they often went into domestic service. Perhaps as many as 175,000 women from other countries worked as servants in the Netherlands in the interwar period.[45] Toward the end of the 1920s, German emigration officials and women from the German Societies for the Protection of Girls began supervising the departure of German girls to the Netherlands more closely, and at the end of the 1930s the German Nationalist Socialist government implemented the Action for the Collective Return of German Maids, summoning them back to the "homeland" under threat of losing their citizenship.[46]

The Dutch took unprecedented measures to register and supervise foreigners from 1918 on, passing a law to ensure that any foreigner who entered or left a Dutch municipality registered with the police.[47] Authorities could and did expel women for being "immoral," but at least one historian suggests that Dutch authorities were often more tolerant than that and sided with German immigrant women in disputes, either because the officials needed consent from the Central Aliens Office in the Hague before they could expel women; because they did not want conflicts with diplomatic representatives of the countries concerned; or because of paternalism.[48]

Still, the numbers of women repatriated by the Dutch, as reported to the League of Nations, was much higher than the number or repatriated women in most other countries, including ones with larger populations of immigrant women in prostitution, such as France. Prior to World War I both Dutch reformers and Dutch officials did emphasize voluntary repatriation, in which the state paid for the return trip of women who wished to go back to their country of origin. The state's own reports to the League of Nations in the interwar period, however, show that officials went beyond this policy. Rather than simply repatriating victims of trafficking, state officials also used the accords as justification for deporting women suspected of prostitution, that is, immigrant women "without means of support" and those who were "leading an immoral life."[49]

Anti-Trafficking Efforts in the Dutch Colonies

The Netherlands' colonial empire was smaller than that of France, and its long-standing presence in the Indies had been characterized by a regime of indirect rule and an associationist approach to race and ethnicity that adjusted Dutch colonial policies toward different ethnic groups in order to preserve some aspects of local culture.[50] In the Dutch East Indies this meant that officials needed to attend to several different groups. In addition to indigenous groups, there was a large Chinese population, numbering 1,233,000 by 1931.[51] Chinese migration to many colonial areas had been stimulated when colonial economies turned toward large-scale agriculture and mining, and governmental authorities started building infrastructures. Also by the early 1930s, there were 72,000 Dutchmen working in the Dutch East Indies, including a large percentage of civil servants; almost as many high-ranking civil servants worked in the Indies as in the Netherlands.[52]

As previously mentioned, concubinage was a long-term and accepted practice, though the Dutch did move away from interracial unions in the interwar period as more Dutch women went to the colonies.[53] Between 1900 and 1930, the number of Dutch women in the Indies rose from 4,000 to 26,000, raising the ratio of men to women from 47-to-100 to 88-to-100.[54] Nonetheless, there remained a high rate of intermarriage—as much as 27.5 percent in 1925 and 20 percent in 1940—and scholars have noted tolerant Dutch attitudes about interracial unions.[55] This toleration was gendered, not surprisingly: unions between Dutch men and indigenous women were acceptable, but unions between Dutch women and indigenous men caused the woman to lose her European civil status and acquire the status of her husband. Yet the children of these interracial unions fared better here than those in other empires, such as in India under the British.[56] They were given European civil status and incorporated into the Dutch colonial administration.[57]

Prostitution had increased greatly in the 1800s, especially after the amendment of the Agrarian Laws in 1870, when the colonial economy was opened to private capital.[58] The expansion of plantations in West Java especially, the growth of the sugar industry in East and Central Java and of plantations in Sumatra, and the building of railroads all contributed. Brothel complexes arose by rail stations, for example, in Bandoeng, in Yogyakarta, and in Surabaya. The latter, a port city, naval base and garrison, and railway terminus, was especially noted for prostitution. Regulation systems were put into place first in such areas.

Regulation had been implemented in the Dutch East Indies since the mid-1800s. In 1852, a central law required regulation in the colonies, and the system was applied in Java in 1857 and throughout the rest of the territory thereafter.[59] Two decades after the central law was passed, it was repealed and replaced with local ordinances that ensured that each residency would establish its own detailed regulations to control prostitution.[60] Surabaya had three brothel *kampong* (hamlets or villages) within which women in prostitution had to operate; Batavia, present-day Jakarta, enacted regulation in 1875, requiring medical officers to visit women in prostitution every Saturday for health checks.[61]

Prostitution was organized along strict racial/ethnic lines in the colony: Chinese women in prostitution serviced only Chinese men, West Sumatran women were not allowed to mix with European men due to strict Islamic codes, and European women in prostitution serviced European men.[62] There was also a subset of Japanese women in prostitution and only they serviced all groups, with some reserved for the use of European men.[63] Japanese at that time had been given a legal status comparable to Europeans as a result of a trade agreement.[64]

Japanese women became prostitutes (*karayuki-san*) by several means: some were kidnapped by traffickers; some went of their own accord, often recruited by returning migrants; and some had parents who agreed to let procurers take them in exchange for a payment. Typically they went first to Hong Kong, Singapore, or Shanghai, and then to the Indies. They reportedly had a brisk business in the Dutch East Indies. In 1895, Penang, the Malay Peninsula, Java, and Sumatra, each had two to three hundred Japanese women in prostitution, and there were forty-one Japanese brothel-keepers.[65]

Dutch officials did not distinguish between European and non-European women in prostitution to the same degree that other countries did in that they applied regulation to both groups.[66] *European prostitute* usually meant a Eurasian woman who serviced European men, but there were also some European women in prostitution among them, including Hungarian, French, Australian, and, more rarely, Dutch women.[67] In Surabaya there were two brothels owned by Europeans that employed European women and catered to European men, a situation similar to that in Batavia, Semarang, and the other major cities in the area.[68]

Although Dutch women originally organized to address prostitution in Dutch metropolitan areas, they soon began to address concubinage and prostitution in the Dutch East Indies as well, working to transport their brand of feminist abolitionism to the colony:[69]

> Dutch women asserted that they could help indigenous women just as they had supported fallen women and wayward girls in the Netherlands. Marianne Klerck-van Hogendorp saw her objections to concubinage as a national continuation of her struggle to have state-regulated prostitution abolished.[70]

They founded a section of the International Abolitionist Federation-affiliated Women's Union at the turn of the twentieth century and went on to hold meetings in Batavia. They developed homes for women there and in Bandoeung, as well as in other towns; protested against the *huishoudster* (housekeeper) system, "which inevitably leads to a life in concubinage"; supported homes for the training and education of children left by their Dutch fathers; and monitored stations and harbors, watching girls who were traveling between Europe and the colony.[71] They protested the importation of Japanese women to Java via Singapore.[72] They also continued to fight regulation and were supported by indigenous nationalists on this issue.[73]

Reformers received a positive governmental response to both their abolitionist and their anti-trafficking efforts in the Indies, in part because their timing coincided with the Dutch Ethical Policy of 1900, which had prompted humanitarian reforms there. Instituted after the election of a liberal government, the policy sought to expand educational opportunities for the population as a whole, to provide for improvements in agriculture, and to resettle indigenous groups from overpopulated Java into the outer islands.[74] The policy had important implications for gender in the Dutch East Indies, as historian Susan Blackburn has noted. Dutch authorities promoted girls' schooling and worked to protect women; they also had concerns about the upbringing of mixed-race children, and prostitution associated with the army.[75] For officials to have implemented the 1904 anti-trafficking agreement "at home" but not in the Dutch East Indies would have been inconsistent in this context. Thus, when government officials set up a central authority in the metropole, they also named the Offices of Justice in Batavia as the central authority on trafficking for the Dutch Indies in 1907.

Reformers also found strong support in Governor General A.W.F. Idenburg, who was appointed to Batavia in 1909, and in Dutch religious organizations in the Indies that cooperated with the International Bureau to press the Dutch government to do something about the trade in Japanese women in the colony.[76] The governor general cited the need to apply the Dutch abolition law uniformly, with no "special circumstances" in the colonies.[77] As early as 1910, routine medical examinations were suspended through his resolution.[78] Concurrently, when the Dutch abolished regulation in the metropole in 1911 through 1913, they also abolished it in the colonies, and they did so against the wishes of colonial military authorities, who wanted regulated prostitution to be maintained.[79] The centralized Dutch morality laws introduced in the Netherlands in 1913 swept away local regulations enacted in 1874, and brothels in the Dutch East Indies were prohibited as of September of that year.[80] The 1913 abolition law led many Chinese and Japanese brothel keepers and women in prostitution to leave for the Straits Settlements, where regulation continued.[81]

There had been resistance from some state officials. When they began to raise the issue of trafficking and abolition in the Indies, the Dutch International Bureau committee reported being told by "experts," whom they did not name:

> But there is no traffic in women in the Indies, none at all; these are illusions, utopias, Western ideas, because the oriental woman has no such ideas; prostitution does her no harm whatever, and later she marries. It is a well-recognised form of earning money, and women do so of their own free will. Do not begin any work in the Indies for it is very, very dangerous to do so.[82]

Nevertheless, when the committee began receiving information about a traffic in Japanese girls to the Dutch East Indies, they publicly reported this allegation at the 1912 International Bureau congress in Brussels. The public admission that the Dutch government had failed to take action on the traffic embarrassed state officials. De Graaf, head of the Dutch International Bureau committee, was subsequently reprimanded by the Dutch minister of justice, who reportedly admonished him, "You have gone too far. What did you say at Brussels? You had no right to speak ill of your country." De Graaf persuaded the minister to take steps against the problem so that he could go to the 1913 International Bureau congress in London the following year and report that the Dutch were doing all they could to combat trafficking in the Indies. The appeal worked.[83] The governmental bureau (that is, central authority) designated at Batavia to combat the traffic allowed de Graaf to report this achievement, as promised, to the International Bureau congress participants at Caxton Hall.

The central authority in the Indies, which in 1915 was under the division of the Department of Justice's Agency for Discipline, Education, and Poverty Relief, collaborated with a variety of other government departments, private associations, and foreign authorities.[84] Its inspectors maintained personal contact with heads of local and regional governments, with the local immigration commissions, with the orphans' court, and with organizations and individuals concerned with protecting women and children. It also subsidized homes for women and girls, kept records of individuals involved in the traffic and keepers of clandestine brothels, worked with police authorities, received descriptions of women in prostitution and of traffickers entering the colony from the immigration commissions at twenty-five recognized ports of entry, and passed on descriptions of suspected persons to seventy foreign authorities, including especially the Singapore Protector of Chinese and the Hong Kong superintendent of police. It also closed brothels when they reappeared.[85]

F.M.G. Van Walsem, the inspector of the central authority, was a tireless anti-trafficking fighter.[86] He confirmed a traffic in Japanese children that had created tension at the League of Nations, and the Dutch government subsequently repatriated the victims at its own expense.[87] He also attended to the traffic in Chinese women, personally collaborating with the Protector of Chinese in Singapore to prevent the movement of women from there. The secretaries for Chinese affairs and the assistant protectors of Chinese in Singapore and Penang often requested the help of the Dutch consul general to return girls to their families after they had been brought to Sumatran brothels, and the consul general almost always cooperated.[88] The Dutch Indies government also warned those in the villages about trafficking scams, such as those involving Indonesian women taken to China as concubines of Chinese men, and parents entrusting children to go to Mecca with persons who would actually sell them to a third party.[89]

Officials with the central authority were also concerned to prevent European entertainers from falling into prostitution. As the League of Nations reported in their study of the Far East, women from the Netherlands, Germany, Austria, and Switzerland went to the Indies in the belief that they could make a great deal of money there, especially in light of the difficult economic conditions in Europe in the late interwar period.[90] Officials required every performer to pay an up-front landing fee, and if the performer's troupe was not trustworthy, they required a deposit to cover the cost of a return fare, requested that troupe leaders deliver itineraries and the contracts of female troupe members to the central authority, and denied entry to troupes with too many under-age performers.[91] This problem was affecting not only European women. In 1922, the Dutch reported forty cases of trafficking in the colonies in which *wayang* theatrical troupes gave performances in the Indies as a pretext for moving Chinese women in prostitution by using false immigration papers and smuggling them in the cargoes of Chinese vessels.[92]

Efforts to combat trafficking and assist women in prostitution were not limited to state officials and those associated with the International Abolitionist Federation. Many reformers, feminists as well as others, provided assistance. The Salvation Army ran homes for girls at Batavia and Semarang for Chinese and indigenous girls; the Young Women's Christian Association maintained hostels for young girls at Weltevreden, Bandoeng, and Jakarta; and the Indo-European Union Women's Organization (*Indo-Europeesch-Verbond Vrouwen Organisatie*), founded in 1931, also had homes for women and girls in danger of prostitution.[93] The Women's League of Peace at Batavia and the International Union of the Friends of Girls (*Union internationale des amies de la jeune fille*) at Batavia were also involved.[94]

Many of the associations involved local and indigenous groups. The Noble Progress Association (*Madjoe-Kamoelian*), founded in Bandoeng in 1914, had European, Chinese, Arab, Indian and native supporters.[95] The Chinese Pure Heart Association (*Ati Soetji*) in Java, modeled on the Chinese Po Leung Kuk Society, aimed at preventing Chinese women and girls from falling into or continuing in prostitution. Founded in 1914 and subsidized by the government, the association ran a home for Chinese girls in Batavia and married out the girls to "men of their own country."[96] Indonesian leaders formed the Association Against the Traffic in Women and Children (*Perempuan dan Anak-anak Perkumpulan*

Pembasmian Perdagangan) in 1930 with participation from the Indonesia Nationalist Party, which saw lax morality as an import from the West. Nationalist parties in the Dutch East Indies, especially Sarekat Islam, were strongly involved in anti-trafficking and prostitution work.[97]

Indonesian women's organizations had developed too late to push for abolition, but they did press the Dutch to follow through on their anti-trafficking measures in the Dutch East Indies. After some early limited efforts, they came together in 1928 to form a unified women's movement, which comprised upper-class Javanese women primarily.[98] They addressed marriage reforms pertaining to polygamy, child marriage, and divorce laws, although these issues brought divisions between secular and religious women's groups.[99] For example, at a 1928 women's congress, conservative women tied the issue of polygamy to prostitution, defending polygamy as preventative, because women could marry instead of become prostitutes.[100] Conversely, radical women, a much smaller component of the women's movement, tied early child marriage to prostitution, suggesting that widowed and divorced girls constituted a large portion of the Indonesian women in prostitution.[101] Like Indonesian nationalists, some women's groups also condemned the practice of concubinage involving Indonesian women and Chinese and European men. In the late interwar period, they asked the colonial government to prohibit concubinage; these women also took part in anti-trafficking efforts.

The central authority had a difficult time overseeing the proliferation of organizations dealing with trafficking and prostitution, although its representatives did attend meetings.[102] Staff also met regularly with the Dutch International Bureau committee. The Netherlands was so active on trafficking and prostitution that it was Dutch reformers who went on to criticize other countries for not addressing these issues in their colonies quickly enough.[103] At the 1921 League of Nations conference, for example, the Dutch delegate called for a universal standard in dealing with the traffic:

> The profession of traffic in women, in whatever country it is practiced, has a definitely parasitic character; this is why the different moral ideas which are peculiar to the colonies must not be taken into account when there is a question of settling the penalty to be inflicted on traffickers. If there is any consideration which determines the penalty to be inflicted, that element must be the same for the East as for the West. He whose task it is to educate people must always draw his inspiration from measures which have succeeded elsewhere, which are not based

on customs which are local or only fitted for Europe, but which are inspired by ideas which belong to the whole human race, and based at the same time on general social conditions. This view is not universally held. . . . It is not only a question of a definitely national interest. It is a question of protecting women in general, whatever be their nationality and whatever be their colour.[104]

The Dutch followed through on this rhetoric. They applied anti-trafficking measures to both European and Japanese women, the Dutch East Indies, and to Japanese brothel keepers.[105] The Japanese Consulate and Dutch authorities together controlled the entry and re-entry of Japanese women in prostitution, so the supply dwindled.[106]

Later, the alleged resurgence in the traffic in Japanese women did cause some difficulty between the Dutch and Japanese delegates at the League of Nations in 1929. The Dutch International Bureau committee strongly denied that there was a traffic in Japanese women, but it did admit that the traffic in Chinese women had been difficult to suppress.[107] It had often repatriated Chinese women, especially in the early interwar years.[108] In 1922, the Dutch reported to the League of Nations that they had repatriated more than fifty Chinese women.[109] Two years later, the Government Office for the Suppression of the Traffic in Women and Girls in Batavia for the Netherlands East Indies reported:

> More than 200 cases of Chinese women imported into the Dutch Indies in order to be handed over to the keepers of clandestine brothels were brought to the notice of the Government Bureau. These women were found in secret brothels during police raids; 75 of them who possessed no legitimate immigration permits were sent back to their country. The remainder possessed a valid entry-card or residence permit or were married to Chinese living in the Netherlands Indies. . . . [110]

The same report states that twenty-three cases of "independent Chinese prostitutes" found without legitimate means of support were expelled from the colony and sent back to China; and that more than eighty independent Chinese women in prostitution attempting to enter the Dutch East Indies were repatriated. Officials saw these women as victims of trafficking as well, reasoning that they had been bought in China when they were very young and remained for some years under the power of their buyer, until they had obtained their freedom and continued to practice prostitution.

The Netherlands was generally considered, by both Dutch officials and the

League of Nations, a success in combating trafficking. When the League extended its special inquiry on trafficking to the Far East in the early 1930s, it concluded that the "traffic in women and children, both outgoing, concerning Malay victims, and incoming, concerning Chinese and European victims, is in the Dutch East Indies reduced to an almost negligible degree."[111] It is perhaps for this reason that when the League of Nations held a follow-up conference on its report on trafficking in the Far East in 1937, it met at Bandoeng. At the conference the League declared itself in favor of abolition.[112]

The anti-trafficking movement in the Netherlands was by all accounts a success, but it nonetheless contained some repressive elements that were only exacerbated as racial concerns became more dominant in the interwar period. As happened in other countries, the implementation of anti-trafficking measures still targeted women and sought to ensure their proper place within nation and empire. In addition to deporting migrant women in prostitution from the metropole and refusing women suspected of being prostitutes entry into Dutch territories, including the Indies, authorities placed Chinese women of dubious morality under surveillance:

> When a case is doubtful, the woman may be allowed in for a certain period, and then we are informed by the Immigration Office that a woman who is suspected has come in, and we give instruction to the police or the domestic administration to keep observation. After a certain period we get a report concerning the kind of life she is living. If the information is not favourable, the paper of admission is not given, or, if it has already been given, it is not prolonged.[113]

They made an exception for minors in prostitution, placing them under supervision of the central authority in the home for Chinese girls at Batavia.

Anticolonial tensions were also thrown into the mix. The effort to bring married Dutch women to the colonies began in the interwar period, to safeguard public morality and suppress anticolonial upheaval, according to its advocates. The International Bureau joined in, arguing that "it is the married women who will civilise our colonies."[114] They saw unmarried Dutch men as the root of the problem and Dutch women as the means of fixing it:

> Either when he lives with his concubine and casts her off when he returns to Europe—depriving the mother of her own children or driving them to the "kampong" and producing thus the problem of the half-caste with all its fruits of bolshevism and anarchy—or when he gives himself to prostitution and by

that means promotes the traffic in women and children, always he exasperates the native population.[115]

As Dutch women went to the colonies to live with their husbands, supporters of Dutch settlement hoped that trafficking, concubinage, and prostitution would die out, and with it the specter of anticolonial nationalism. Plantation workers were of particular concern as the Governmental Bureau of Labour made efforts to increase the number of married workers and the facilities for them to have their families with them on the plantations.[116]

New Dutch settlers exacerbated the tension. Historian Frances Gouda notes that "toward the late 1920s Dutch political rhetoric and action were modulated less and less by humanitarian scruples," especially among increasingly vocal groups of Dutch colonial residents who belonged to the reactionary *Vaderlandsche* (patriotic) club.[117] The new temporary Dutch immigrants to the colonies (known as *trekkers*) brought with them racist views of indigenous groups and withdrew into their own community, displacing the established community of permanent settlers who had adapted to the local culture (*blijvers*). For their part, indigenous organizations, which had always mixed anti-trafficking and prostitution concerns with nationalist ones, increasingly denounced the degradation of women brought about by colonialism and capitalism.[118]

Summary

The Dutch movement was able to gain some ground in its calls for the uniform application of anti-trafficking measures and abolition in the colonies. State officials enacted these measures and promoted them in international circles as part of liberal government reform. Racism was both curbed and institutionalized during the ethical period in colonial politics as the Dutch pursued their own "civilizing mission" in the East Indies.[119]

Influenced by the International Abolitionist Federation, the local movement was relatively autonomous from the state and free to espouse abolitionist views. Dutch Protestant groups were helpful in this case—even the conservative Réveil reformers, who moved from an initial reluctance to organize politically to collaboration with liberals and socialists.[120] Dutch Protestantism was also relatively autonomous from the state.[121] This allowed space for the growth of a local movement with an abolitionist slant.

The International Abolitionist Federation's positive reception in the Dutch case was further strengthened by the small role that regulated prostitution played in the Dutch empire. Prostitution was not perceived by state officials to be vital to state- or nation-building. The Dutch state, liberal and democratic, was already established and its colonial empire was already circumscribed. The state did take on a more active role in colonial areas as part of their *mise en valeur* at the turn of the twentieth century, but the Dutch were not then engaged in expansionism, nor were they involved in the reordering of territorial boundaries in the aftermath of World War I.[122] As a result, there was less concern with officially organizing and controlling prostitutes in the Netherlands compared to France or Italy during the same period.

In addition, important pressure from Indonesian nationalists helped to convince the Dutch to address interracial sexuality in the form of concubinage and prostitution. Indonesian nationalism was launched after 1900, and nationalist groups strongly opposed concubinage that involved Chinese men as well as Europeans, and they fought against prostitution. Indonesian women's organizations tended to follow their lead. Dutch officials may therefore have been concerned to apply anti-trafficking measures in an attempt to contain anticolonial tensions and defuse racial conflicts between Javanese and Chinese groups in the Dutch East Indies. Officials were also able to use the Netherlands' anti-trafficking record to defend its imperial regimes as more moral and, presumably in their perspective, more justifiable than others'.[123]

Influenced by feminists and reformers on the ground in the Dutch East Indies, and less concerned than other state officials about the control of regulated prostitution for empire, the Dutch government abolished regulation and implemented anti-trafficking measures universally. It did so early, prior to the increased ethnonationalism of the interwar period. Like other countries in the interwar period, however, Dutch officials also began to concern themselves with the movement of migrant women suspected of prostitution, not only to protect them from being exploited within Dutch territories, but also out of concern to maintain morality and bolster the image of the Dutch state internationally and in the Dutch East Indies. State officials not only paid for the voluntary repatriation of women, but also deported women suspected of being prostitutes and denied others entry into Dutch territories. Feminist involvement had tempered these tendencies prior to World War I, but even at this point anti-trafficking efforts balanced on a fine line between the protection of women and the control of their mobility and sexual activity.

6 International Bureau Reformers and the French Movement

FRANCE WAS BOTH A SUPPLY AND DESTINATION COUNTRY in the international traffic in women. French emigration was small compared to that of countries such as Italy, but French emigrants did go overseas and to the colonies, and women were an increasing proportion of these migrants in the interwar period.[1] About one-fifth of French emigrants went to French colonies from 1850 to 1925, and many also went to Belgium, Switzerland, Spain, and other European countries.[2]

One component of this migration involved women in prostitution, which the 1927 League of Nations trafficking report confirmed. French prostitutes were found overseas, in South America, North America, and the colonies, although state officials disputed this in international forums, claiming that French-speaking women in prostitution were passing for nationals; but researchers for the League of Nations report defended their findings.[3] France also supplied European markets, especially the brothels of Belgium, Holland, and the Russian Empire. In 1902, for example, the Netherlands had eleven French brothels, four of which imported the women directly from France and sold them again after a few weeks to other brothels. They were sold to brothels outside of Europe as well, especially to those in South America.[4]

As an immigration as well as emigration country, France also had an increasing number of non-French men in the metropole, which contributed to its reputation as a destination country for migrant women in prostitution. The 1870s brought incoming refugees from the Franco-Prussian war and the annexation of Alsace Lorraine by Germany, and workers from neighboring European countries.[5] Over time, Italian, Belgian, Spanish, and Polish labor migrants settled in France, and all intermarried except the Polish, contributing to a permanent immigrant population.[6] With World War I, colonial men also arrived, as soldiers and factory workers. In the colonies, France assimilated Algerian Jews in 1870, and working class Italians, Spanish, and Maltese in Algeria were given French citizenship.

The movement of women for prostitution constituted one small component of these overall migration trends and led to a number of migrant women in prostitution in the metropole. In some areas in the 1880s, such as Marseilles, up to 25 percent of the women in prostitution were from another country, and they included Italian, Spanish, Swiss, and German women as well as women from Austria and Belgium.[7] Recruitment for state regulated brothels was in fact linked to the traffic in women as early as 1902. The records of the Paris police show that, at least at that time, traffickers were individuals involved in regulated prostitution who worked to supply the system, especially brothels.[8] They included brothel owners, madams and their husbands, procurers and solicitors working for a particular brothel, hotel owners, wine merchants, proprietors of employment agencies, and managers of theatrical companies, often French but including Belgian, Russian, and Jewish individuals.[9] Thirty-four Parisian establishments contained women and girls from the Levant (that is, the Middle East, likely Syria and Lebanon), Galicia (a historical region of Central-Eastern Europe now divided between Poland and the Ukraine), South America, Belgium, and Russia, as well as French women and girls from the provinces.[10]

Anti-Trafficking Efforts in the French Metropole

In France, as in the Netherlands, International Abolitionist Federation reformers were among the first to organize. They were invited initially not by religious supporters but by feminist Julie Daubié, the first women in France to receive her baccalaureate; she worked on issues of education, poverty, and paternity. Along with noted French feminist Maria Deraismes, Daubié was involved in organizing against regulation in the 1860s, and as Josephine Butler began her efforts in Great Britain, Daubié translated Butler's works for French audiences. Supported by Butler herself and then led by the French liberal economist Yves Guyot and a small band of Protestants in the predominantly Catholic country, abolitionists in France started off with some optimism but failed to gain momentum. At least one historian has suggested that abolitionists faced an uphill battle in taking on regulation in France because of the lack of a central law, which meant that reformers had to fight separate battles in each municipality, but this was also the case in the Netherlands, where reformers nonetheless found success.[11] It is true, however, that, as the heralded international model for the state regulation of prostitution, which had been implemented under Napoleon in the early 1800s, the French system was long-standing and entrenched.[12]

International Abolitionist Federation reformers certainly worked hard in French metropolitan areas, continually attempting to organize and bolster the movement there; Butler visited three times between 1874 and 1880.[13] During her initial visit, she met with the director of police, M. Lecour, who invited her to visit the notorious prison infirmary Saint-Lazare, which housed sick women who had been involved in prostitution. Several months later she toured it, and was appalled at the terrible conditions. French women had formed an association to assist women and girls released from Saint-Lazare, to help integrate them back into society; it provided clothing, housing, and job training for the women and girls, most of whom were between sixteen and twenty-one years old. It was the women who founded this society who would take part in the original French committee to abolish regulation, the French Association for the Abolition of Regulated Prostitution (*Association français pour l'abolition de la prostitution réglementée*), formed in 1878 with the hope of closing the prison. Many reformers would reaffirm a commitment to abolition over purity reform approaches to prostitution as the movement in France unfolded.[14]

Butler attracted various people during her visits to France: republicans, radicals, socialists, students, workers, Protestant pastors, a Catholic former senator, as well as a few Catholic women.[15] She attracted crowds of from one hundred to two thousand people.[16] Alarmed, the police prevented Butler and French abolitionists from holding some of their meetings, and they sent police to observe and record the activities in others.[17] Undaunted, the abolitionists pressed on. In an attempt to reach out to working women, Butler framed the issue of regulation in class terms, arguing for legitimate and well-paid work for women and pointing out that rich men did not give their daughters up to prostitution. The International Abolitionist Federation even funded a project to form local cooperatives of washerwomen, seamstresses, and hairdressers, among others.[18] Most socialists nonetheless remained aloof from the movement.

Not so republicans, such as Yves Guyot, formerly minister of public works and then a member of the Paris Municipal Council. He worked diligently against the morals police (*police des mœurs*) who were in charge of prostitution, and led a campaign against them in Paris in 1876. Unfortunately this led the Ministry of the Interior to take over jurisdiction of the system in 1884.[19]

The International Abolitionist Federation collected money to pay for the fines Guyot incurred in the process.[20] Guyot also helped to found the French Association for the Abolition of Regulated Prostitution, referred to earlier.[21] The government originally denied authorization for this branch of the International Abolitionist Federation to form, but relented when some prominent members used their influence to obtain approval from authorities in 1879.[22] The chapter soon divided between liberal Guyot and more conservative Protestant reformers, such as Tommy Fallot, who wanted to deal with issues of pornography and public decency.[23] He founded the French League for the Improvement of Public Morality (*Ligue française pour le relevement de la moralite publique*).

The movement did not flourish under these circumstances and it was slowed by other factors as well. In comparison to women's groups in the Netherlands, such groups in France were not involved in the abolitionist movement in large numbers, and French "difference feminism" proved less receptive to the liberal feminist arguments of the international abolitionists.[24] The few feminists involved in the movement were mostly Protestant, and some, such as Maria Deraismes, who became vice president of the French Association for the Abolition of Regulated Prostitution, actually moved away from Guyot and toward Pastor Fallot's organization. Others continued in their charitable work, including many Catholic women. Still others put their efforts into socialism, where they were subordinate to male leadership.[25] There was some support from radical and socialist men, but the latter remained fairly quiet on the topic of prostitution.[26]

The movement was also hampered by conservative male Catholic reformers within France prior to the arrival of William Alexander Coote and the International Bureau, who worked to reform regulation rather than abolish it. Catholic Senator Rene Bérenger, who served from 1876 to 1895, was a regulation supporter who was also active on issues of obscenity. He introduced a bill outlawing public soliciting that was targeted at women in prostitution. Guilty women would be sentenced from six months to one year in prison, and women could be medically examined at the time of arrest and sent for obligatory treatment even prior to any conviction. The measure also sought to prosecute pimps and those who procured women by violence or fraud.[27] Not only would this attempt at "neoregulationism" be supported by the International Bureau, but it would also come to divide women reformers in France, many of whom would go on to work with Bérenger on the League for Public Morality (*La Ligue de la moralite publique*) and on his French International Bureau committee, the Association for the Repression of the White Slave Trade and for the Protection of Young Women (Association pour la répression de la traite des blanches et las préservation de la jeune fille).[28]

Nationalism was often invoked by those who opposed feminist abolitionists in France. They charged that French abolitionists were merely front organizations for the International Abolitionist Federation, and that the English-controlled International Abolitionist Federation did not understand the unique circumstances of France.[29] Regulation supporters variously accused feminists of being irrational, utopian, hysterical, prudish, repressed, too liberal, and too focused on the individual and not enough on national unity. They argued that abolitionism was being spread by a foreign "brigade of British, Swiss, and Belgians, aided by a few French," or it was being propagated by the British possibly to spread venereal disease and win the colonial race.[30] Abolitionism was "born of English prudery, of mystical Protestantism."[31] The International Abolitionist Federation's brand of liberal feminist abolitionism was a danger to the French nation and empire.

In spite of such rhetoric, Butler and the International Abolitionist Federation found their own formidable supporter, French secular feminist and journalist Ghénia Avril de Sainte-Croix, who became involved in 1898 and revitalized French feminist abolitionism. She remained active on the issue until the mid-1930s.[32] Sainte-Croix had gone to London for the 1898 International Abolitionist Federation congress and met Josephine Butler, who became a role model, friend, and mentor.[33] A French branch of the International Abolitionist Federation was reestablished that same year and Sainte-Croix became the secretary-general in 1900. At the same time she founded an association that provided lodging, job training, and health care to young women in hopes of preventing their involvement in prostitution.[34] She would eventually become chair of the International Council of Women's committee on trafficking, and later, vice president of the organization.[35] Many International Abolitionist Federation committee members were also members of the French Council of Women.

Although the International Abolitionist Federation committee gained momentum in France at the turn of the century, finally incorporating women's groups such as the National Council of Women and some socialist support, it was actively challenged by the International Bureau. Coote traveled to France in 1899 and met with Bérenger to form a national committee with the senator as president.[36] Under Coote's direction, the French International Bureau committee focused on the white slave traffic, immoral literature, and alcoholism, detracting from abolitionist members who wanted to target France's system of regulated prostitution and its connection to the traffic.[37] Bérenger purposely included regulationist supporters on the committee and worked both within France and in international circles to defend state regulation. He also worked persistently for the criminalization of those who transmit venereal diseases, arguing the need to move ahead with such legislation lest other European countries do so ahead of France; it was a matter of national pride.[38]

Coote reported that the formation of the International Bureau committee was a "most trying experience" because "those friends of the [International Abolitionist] Federation with whom I had laboured for years did not then see eye to eye with me."[39] Both in the committee and in international settings such as the International Bureau meetings held in 1905, 1906, and 1909, Bérenger consistently attempted to thwart feminist abolitionists. At the 1906 International Bureau congress in Paris, for example, Sainte-Croix raised the issue of regulation and Bérenger first attempted a veto and then tried to refuse her the floor.[40] She nonetheless managed to obtain positions that allowed her to promote abolitionist views, such as her appointment to the Extraparliamentary Commission assigned to investigate the morals police (1904 to 1908) and her position on the League of Nations' Traffic in Women and Children Committee during the interwar period.[41]

State officials in France, as in other countries, warmly embraced the International Bureau. The Bureau was able to have the French Government convene an international conference in 1902 with the aim of creating the first international convention to combat the "white slave trade." Successful follow-up meetings in 1904 and 1906 were also held in Paris, the latter under the patronage of the president of the French Republic and with the ministers of foreign affairs and the interior as honorary presidents.[42] Béranger was at the center of the efforts, bringing together key French officials and reformers to work on the development of international accords.[43]

The strong connection between the state and the International Bureau was reflected in the number and variety of governmental delegates that France sent to International Bureau congresses, as well as in the composition of the International Bureau committee itself. Ministers plenipotentiary of foreign affairs (including Professor Louis Renault, who won the 1907 Nobel Peace Prize for his contributions to international law); representatives of the Home Ministry, including the prefect of police and the director of public safety; and representatives of the Ministries of Justice and Public Works attended the 1906 International Bureau congress, for example.[44] The International Bureau's national committee included not only the former senator Béranger, but also a former deputy and barrister at the Court of Appeal, a law professor from the Academy of Moral and Political Sciences, members of the Higher Council of Public Assistance, and Catholic women involved in rescue work.

Béranger's dogged insistence on dealing with the white slave traffic was a calculated and successful move. Abolitionist attempts to protect women in prostitution via the elimination of gender-specific regulation policies were transmuted into a concern with protecting only those women and girls who had been forced into prostitution in foreign lands by violence or fraud. This focus allowed proregulationists to quell any public discontent with the French brothel system by providing assurances that the brothels contained only adult women who wanted to be prostitutes and were not being exploited.

Ironically, the anti-trafficking measures that France promoted were used as a means of further bolstering and legitimizing their regulation system. Rather than treating all procurement as a crime, in keeping with an abolitionist framework, France did so only with minors. To do otherwise would have jeopardized the operations of the brothel system.[45] As one historian of France concluded, "Senator Béranger and his fellow neo-regulationists strengthened their case for greater and more effective regulationary controls."[46]

Such regulation was not limited to prostitution. The French International Bureau committee also focused on the sexual morality of women and girls. The members did concern themselves with the movement of women and girls working as entertainers, who were recruited by theatrical agencies for music halls in France and Algeria.[47] In 1908 they also promoted legislation to send underage girls in prostitution to reform school. However, by this time they were expanding their scope by facilitating arrests for "improper performances" at the music halls in Paris, and continuing Béranger's interest in obscenity by organizing an international congress for the suppression of pornography.[48]

Feminists continued to protest regulation, but because of their stance on state power, they were a minority, and French women remained at odds. Catholic women involved in rescue work took issue with feminist abolitionism and its secular message of women's equal rights. Privileging their "Frenchness" in order to secure their place in the French nation and combat what they understood to be the dangerous secularization and internationalization of the French state, these women focused on increasing the morality of the French state, and they supported the French International Bureau committee.[49]

The tension spilled over into the international realm. In the League of Nations Traffic in Women and Children Committee, after Sainte-Croix put forward a proposal that all voluntary organizations assisting girls should coordinate their efforts, the representative of the Catholic Association for the Protection of Girls publicly questioned why the feminist International Women's Suffrage Association was helping girls in France, and asked what connection the suffrage question could have with the traffic in women and children.[50]

These divisions between women played out along several lines—Protestant versus Catholic, secular versus religious, and liberal versus conservative. In 1926, Marcelle Legrand-Falco, the widow of a general and a trained nurse who had been active in assisting women and girls released from Saint-Lazare, founded the Temporary Union against Regulated Prostitution (*Union temporaire contre la prostitution reglementée*). Conceived as an umbrella abolitionist group, the Union attracted conservative feminists, Protestant and Catholic reformers, physicians, jurists, and politicians.

The Union became a rival to the French committee of the International Abolitionist Federation. Congruent with the French International Bureau committee, it supported proposed legislation to reinforce registration and medical surveillance, and its members were willing to work with regulationists. Legrand-Falco herself backed the criminalization of soliciting and the transmission of venereal disease. Sainte-Croix and her supporters disagreed. They believed that the Union had betrayed the true legacy of Josephine Butler.[51]

These divisions weakened the feminist abolitionist movement and gave the French government the ability to put forward an anti-trafficking agenda that would not conflict with regulation. State officials took on their efforts with enthusiasm, helping to fashion the international legal framework for combating the traffic in women at the first international congress of 1902, with sixteen states participating. Louis Renault helped to craft the language, defining *trafficking* in such a way as to ensure that regulation was not called into question and that no changes to French legislation would be necessary.[52] Voluntary adult prostitution, whether migratory or not, was outside the scope of the international accords finalized in 1904 and 1910.

The French government acted quickly on the first two international accords. It created in the Ministry of the Interior a central authority for trafficking: the Office of the White Slave Trade (*Bureau de la traite des blanches*), later subsumed under the Department of General Security (*Direction de la Sûreté générale, Contrôle des recherches judiciaries*).[53] The central authority reported

that it refused to deliver passports to French women and girls who were suspected of prostitution, and it arrested some traffickers attempting to leave
France with French women.[54] Yet it did little to prevent the entry of migrant
women into prostitution in the metropole or the colonies, nor did it repatriate French or other women involved in migrant prostitution.

World War I only worsened matters for abolitionists as men from French
colonies came to the metropole. More than six hundred thousand soldiers
from French colonies had been conscripted for the war,[55] including 172,800
soldiers from Algeria, 60,000 from Tunisia, 37,150 from Morocco, 48,922 from
Indochina, and 163,602 from French West Africa.[56] Along with men recruited
for factory work and immigrants from neighboring European countries, these
soldiers were increasingly visible in the French metropole.[57] Italian immigration, for example, began prior to World War I and peaked in the interwar
period, followed by immigrants from Greece, Algeria, Morocco, and Spain.[58]
Police authorities worried about the growth of clandestine prostitution, in
part because women were thought to cross racial and ethnic lines in servicing
these men, as well as American, English, Hindu, North African, Senegalese,
and Annamite soldiers.[59]

After the war, the specter of clandestine prostitution gave the French government and regulationist supporters an impetus for increasing control over
prostitution amid the growing xenophobia of the interwar period. The numbers of women in regulated brothels in Paris had declined, from 5,283 registered women in 1918 to 4,145 women in 1924, prompting ongoing fears about
uncontrolled sexual liaisons.[60] French International Bureau reformers and state
officials recoiled from the prospect of a laissez-faire approach to prostitution
that would allow unsupervised sexual relations between French women, colonial subjects, and immigrant men from other European countries.

Regulation was then defended as a way to segregate undesirable European
immigrants and men from the colonies, to ensure that they each had access
to their "own" prostitutes and would not act out their sexual desires by raping French women or patronizing brothels staffed by French women. Ensuring
a supply of women for each ethnic group presumably entailed the transport
of women from the colonies to the metropole. Some regulation proponents,
for example, lamented the fact that there were only two regulated brothels for
"Arabs" in the entire city of Paris, even though police reports indicated that
"Arab" rooms were sometimes set apart in French brothels to meet demand.[61]

French officials also continued to promote regulation in international circles. As the anti-trafficking agenda was being negotiated in the League of Nations Traffic in Women and Children Committee, state delegates maintained their defense of regulation for purposes of public health and social order. French sovereignty over domestic prostitution was at stake, and in continued spats with the representatives of Great Britain as well as with others who advocated an abolitionist agenda with regard to future anti-trafficking conventions and activities, France repeatedly stressed the difference between forced trafficking and voluntary prostitution.[62] At the 1921 League of Nations conference, for example, the French delegate claimed the following:

> Well, the experiment has been made. It has often been made. It was made during the war. All the military doctors were unanimous in declaring that regulation was an absolutely necessary evil and tended to diminution of disease. Some people desired to suppress the brothels in order not to hurt our sensitive feelings, but I would ask them first to think of those who contract terrible diseases which may perhaps be transmitted to their families and which may affect the health of their children.[63]

The distinction between forced trafficking and voluntary adult prostitution was maintained in the 1921 convention against the objections of the Dutch.

Even after Bérenger died in 1915 and Coote in 1919, the ties between the International Bureau, its French committee, and the French government remained intact and provided a united front at the League of Nations when it took up trafficking work. Law professor and minister plenipotentiary Louis Renault, who had been present as a government delegate at earlier International Bureau congresses, became the French delegate to the League of Nations Traffic in Women and Children Committee.[64] Renault's representative on the committee repeatedly defended regulation at the League of Nations and was often in dispute with the representatives of other European countries over the issue of prostitution within France's territories.

Whether engaged in struggles over regulation with the Traffic in Women and Children Committee delegate from Great Britain or contesting with the Polish delegate's claims that female Polish agricultural workers were being moved into French brothels in 1925, French officials at the League of Nations consistently sought to defend their ability to maintain brothels with foreign prostitutes as long as they were voluntary. At the International Bureau congress of 1924, for example, a French International Bureau delegate, who had also acted as director of the French central authority that oversaw trafficking

matters, strongly objected to the League of Nations proposal to prohibit foreign women in regulated brothels:

> It would encroach on the rights and prerogatives of those authorities who alone
> are in a position to judge as to what the internal system of prostitution should
> be and the system to be applied to foreigners; they alone can decide as to what
> measures should be taken with regard to them, according to the interests and
> exigencies of the country in question, its circumstances and internal legisla-
> tion, the mentality of its people, the state of public opinion and many other
> considerations.[65]

There was no pretense about the ability to protect women better though state
regulation, only a defense of state sovereignty.

France adhered to the 1921 convention in 1926 but did little throughout
the interwar period to prevent the entry of migrant women for prostitution
or to repatriate them. As described in Chapter Five, France did eventually
agree to the 1923 League of Nations proposal (put forward by the Polish
delegate) to prohibit foreign prostitutes in regulated brothels, but only after
strenuously and unsuccessfully attempting to oppose it. They then limited
new arrivals and allowed established prostitutes to remain. A French report to
the League of Nations Traffic in Women and Children Committee indicated
that one prostitute from Luxemburg had been expelled in 1924, and they had
not repatriated any women in prostitution to other countries, though several French women had been repatriated to France from Spain, Havana, and
the United States.[66] The 1925 French annual report to the League of Nations
Traffic in Women and Children Committee states that there was "nothing to
report" for French colonies and mandated territories in relation to trafficking
offenses discovered or women repatriated.

French officials also continually defended the implementation of brothels
for French troops in occupied areas of Germany during the interwar period,
despite international pressure on the French government to stop the practice.[67]
When the issue finally went to the League of Nations Traffic in Women and
Children Committee, it was dropped, over the objection of the British delegate, on the grounds that a German representative was not present. France's
regulation system remained intact. Ironically, some in France would later complain about men from Great Britain using French brothels at the beginning of
World War II, which caused indignation among some sections of the French
population. Even then it was not the exploitation of women in brothel pros-

titution that was deemed unacceptable. Rather, it was cross-national mixing: "Some French people said, either in sorrow or anger, that the British should have brought English girls for these purposes instead of using French women if these brothels were necessary."[68]

French abolitionists continued their struggle against regulation in the interwar period, but Sainte-Croix was busy in international organizing and the French International Abolitionist Federation committee floundered. Legrand-Falco's Union was more active, with University of Strasbourg professor Paul Gemaehling participating.[69] They had success in closing a few brothels at the municipal level—for example, in Grenoble, Mulhouse, and Roubaix—but no legislation against regulation was enacted at the national level.[70]

War intervened on the side of regulationists. In Vichy France, the regime not only increased regulatory activities but even moved toward the "official recognition" of brothels, a step toward making prostitution an authorized form of commerce.[71] In Paris in 1941 there were thirty-two brothels for German military men.[72] In Grenoble, prostitution was reestablished during the war. One member of the Union, on its Catholic committee, became a Vichy supporter while other members joined the resistance and were killed by Nazis during the occupation.[73]

After the war, the association of regulated brothels with the German occupation and the Vichy regime undermined the proponents of regulation who wanted to reestablish the brothel system. Many members of the resistance who became important figures in politics after the war opposed regulation. One of them, Marthe Richard, was one of the first female politicians in France and a member of the Mouvement Républicain Populaire, the new party founded by social-Catholic leaders of the Resistance at the end of 1944. A newcomer to the issue of abolition, Richard proposed legislation to end regulation.[74] The provisional government then, in 1946, proposed its own laws, which were opposed by abolitionists. The laws punished soliciting, dropped provisions for the establishment of centers to help women in prostitution, and established a national index of prostitutes.[75] This system continued for fourteen years, until France finally ratified the 1949/51 United Nations trafficking convention in 1960.[76]

Anti-Trafficking Efforts in the French Colonies

From the 1870s through the early twentieth century, France was second only to Great Britain in colonial lands and population. Scholars have noted France's strong bureaucracy and system of direct rule in the colonies, including the

well-known French policy of assimilation that attempted to override local cultures.[77] French enthusiasm for assimilation was already in decline by the 1870s
and had all but disappeared in the interwar period in favor of associationist
policies in colonial areas.[78] This was not the case, however, when it came to the
issue of regulated prostitution, which the French directly maintained in colonial areas throughout the interwar period, despite ongoing pressure from Great
Britain and others in the League of Nations, the efforts of feminist reformers,
and the dissatisfaction of indigenous groups in colonial areas.[79]

The French carved out spaces for prostitution throughout the empire and,
just as in the metropole, government officials were unwilling to compromise
their systems. The French government did not apply the 1904 agreement to its
protectorates or the 1921 anti-trafficking convention to its colonies, protectorates, or mandates. Nor did the French abolish regulation in those areas where
it had been established, including Algeria, Morocco, Tunisia, and Indochina.
Regulation was typically implemented immediately after French occupation of
a territory in order to better service the military. Ongoing pacification cam-
paigns meant that the French military remained in colonial areas for an extended period, ready to repress uprisings such as those in Algeria, Morocco,
and Vietnam.

In Algeria, General Bourmont issued a law on August 11, 1830, barely a
month after he landed, mandating a monthly medical visit for women in prostitution and their registration.[80] The French also applied the system to indigenous women, who did not consider themselves prostitutes in the Western
understanding of the term. The Nailiyat (women of the Ouled Nail tribe) were
dancers who engaged in sexual activity with members of their audience for
remuneration in their own homes before eventually marrying. Officials classi-
fied them as prostitutes and issued them cards, segregated them, and restricted
their freedom of movement.[81] The police ensured that they were literally prisoners either of the cafes where they performed or of the windowless rooms
where they were made to live.[82] They became tourist attractions for Frenchmen and were advertised by France's travel agencies; according to one Algerian
historian, a French office for the promotion of tourism (*Syndicat d'Initiative
de Bou Saada*) began to determine the contents of the Nailiyat's performances,
insisting that they appear naked before their visitors.

The Nailiyat and other indigenous women in prostitution in Algeria did
not initially service European clients, but poverty intervened, leading to an increase in prostitution and some interracial mixing.[83] Perhaps for this reason, or

simply in keeping with general segregationist policies, the governor general in Algeria in 1898 proposed the creation of special neighborhoods for women in prostitution, separated according to race.[84] In 1937 there were more than eight hundred women in prostitution working in Algiers, with two hundred and fifty in brothels and others working elsewhere in the allotted areas.[85] Segregation was also the norm in Tunis, where Muslim women were kept for Muslims and Jewish and other Mediterranean women were kept for foreigners. Police allotted certain days to French army men in the Foreign Legion (*legionnaires*), and other days to colonial subjects who served the army as riflemen (*tirailleurs*).[86]

Regulated prostitution was so important to the French that the government sold bonds to raise money for brothels in Morocco.[87] The inauguration of an enormous brothel in Fes in September 1925 was celebrated as a municipal event, with a public reception.[88] Colonial authorities eventually fully segregated prostitution, working with a private company to create an indigenous "red-light" district, the Bousbir, in Casablanca in the interwar period. The Bousbir was like a state within a state, built as a big rectangle, with military and police guards at its single entrance. It lacked basic necessities for women, such as running water, electricity, and even toilets, yet this *quartier reserve* model was heralded by French officials and exported to other African cities, supported by public funds.[89] Each town had its special district set apart for prostitution.[90] Proud of the model, the French built one for exhibition at the 1933–1934 World's Fair in Chicago.[91]

The French maintained brothels in Indochina as well.[92] Resident-General Paul Bert introduced the regulation of prostitution in Tonkin in 1886, within a year of its becoming a protectorate, first in Haiphong and subsequently in Hanoi.[93] By the interwar period, the stipulations came to include the registration of every woman of any nationality practicing prostitution, with a minimum-age limit of eighteen for "Asiatics" and twenty-one for Europeans; enforced registration if the woman was "known to practise prostitution"; and the prohibition of solicitation, including the restriction that prostitutes were not to enter cafés or drinking shops or practice prostitution outside of the brothel or their lodgings.[94]

Many women, both migrant and local, were found in the brothels. There were two hundred Vietnamese women and twenty-five French women registered in Saigon in 1930, and two French licensed houses.[95] In Hanoi there were an estimated 800 prostitutes, out of which some 350 were clandestine while 156 were Vietnamese women living in twenty licensed brothels.[96] Officials claimed that there were no French prostitutes in Hanoi, although they admitted that there had been Eastern European and Russian women. Other areas of Indochina had mixed Eurasian, Chinese, and Japanese women in prostitution. Officials eventually established a *quartier reserve* in Saigon in 1934 and proposed one for Hanoi in 1936.

As in other areas of the French empire, colonial doctors in Indochina defended the need to protect French men from the possible negative health consequences of unregulated interracial sexual relations, and their writings often depicted French men as "victims" of debauched local populations of women, men, and boys.[97] To the French, the prostitute could be and was any Vietnamese woman, exemplified by the French use of the word *congai* (young woman, girl, or female child in Vietnamese) to mean "whore."[98] In times of flood, drought, pestilence, and war, a ready supply of women and girls was available to work in brothels, and young daughters were sometimes sold as prostitutes.[99]

World War I brought revolts and instability to the French empire, and like the Dutch, French officials began to encourage female nationals to go to the colonies in the hope of civilizing those areas.[100] Employment and marriage bureaus assisted in moving French women to Indochina in the 1920s.[101] Still, state officials continued regulation. In 1926 there were 157 brothels in the colonies alone, not including protectorates and mandated areas.[102] Regulation continued to be implemented in the latter as well, such as the newly acquired mandates in the Levant in the 1920s. General Gourand commissioned a cafe owner in Beirut to create a chain of brothels for France's troops, requisitioned a building for the installation of the first brothel, signed a 100,000 franc bond from the treasury to finance the project, and drew up the regulations governing it.[103]

Officials also continued to ignore trafficking in the colonies, reporting on few cases in the interwar period and maintaining the right to have foreign prostitutes in brothels. It was only under pressure at the League of Nations that France finally agreed to forbid foreign prostitutes in brothels in Algeria in 1925, decreasing the number of Spanish women. In the same year they reported on one Dutch woman whose pimp was made to leave the colony while she herself became the mistress of a Dutch businessman in Saigon; they also claimed to have thwarted attempts by a Polish brothel keeper from Bangkok to recruit prostitutes or young French girls in Saigon. She was in Saigon, they explained, because Thai authorities would not allow the entry of Russian prostitutes from Shanghai, which was her usual source country.[104] In 1926 they reported that no cases of traffic in European women had occurred in Indochina, and that trafficking of "haf'castes" had become less frequent.[105] At the same time they sought to encourage the emigration of women from France to Indochina to contain the frequency of mixed-race unions.[106]

French governmental delegates to the League of Nations suggested that abolition in Indochina, which was occupied by the military, could occur only if it was preceded by changes in the "milieu social." They argued that for abolition to be successful, what was needed first was the general education of women, then the raising of their legal status and the establishment of medical, social, and other measures. As for North Africa, colonial administrators continued to defend the system, arguing that "ethnic conditions are not exactly the same, and metropolitan French laws will not change the natives' ancestral customs."[107] Even as late as 1944, the prefect of Algiers ruled that women could be registered without their consent if issues of morals and public health demanded it.[108]

Later, in 1948, British abolitionists reported that "reserved quarters" for women in prostitution still existed in French North Africa:

> to prevent clashes among soldiers admission to these quarters is usually granted in rotation to the different units of each garrison—Senegalese, North Africans, Europeans, etc. . . . the reserved quarter in Casablanca has been regarded as a model; in it the medical authorities came nearer to realizing their ideals than anywhere else, and its attractions were "renowned throughout the world."[109]

The system remained remarkably resilient.

French feminists such as Sainte-Croix fought rather single-handedly against trafficking and prostitution in the French metropole, without the popular groundswell of support that had occurred in Great Britain or the Netherlands, and they seem to have found even less interest in the issue of regulation in colonial areas. Julie Daubié, the French feminist who had opposed regulation in France and helped to organize an abolition campaign in the 1860s, did critique the system in North African colonies. She charged that the French had introduced rampant prostitution and venereal diseases and said that French morality was in some ways inferior to that of indigenous peoples.[110] A few French colonial settlers also protested against regulation in the colonies, sending abolitionists information about the abuses of the systems in the early 1900s, such as when authorities arbitrarily arrested Vietnamese women or registered a girl of thirteen in Algeria.[111]

Sainte-Croix was clearly cognizant of regulation in the colonies, and she was likely among those who critiqued it, but there seems to be little evidence at present that she or other feminists attempted to organize in French colonial territories. The number of French women in colonial areas, which was lower than the number of Dutch women in the Indies, must have played a role in hindering a French feminist response to trafficking and prostitution in colonial areas. By 1915, the percentage of European women in the Dutch East Indies was 40 percent, but a comparable percentage was not found in Indochina until 1937.[112]

There were more French women in Algeria, but imperialism and religious differences still limited the possibilities for joint action by French and Algerian women in the interwar period.[113] When French feminists in the 1930s did call for the extension of rights to Algerian women, prostitution was not a priority. They were concerned about Arab and Berber women's inferior status, and they raised issues of child marriage, illiteracy, poverty, and legal discrimination, arguing that French law should fully apply to them.[114] Educated urban Muslim women responded to the implication that European laws and culture were superior by allying with indigenous men to insist on their free exercise of religion.[115]

Furthermore, among the French who critiqued regulation in colonial areas were the conservative reformers associated with Protestant Pastor Fallot, who spun the issue in imperialist and racial terms rather than framing it as a feminist concern. They worried about European women in Saigon catering to Chinese and Indochinese men or such women in other areas servicing Senegalese and "other tribes."[116]

> How do you expect the blacks, yellows and browns to respect honest women when they can for five francs, and even less, make advances to a woman of the same color as the wife of the doctor, of the officer, of the general, or of the governor?[117]

At stake was imperial prestige; the right to rule was to be guaranteed through the protection of French women's bodies.

It was not until the 1930s that the French began organizing on the issue of regulation in the colonies, and it usually involved small groups of physicians, journalists, Catholics, and Protestants. Legrand-Falco's Union supported local movements by encouraging them to affiliate with her organization, and she lobbied colonial administrators and undertook a tour of North Africa, visiting the indigenous hospital in the red-light district of Tunis and setting up a local section of the Union.[118] The Union also arranged a conference tour in Algeria, where new sections were being formed. The secretary-general of the French committee of the International Abolitionist Federation also undertook a documentary voyage to Morocco.

Indigenous women involved in prostitution protested French regulation at times. In Tunis in the early 1890s, eight hundred native courtesans signed a petition complaining of their registration as prostitutes, and sixty Vietnamese prostitutes rioted in 1912 when authorities arrested and attempted to inspect them.[119] Indigenous women's movements had not yet emerged in French North Africa or colonial Vietnam, however, and the cause of prostitution was often taken up by indigenous men rather than women. Prominent Tunisians complained of the introduction of regulation in the capital in 1885, for example, and the Muslim middle-class of Marrakech protested the *quartier reserve* there.[120] Later, in the 1930s, youth groups in Morocco and Algeria would protest the establishment of *quartiers reserves*, and Syrians in Homs and Damascus would call for the imprisonment or expulsion of a prominent brothel owner.[121]

Regulation was often criticized by nationalists, who claimed that the French administration organized the brothel business as an attack on indigenous society.[122] For example, Emir Khaled, forebearer of Algerian nationalism, denounced the colonial administration for tolerating, if not encouraging, prostitution. He criticized the prostitution of girls under "the indifferent eye of policemen and vice squads."[123] Both secular and religious nationalists portrayed prostitution as a "Western ill," criticized mixed marriages between Algerian men and French women, and advocated lowering the dowry in order for Algerian men to be able to afford to marry within their group.[124]

Indigenous opponents of regulation often argued that the French imported prostitution and they juxtaposed their own moral practices to the immoral activities of the French. In Muslim areas, they argued, women were always under the protection of fathers, husbands, or brothers, unlike in France. In Vietnam, they charged, the French had created prostitution by educating girls who were no longer happy with their traditional roles. For these critics, colonization had undermined the authority of indigenous men.[125]

Moreover, as the examples in this chapter show, women in many nationalist movements were constructed as the guardians of traditional culture, leading to the status quo in gender relations rather than fundamentally challenging them.[126] Women in colonial Vietnam faced a situation similar to that of women in Algeria in juggling emerging feminist and nationalist projects. Early women's organizations had developed in the interwar period and focused on work skills and education for women and girls.[127] Gender reforms were also taken up by Vietnamese nationalists, and women joined nationalist groups, but women's issues were eventually seen as ancillary to the nationalist movement.[128] Secular nationalists usually called for only limited women's rights, and women were not typically represented in the leadership of either secular or religious nationalist movements.

Although women often found their emerging feminist and nationalist interests in potential conflict, the issue of prostitution could have, and perhaps did, provide a bridge between them. During the Algerian Revolution (1954 to 1962), nationalist criticism of indigenous women's sexual exploitation grew more pointed as they denounced French administrators who forced women into prostitution as a means of humiliating and disciplining Algerian men. They accused French officials of condoning the kidnapping of daughters of notable Algerian men who failed to cooperate with colonial authorities and forcing them into mobile brothels for use by French soldiers. They also charged that colonial police frequently rounded up women for identification control and then sent them to brothels for failing to produce a proof of their identity.[129]

International groups eventually made similar claims, again calling for the abolition of regulated prostitution. By 1958, International Bureau reformers in France finally declared that "the illegal continuance of tolerated prostitution in Algeria was contrary to the projects for the emancipation of the Moslem woman and opposed to the traditions of Islam, Christianity, and Judaism, and to the dignity and respect of the human person."[130] Others, such as the Movement for Colonial Freedom, criticized France for maintaining brothels in Algeria, Tunisia, and Morocco: "under the eyes of the protecting power, France, and in spite of United Nations agreements to suppress the traffic in persons . . . it is still lawful for both Frenchmen and Algerians to operate brothels in Algeria, while they cannot do so in France."[131]

Citing the continued military presence in North Africa (like Indochina) and the lucrative income for local rulers, who ran combines that operated expensive brothels catering to Europeans, nationalist groups and their supporters pointed out the hypocrisy of French regulation policy and blamed it for a traffic in European as well as local women. They argued that local officials falsely arrested women in order to replenish the supplies of prostitutes in Morocco and Indochina. Morocco also lowered the age of consent for girls, presumably to increase supply. The International Abolitionist Federation protested to the French government, as reported in an International Bureau meeting in 1955, because the age was reduced to sixteen, in violation of the 1910 international convention.[132]

The tug of war over women's bodies and sexuality in Algeria was fought between French colonial supporters and anticolonial nationalists, but this not only pitted French against Algerian men. Algerian collaborators with the French also allegedly kidnapped young women as a vindictive measure, allowing parents who could trace their daughters' whereabouts to buy them back.[133] Still, the traffic in women for prostitution gave the colonial administration a powerful tool of social control over the indigenous society.[134] Given this, it is not surprising that when the United Nations took on anti-trafficking work after World War II, former colonies were among the strongest supporters of a new anti-trafficking convention. Algeria adhered to the 1950 United Nations anti-trafficking convention in 1963, the year after it gained independence, and Morocco adhered in 1973. By that time, Algeria was a sending country to France.

Summary

The importance of prostitution to the French state was affirmed by both anti-trafficking reformers and state officials in France. The anti-trafficking movement was little influenced by International Abolitionist Federation reformers' efforts to sway it toward abolition and to prevent the state from intervening in women's but not men's sexual activity. Liberal feminism was hampered in France, in part, as historian Karen Offen explains, because nationalism made individualist feminism an untenable strategy for women.[135] Splinters between liberal and conservative women prevented common action. Catholicism also hindered International Abolitionist Federation efforts, both because Catholic groups acted in ways that reinforced national differences and because they refused to challenge the state.

Neither state officials at the League of Nations nor French International Bureau leaders admitted any connection between regulated brothels and the traffic in French or other women. Despite signing all three conventions, France seemingly did little to address the traffic in its territories aside from preventing the unsupervised emigration of some French women. State officials actually condoned the movement of some women from colonial areas to the metropole when they were thought to be necessary to service local populations of immigrant men. French state officials wanted to retain the ability to keep other European women in its brothel system and gave up this option only under intense pressure from the League of Nations.

Similarly, in the colonies, the movement of women between brothels was allowed, and French brothels, some with European women in them, were maintained. French officials put into place measures to segregate brothels by ethnicity, or at least to separate out rooms for the use of French rather than indigenous men. France's prostitution policy—and its selective application of anti-trafficking accords—shows an increasing preoccupation with race throughout the interwar French empire. Sexual relations between French and Africans were increasingly condemned and the ideal of white families was reinforced. There was more concern about miscegenation and the consequences for French rule. Concubines were banned and enthusiasm for white endogamy rose.[136] At the same time government officials took pains to defend their right to control prostitution and to control the movement of French or other women involved in it. There was no desire to stop trafficking, only to control it.

Prostitution played a much larger role in state- and empire-building efforts in France than it did in the Netherlands, for a longer period, and it was well-integrated into the administrative structure of the state. Prostitution was seen as a necessity for men who could not remain continent outside of marriage; the state regulation of prostitution was believed to be vital for public health and social order, and state officials and their supporters believed this to be true in both metropole and colony.

The importance of the military in French imperialism only exacerbated these beliefs. The continued need for military presence to control colonial unrest coupled with depopulation concerns made state officials increasingly receptive to measures by which they could control racial segregation. With conscripted men from the colonies in the French military, both state officials and nationalists desired to provide controlled outlets for their sexual activities. Trafficking, while considered regrettable when it involved coercion, did not threaten the integrity of the French nation-state or its empire.[137] On the contrary, it could help to secure it.

7 Italy's State-Driven Movement

ITALY WAS A MAJOR EMIGRATION COUNTRY from the late 1800s on and a sending country in the international traffic in women. Italians went overseas to North and South America, and to other countries within Europe, including France, Switzerland, and Germany, and women were up to 25 percent of those emigrating at the end of the nineteenth century.[1] From 1901 to 1915, Italian emigration peaked, and after 1920 the flow shifted from overseas to other countries in Europe. Throughout this period, one aspect of this migration involved the movement of Italian women into brothels abroad. Along with Polish, French, and German women, Italian women were in prostitution in Argentina, Mexico, Uruguay, Brazil, Algiers, Tunis, and Egypt.[2]

Italy was not a major receiving country for the traffic in women, but like France it did maintain a system of regulated prostitution in metropolitan and colonial areas, and it had a proportion of women from neighboring countries in its brothels at home. In 1875, for example, 29 percent of the registered women in prostitution in Venice had been born in another country, and from 1880 to 1885 nearly a quarter of registered women in prostitution in Bologna were from another country, typically Austria, Germany, and France.[3] In the interwar period, women in prostitution continued to come from these countries, as well as from Yugoslavia, Hungary, and Czechoslovakia.[4] Italian brothels in colonial areas included Italian, other European, and indigenous women.

Anti-Trafficking Efforts in the Italian Metropole

Regulation had been adopted by Prime Minister Cavour as a component of Italian unification in 1860, and Italian regulation was explicitly modeled on the French and Belgian systems.[5] Cavour modified the system in Italy, centralizing it rather than copying the municipal organization of the other countries, so regulation was directed by the Ministry of the Interior. It was promoted not only on the premise that it would safeguard the health of the army and the Italian people, but also on the argument that it would professionalize prostitution, minimize its connection to crime, and provide protection to women in prostitution. The state fixed the prices of each brothel and the percentage of profit the owner could take from women in prostitution; disputes between madams and prostitutes were to be referred to the Health Office for arbitration.[6]

In practice, in Italy as elsewhere, regulation created difficulties for women who wished to leave brothels, and subjected them to police control.[7] The movements of women in prostitution were greatly restricted and surveillance of them was normalized. They were prohibited from walking through neighborhoods near their brothels and from going outside in the evenings without just cause, and they had to get permission from the police to change residence, leave their brothel for more than three days, enter a hospital, or leave prostitution.[8] They had to undergo compulsory medical examinations twice a week. Women sometimes protested regulation in Italy, as they had in other countries, and abolitionists in 1887 sympathetically reported on a riot by women in a lock hospital in Naples.[9] The women drove out the nuns who provided nursing care, sacked the hospital, and "maintained a regular siege against a company of soldiers and a picket of carbineers."[10] Abolitionists hailed the "rebellious spirit" of the women.[11]

Abolitionists focused their attention on Italy early in the movement, but despite their efforts they found little purchase. The anti-trafficking movement in Italy did not begin with an initial surge of support from women's groups as it did in the Netherlands, nor was it usurped by purity reformers affiliated with or sympathetic to the moral approach of the International Bureau as it was in France. The initial proponents of abolition in Italy were the radical leaders of the Risorgimento, the movement for Italian unification, and their supporters. Josephine Butler had personal connections to Italy through her sister, who had married into a Swiss Italian family, and she had hosted one of the leading figures of the Risorgimento, Giuseppe Mazzini, at her house in Oxford even before regulation was passed in Italy.[12] Mazzini subsequently wrote to her about it.

Butler was particularly active in Italy, just as she had been in the Netherlands and France, and she visited the country several times beginning in 1874.

Drawing on her ties, she encouraged the formation of an International Abolitionist Federation committee. There was some initial success; the abolitionists reported the formation of an Italian committee in Rome in 1876, with supporters of the republican movement inspired by Mazzini.[13] The abolitionists then provided a grant to the Rome committee to bolster its efforts.[14]

Butler and the local committee leader, Giuseppe Nathan, attempted to broaden their base by lecturing to audiences including professors, students, judges, physicians, officers of the army, women, and working-class men. They focused particularly on the working class, speaking to associations in Milan and Genoa, for example. These groups were receptive, and the abolitionists won the support of a working men's congress representing sixteen hundred societies throughout Italy who agreed to oppose the establishment of new brothels in workmen's quarters.[15] Some also resisted the police registration of their daughters or refused to allow them to be taken by authorities.[16] In Tuscany and in Florence, Butler reported, fathers and brothers physically fought with the police.[17]

As in France, however, one missing ingredient was the early participation of women's groups. Italian feminists did not organize until the 1890s, and the few women who were interested in abolition comprised a very small circle of Protestant and Jewish women, some of whom were British and had married Italian men. These feminists did support Butler. Anna Maria Mozzoni, a pioneer of nineteenth-century Italian feminism, was involved in abolition. She agreed to head an International Abolitionist Federation committee in Milan in 1874.[18] She went on to help create the socialist party, founded in 1892, although she did not enter it, and she fought for women's rights, forming the League to Promote the Interests of Women (*Lega Promotrice degli Interessi Femminili*) in 1881.[19] Sarah Nathan, a supporter of Mazzini, also became involved in abolition, and it was her sons who helped Butler to organize and form the first central International Abolitionist Federation committee.[20]

Catholic women in Italy shunned the abolitionist movement, believing that prostitutes required redemption rather than liberty.[21] Catholic associations dedicated to the protection of girls were active but, as in France, found little common ground with liberal feminist abolitionists. Instead, they flocked to the issue of trafficking. As historian B.P.F. Wanrooij states, "the Catholic approach was more moralistic and did not always distinguish between the protection of women and the repression of their freedom."[22] Catholics tended to concern themselves with trafficking, pornography, and public indecency rather than regulated prostitution.

International Abolitionist Federation reformers were also hampered by the characterization, circulated in France as well, that abolition was an "English eccentricity" that failed to understand that individual freedoms were secondary to the public health needs of the nation.[23] Feminist abolitionism was discredited as a foreign idea, alien to Italian culture. In its place, neo-regulationist discourses gained popularity, which was possible without a network of feminists to counter it. As in France, neoregulationism appealed to conservative moral reformers on the ground, aligning them with the ideas and strategies of the International Bureau rather than the International Abolitionist Federation. Regulation reforms implemented in Italy in the 1880s freed women from compulsory medical examinations and allowed them to be treated in general hospitals or privately, though they continued the registration of brothels, and the police control and gathering of information about individual women remained intact. Yet even these reforms were overturned in 1891.[24]

The International Bureau did not fare much better in Italy. The initial response to Secretary Coote's visit in 1899 was not very enthusiastic, but he persisted and managed to convene a meeting with the mayor of Rome.[25] By 1900 he had been successful in organizing an International Bureau national committee in the city, with the consent of the Italian government and with Senator Luigi Luzzatti as president. Luzzatti, a Jewish liberal political leader and an economist, was known for his advocacy of minority rights. He also became the first Jewish Italian prime minister of Italy in 1910.

Under Luzzatti, the Italian Committee Against the White Slave Trade was active for a short time, founding chapters in Genoa, Milan, Naples, and Messina.[26] Yet only the Milan chapter, which had some involvement of feminists, remained active. Its vice president was Ersilia Majno Bronzini, who helped to establish the Asilo Mariuccia, a reformatory for wayward girls that was ran under the auspices of the Women's Union (*Unione Femminile*), a feminist organization. The Milan reformers focused particularly on the protection of children. By 1908 Coote needed to visit Italy to revive flagging interest in anti-trafficking work and to reconstitute the national committee's headquarters in Milan instead of Rome.[27]

Although popular support for the anti-trafficking movement was weak in Italy compared to the Netherlands and France, it did have some adherents, and state officials did take notice. The government sent delegates to the conferences that developed the 1904 and 1910 accords, as well as to other International

Bureau congresses and conferences (see Table 3.2). The chief of the Division of Public Security, who promised to repress the traffic, directed prefects to conform to the spirit of the two international accords and put special emphasis on the protection of minors.[28] Government officials also attended International Bureau congresses. In 1913, for example, the first secretary of the Ministry of the Interior attended the International Bureau congress as the government representative.[29] That same year, Public Security agents began to more thoroughly vet foreign prostitutes, after being requested to do so by the Ministry in Rome.[30] They interviewed women in prostitution to ascertain if they were victims of trafficking and to ask if they knew of any cases.

After World War I, state interest in the anti-trafficking movement continued as the League of Nations held its 1921 conference and an Italian governmental delegate, Marquis Paulucci de Calboli, was appointed to the Traffic in Women and Children Committee. Like French officials, he too opposed the Netherlands' suggestion that the League of Nations' anti-trafficking agenda should include the goal of abolishing regulation.[31] Two years later, in 1923, at the second League of Nations Traffic in Women and Children Committee meeting, he presented to the committee a telegram from Mussolini, who wished to notify them of his draft decree instituting new legal measures for the suppression of trafficking. The decree punished trafficking, provided for the regulation of "women's labour exchanges," and created a central governmental office for the suppression of the traffic.[32] The central office was placed under the Ministry of the Interior and Police Administration.[33]

Some popular support was also mustered that same year when a committee was established at Trieste. The committee members wrote to the International Bureau to report that they had held meetings and spoken "with much appreciation of Signior Mussolini's practical interest in the Suppression of the Traffic."[34] What Mussolini was actually doing, however, was suppressing clandestine (that is, "unregulated") prostitution and forcing women into state-regulated brothels. From 1923 to 1926, he had police target women to ensure compliance with compulsory health checks and with other requirements of regulation; those found violating the rules could be sent to prison and released with one-way tickets to their hometown.[35]

State officials, rather than international voluntary association reformers, continued to dominate anti-trafficking efforts. At the 1924 Sixth International Bureau Congress, the Italian committee was represented by only of its two members, and their attendance at the 1927 International Bureau congress was equally paltry.[36] The interwar secretary of the International Bureau lamented the state of affairs in Italy:

> There is nothing in Sicily and throughout Italy there is at present no possibility of any effective work being done except through the authorities. The National Committee there at present really comes down to a home for girls at Milan. . . . See how unsatisfactory we are.[37]

It cannot have helped matters for the International Bureau that the one place where a national committee remained was where feminists had been actively involved.

Feminists also despaired of the conditions on the ground in Italy. After visiting Rome in 1933, the secretary of the British committee of the International Abolitionist Federation reported:

> The women feel, too, they are not as united as they were, but then, all Societies that are not of State-organisation have been dissolved. The President of the former Abolitionist group dare not even have two or three people in her drawing-room to discuss the subject. The Alliance for Equal Citizenship, before its dissolution, presented a memorial to Government asking for the closing of the licensed houses . . . but they are unable to give voice to their views on public matters as they have been told they must confine themselves to their professional unions ("Syndicates") as their sole channel of expression. But these can only deal with professional matters.[38]

The aspirations of both abolitionists and the International Bureau were thwarted as societies not organized by the state were dissolved.

State authorities never waivered in their interest, however. Marquis de Calboli regularly attended all of the League of Nations Traffic in Women and Children Committee meetings through at least 1929, before another Italian delegate took over. Italy also regularly sent reports to the League of Nations that showed trafficking arrests and repatriation figures for women in prostitution. Their reports showed little activity pertaining to trafficking, but much involving the repatriation of women. For example, in 1924, authorities repatriated fifteen victims of trafficking and fifty foreign women in prostitution, and refused forty-two women admission at the border.[39] The following year, 386 Italian minors in prostitution were repatriated to their own homes, seventeen foreign women in prostitution were deported, and four migrant women were sent back at the frontier.[40] Authorities' preferences for voluntary prostitutes from other countries is perhaps best indicated in their report of 1927, which states that they questioned 204 alien prostitutes but did not repatriate them because they were not trafficked; they did, however, repatriate 597 underage Italian girls in prostitution.[41]

The repatriation of Italian girls was likely bound up in Fascist population policy. In addition to their pronatalist policy and emigration control, Italian Fascists also enacted programs of controlled internal colonization and migration that included discouraging movement to the cities.[42] They coupled their efforts to organize women voluntarily through social activities with more oppressive and direct control of women's freedom of movement.[43] Repatriation figures reported by Italy to the League of Nations increased in the late interwar period, surging higher than in any other country, and nearly all of the cases were "internal," meaning they involved only Italian subjects. Italian officials reported "883 minors, including 2 foreigners (Yugoslavs), repatriated, who were engaged in prostitution" in 1931.[44] For 1933 to 1934 they reported that "there were 1,182 prostitutes under age sent back to their home communes" and "three foreign women repatriated."[45]

Like France, Italy took some steps to prevent the uncontrolled movement of their "own" women while doing little to address foreign prostitution in their territories, and Italian state officials consistently opposed efforts to abolish state regulation. The regime even made several highly visible "roundups" of women on the street and had them confined to brothels.[46] Brothels were strictly policed under the Fascists: solicitation was patrolled; rules of the licensed houses, such as no dancing, were enforced; and the houses were closed during Fascist demonstrations, with guards posted at the doors.[47] As a result of continued efforts by Italian feminists, whose numbers had grown in the interwar period, some eleven brothels were closed as an experiment, but twenty-six others remained in Rome.

It was not until 1948 that feminist abolitionists gained political support, but the end result was not as had been anticipated. After women had received the vote in 1946, they elected forty-four women to Parliament, including Angelina Merlin, a newly elected senator from the Socialist party who had been an anti-Fascist and a Resistance leader.[48] Signora Antonietta de Silvestri, then president of the Milan Branch of the International Alliance of Women, drafted an abolition proposal and encouraged Merlin to present it to the Senate.[49] She did so. The proposal sought to abolish brothels and prohibit trafficking, but also to provide treatment for venereal disease without compulsory health checks, to abolish the morals police, and to criminalize brothel keeping.

The original proposal was meant to leave prostitution legal while criminalizing those third parties who exploited women, including pimps and brothel owners, and to do away with regulation.[50] After Merlin partnered with Catholic Christian Democrat Senator Boggiano-Pico to revise the proposal, however, the new version allowed compulsory rehabilitation of women in prostitution, kept the morals police, and even included language that left open the possibility of women having to remain in debt to brothel owners. Against abolitionist doctrine, the focus was on women particularly, and the tone became disciplinary, not protective, as women in prostitution were cast as criminal.[51]

Anti-Trafficking Efforts in the Italian Colonies

Italy came late to colonialism and, from the late 1800s on, sought to create an empire. In the process, as other imperial powers had done, it established systems for attending to the presumed sexual needs of Italian men. The archives of the International Abolitionist Federation and the International Bureau yielded little discussion about trafficking and prostitution in colonial areas occupied by the Italians, and there are few historical narratives, but we do know something about the way Italian officials sought to organize sexual activity in Italian East Africa, particularly Eritrea and Ethiopia. After Italy occupied Eritrea in the 1880s, both concubinage and prostitution were accepted practices for Italian men of all classes. They formed unions with indigenous women and at first the government allowed children of these unions to have citizenship status.[52] This policy changed with the rise of fascism and the conquest of Ethiopia in the 1930s, as Italy enacted a variety of racial laws and embarked on Mussolini's program of "demographic colonization."[53]

Italian authorities outlawed concubinage and recategorized mixed-race children as Africans rather than as Italian citizens. They closed places of public entertainment to Ethiopians, segregated movie theaters, and prohibited Italians from performing humble jobs, such as porter or shoe-shine boy, because those jobs were to be held by Ethiopians.[54] In commercial shops for whites, an Italian could not serve an Ethiopian; instead, special Ethiopian attendants performed the task. If an Italian was found performing degrading work for an Ethiopian subject, he could be fined up to five thousand lire.[55]

The pattern in both Eritrea and Ethiopia was to encourage Italian male settlers, tolerate concubinage, and later to discourage interracial marriage and promote prostitution as a strategy to end interracial domestic arrangements. The well-known general Rodolfo Braziani, who led the 1935 war against Ethiopia, clearly articulated this campaign to delegitimize interracial domestic arrangements in favor of institutionalized prostitution. In his words:

> From a moral point of view let me remind you of the civil and economic and sometimes sentimental complications that occur when the [African] woman gets pregnant. . . . Headquarters and the Regional Authorities will do everything to meet this necessity [sexual relations] by establishing wherever possible brothels in all localities that are still without them.[56]

Authorities proceeded to open brothels, stocking them through coercion when necessary. A Hungarian physician in Addis Ababa reported seeing houses converted into brothels and indigenous women forced into them.[57] As other European imperial powers had done, the Italians segregated the brothels, some with Ethiopian women and girls for use by Italians only, and others for indigenous men recruited into the Italian army.[58]

The importance of prostitution to the state caused contradictions for the Fascist regime as they attempted to enact racial purity measures. To prevent interracial sexual relations, state officials needed Italian women in prostitution for Italian men, yet this would impinge on the image of Italian moral superiority. At first, colonial authorities opted for measures to increase the number of Italian prostitutes. The Italian Madame Mira was recruited to help set up Italian brothels in Ethiopia; although she traveled to Asmara and Addis Ababa, there remained a shortage of Italian women in prostitution.[59]

The authorities grew increasingly uncomfortable with their efforts to recruit Italian women for prostitution. Plans to establish mobile brothels to service Italian workers in the provinces were abandoned, for example, because "the fascist commissioner for labour and other party luminaries . . . argued that in areas where European families had not yet arrived it would be detrimental for the prestige of the Italian race if the Italian woman would be seen for the first time in the shape of the prostitute."[60] They then tried another option: importing other European women for colonial brothels:[61]

> for reasons of racial prestige, it was undesirable that the first contact between the Ethiopian world and the Italian women should be through "bought women." Attempts were therefore made to import French prostitutes, but when six such women were ordered from Marseilles in July 1936, this was frustrated by the French authorities at Jibuti who, according to Poggiali [a reporter for the *Corriere della Sera*], argued that if "white prostitution could offend the prestige of the Italian race we cannot permit it to offend the French race. If you

want women of ill repute take those of your own house." Reliance was thereafter placed mainly on Italian as well as Ethiopian women, who constituted the bulk of the women in prostitution under fascist rule.[62]

British abolitionists affiliated with the International Abolitionist Federation at the time confirmed this account.[63] As they concluded, "This is one way of ensuring 'racial purity,' by encouraging a traffic in white women but not Italian!"[64] British abolitionists also noted that Italians were not alone in their behavior. The British had employed the same strategy in Singapore, where Hungarians, Poles, and Russian Jews—the "frail army of white women recruited by professional pimps from the poorest population of Central and Eastern Europe"—had been found while the British administration maintained a ban on British women in prostitution in the area.[65]

Italian officials opted for other European women when possible and settled for local women when necessary, but they never questioned the necessity of regulated prostitution in the colonies. They did, however, simultaneously work toward the settlement of Italian families by encouraging the emigration of Italian women to colonial areas. Fascists provided special courses to train women for their role in Italy's "place in the sun" as colonial wives.[66] As with the French, the Italian effort was not successful. The numbers of Italians in the colonies did grow. In 1935, the Italian community in Eritrea increased more than tenfold. Prior to 1935 there were fewer than five thousand Italians, including the military, but by the end of 1935, fifty thousand Italian workers had migrated to Eritrea.[67] In Ethiopia, the Italian community was created from scratch in a matter of months, and in 1920 it totaled sixty-two thousand, military excluded.[68] Despite this growth, women did not settle in great numbers.[69]

The activities of Italian authorities regarding prostitution in the colonies seems to have been overlooked by most Italians and by the international community. When the issue of trafficking was raised with regard to Italy, it typically pertained to the movement of Italian women to South American brothels, particularly those in Argentina, or to Egypt. As early as 1885, for example, Italian associations in Alexandria, Egypt, protested against prostitution there. Italian abolitionists reported to Josephine Butler:

> Italian men are the procurers; Italian men are the proprietors of the brothels; Italian women are the prostitutes, and the most hideous, the most shameful trade in these women is carried on between Alexandria and Italy. . . . Suffice it to say that the number of Italian prostitutes in Alexandria is over five hundred, without

counting those spread among the lower classes of society; while among the Greek colony, two-thirds larger than our own, the number is so insignificant as to remain unknown, and the Austrian and Russian colonies, which formerly supplied by far the greatest amount of prostitutes, have, owing to the assistance given by their respective Governments, been entirely rid of this impure element.[70]

Years later, the League of Nations would again note the movement of Italian women to South America and Egypt.[71]

Summary

Neither the International Abolitionist Federation nor the International Bureau gained much popular support in Italy, compared to the Netherlands and France, and state officials were free to take over anti-trafficking activities and fashion them in their interests. As in France, the International Abolitionist Federation unsuccessfully attempted to organize, though they drew support from liberals, from the small group of feminists that existed in the late 1800s, and from some socialists and members of the working class. Catholic women and men again avoided the movement, and regulationists were able to put forward neoregulationist proposals for the reform rather than the abolition of state regulation. The International Bureau also had difficulties mustering popular support, but it was received well by the government, which took over anti-trafficking work and only increased control over regulation in metropolitan and colonial areas.

Clearly state officials never intended to suppress the traffic in indigenous or European women in the colonies, despite Mussolini's pronouncement to the League of Nations. On the contrary, under Fascist population policy, women's sexual labor was but one type of labor needed for the metropolitan and colonial areas. Over time, with increased concern about imperial prestige and race-mixing, Italian officials attempted to import other European women for brothels in colonial areas. When this was not possible, indigenous women were recruited, with force when necessary. Other administrative measures could also be used to help stock the brothels. When Italy signed the 1921 League of Nations trafficking convention, it included a declaration lowering the age of consent from twenty-one to sixteen for the colonies. Italy maintained the legitimacy of state-controlled prostitution, and by lowering the age of consent they could ensure a larger supply of "adults." In the context of active colonialism, Italy sought to maintain both the regulation of prostitution and the traffic in women.

8 The Politics of Trafficking

WITH ITS FEMINIST ORIGINS, the international movement to combat the traffic in women for prostitution began as a means of arguing for women's universal right to be free from state control and sexual exploitation in state-regulated prostitution markets. The women and men affiliated with the International Abolitionist Federation were attempting to develop a universal liberal feminist agenda to help women and girls, one that challenged state regulation around the world. There were a few early successes: the movements in Great Britain, the home of the International Abolitionist Federation, and the Netherlands were heavily influenced by and involved with abolitionists. In the end, however, the International Abolitionist Federation's agenda lost out to the explicitly nationalist calls made by the men and women of the International Bureau. It was purity reformers and affiliated state officials who had much more success in influencing prostitution reform efforts on the continent, in France, Germany, Belgium, Spain, and to a lesser extent, Italy and Hungary. In all countries where they were active, international purity reformers helped to organize morally conservative local reformers and the state officials who funded them and in some cases gave them quasi-governmental status.

Purity reformers could have opposed state officials' authorization of prostitution through regulation, but they did not. State regulation created a moral dilemma for them, because they acknowledged prostitution as an "evil" yet were also opposed to any efforts to reduce governmental control over prostitution. Internationally and nationally, they chose to sidestep the issue of regulation in favor of working with state officials to nationalize and suppress prostitutes themselves. State officials, who had strongly opposed abolitionist efforts in most countries, often using police repression to try to stop the movement, embraced the International Bureau and their anti-trafficking agenda.

As the international anti-trafficking movement came to be dominated by purity reformers and state officials, it began to lose its focus on the protection of women and instead stressed the need to control women's mobility and sexual activity. Under the banner of an international organization, the International Bureau actually worked with state officials to address prostitution in national rather than universal terms: developing international conventions against the traffic in women in order to protect "their" women from being prostituted by foreign men; cleansing their streets of foreign women in prostitution, with police assistance when desired; increasing the legal means by which the state could enforce sexual morality, and defending the right of state officials to control domestic prostitution as they saw fit.

Aside from showing the complex positions of the international voluntary associations in relation to each other and to state officials, the politics of the first international anti-trafficking movement demonstrate state interests in the control of women's bodies and sexual activity, and the importance of sexuality in national, imperial, and state-building projects. State officials were intricately involved both in pressing for the creation of anti-trafficking conventions and in implementing them locally. As part of an increasing overall concern with ethnic and racial endogamy in the face of growing nationalism and colonial endeavors, trafficking and prostitution became important issues to imperial states.

The anti-trafficking accords not only allowed officials to control legitimately the emigration and immigration of women, particularly those whose sexual activity was deemed either necessary or dangerous to the nation or empire. They also provided states with a means of ensuring the legitimacy of regulated prostitution systems. With anti-trafficking procedures in place, state officials defended state-regulated prostitution, characterizing it as involving only women above the age of consent who worked voluntarily.

Moreover, anti-trafficking measures lent themselves to increased state oversight of prostitution as officials argued that close scrutiny was necessary to prevent abuses. It should be noted that the International Abolitionist Federation's stance toward trafficking and prostitution also necessitated some increased infrastructural power for states, though both they and their detractors uniformly understood their "laissez-faire" approach to prostitution as a challenge to state power. Their efforts to fight state regulation of prostitution around the world often landed them on the same side as anticolonial nationalists, and in metro-politan areas they often drew the interest of those who opposed state involve-ment in other aspects of daily life.

The feminist abolitionist stance against state regulation nonetheless envi-sioned a limited role for state officials in criminalizing the third-party orga-nization of prostitution and in closing brothels, though they opposed further state involvement such as criminalizing the act of prostitution or creating laws to enforce morality. Both international voluntary associations, then, were fight-ing for increased infrastructural control over some aspects of prostitution, but the International Bureau's vision was much more expansive, and it left state-regulated prostitution systems under the control of state officials. It is not sur-prising that state officials responded to this agenda.

Anti-Trafficking Efforts Within Countries

The case studies in this book show, first, that the organizing efforts of the differ-ent international voluntary associations did affect the character of local move-ments in particular countries. Where emerging feminist abolitionists were able to organize successfully, such as in the Netherlands, the movements remained relatively autonomous from the state and were in a better position to press for changes to state policies. Where International Bureau reformers and affiliated conservative moral reformers dominated the movement, as they did in France, or where popular support was lacking, as it was in Italy, state officials took over anti-trafficking efforts and used anti-trafficking measures in service of nation and empire, to control women's migration and legitimize state-regulated sys-tems of prostitution.

In this respect, the Dutch came closest to realizing feminist abolitionist goals, and supporters of the International Abolitionist Federation helped to pressure the state to change its policies regarding prostitution. This was not typical. The early and positive reception of the International Abolitionist Fed-eration's liberal feminist stance on prostitution was not replicated in France or Italy, and even if it had been, the outcome of feminist pressure to challenge trafficking and prostitution depended also on a country's imperial trajectories and its interests in maintaining control of women's sexual labor.

In the case of the Netherlands, the International Abolitionist Federation was able to help move local reformers from religious charitable work to a po-liticized, feminist agenda, incorporating Dutch reformers into the international voluntary association to a greater degree than those from the other countries.

Emerging feminists allied successfully with already established Protestant charitable and reform groups, including women's groups that were organized separately from those of men.[1] The relative autonomy of these groups from the state, rather than anything intrinsic to Protestantism, seems to have been important in fostering the linkage, helping to provide the basis for a strong movement in the Netherlands that tempered its nationalism to a larger degree than those in France or Italy. Protestant groups did not always provide a warm welcome to the International Abolitionist Federation. In Germany, for example, where German evangelical groups were particularly nation-statist, they actively fought feminists affiliated with the International Abolitionist Federation and embraced the International Bureau.[2]

In France and Italy, feminism was slower to develop as an organized movement, and women struggled to accomplish their political goals, not only with regard to trafficking and prostitution, but in other areas as well. In both countries, at late as the interwar period women had not yet even been granted suffrage. French Protestant philanthropists "gradually became receptive to feminism in their struggle against prostitution . . . ," but they were hampered by Catholic groups hostile to the association between Republican anticlericalism and liberal feminism.[3] The strength of French nationalism also created difficulties.[4] Italian abolitionists were likewise often Protestant in a Catholic country, and as in France, Catholic groups preferred the International Bureau's anti-trafficking agenda to the International Abolitionist Federation's abolitionism. Abolitionism was also seen as a challenge to the recently unified Italian state.[5] These circumstances contributed to the likelihood that state officials would respond more positively to the International Bureau's trafficking and morality agenda than to the agenda of the International Abolitionist Federation.

Second, the case studies show the importance of different imperial trajectories that led the Netherlands, France, and Italy to have varied levels of concern with controlling interracial sexuality through prostitution. France and Italy were engaged in the active expansion of their colonial empires from the 1870s on. For France, the expansion of empire in North Africa and Indochina was tied to French renewal and to efforts to prove French prestige and national grandeur.[6] Italy's late expansion into Africa, which was continued under fascism, became an important component of Italian nationalism.[7] World War I only increased French and Italian ambitions for territory, but the Netherlands was not expanding its territory, nor did it take part in the war. The Dutch were instead focused on maintaining the territories they already possessed.[8]

These different imperial agendas bolstered the importance of the military for France and Italy compared to the Netherlands. The Dutch faced increasing unrest with the rise of nationalist groups in the Dutch East Indies from 1900 on, but they were not coping with the same level of resistance as the French encountered in their colonies, nor were they engaged in new conquests like the Italians. The strong role of the military in French and Italian imperialism, and their heavy use of indigenous men in the colonies to increase the reservoir of colonial soldiers, meant that prostitution was a salient issue to both French and Italian authorities.[9]

In all three cases, military authorities had condoned concubinage as a means of providing for the presumed sexual needs of men, and all had allowed the children of mixed-race unions to be categorized as citizens if claimed by their fathers. Then, in the interwar period, they all began to evince increasing concern with interracial sexual activity, and worked to prevent concubinage and interracial domestic arrangements. The Dutch eventually allowed interracial marriage, however, thereby offering some protection to indigenous women through the marriage contract.[10]

All of this points to a suggestion that the Dutch case was unique in its tolerance of interracial mixing and therefore less concerned to control it through state-regulated and segregated prostitution systems.[11] It is not that the Dutch were less prejudiced than the French or Italians; in fact, considerations of race permeated colonial life in the late nineteenth century.[12] Rather, it is that race and ethnicity were not as salient in delineating the boundaries of the Dutch nation and empire compared to other European countries during this period. Unlike Italians, who recategorized mixed-race persons as Africans rather than citizens, mixed-race Dutch groups in the Dutch East Indies were not deprived of their citizenship.[13] A less prominent role for the military and less insistence on the need to maintain racial boundaries provided a more receptive environment for abolitionism. Organizing just prior to the development of the Dutch Ethical Policy at the turn of the twentieth century, Dutch reformers were able to argue for abolition in the colonies as part of Dutch colonial reform; and with less need to maintain foreign women in prostitution, Dutch officials could take steps to deal with trafficking.

Reformers affiliated with the International Abolitionist Federation in France and Italy faced a different situation. With French governmental officials worried not only about the health of the colonial military but also about the influx of immigrant groups and those from the colonies, ethnonational concerns were much stronger. In many ways the Italian case was similar to the French: state officials were convinced of the importance of state-regulated prostitution for the health of the military and of the civilian populations in both metropole and colony; there was strong interest among state officials in the potential use of anti-trafficking measures to bolster the legitimacy of their brothel systems; and there was increasing concern with controlling interracial sexual activity in the interwar period as one means of reinforcing or securing the prestige of colonial rule. This was not the case in Italy at first; Italian officials were not particularly concerned about ethnicity until fascism developed, and with it efforts to expand the Italian population through colonization.[14]

I do not wish to argue, however, that the unique context of the Dutch efforts reflected only altruistic motives on the part of the Dutch government as opposed to the French or Italians. Dutch officials were faced with a groundswell of action on trafficking and prostitution in the Indies, with the growth of organizations that included Dutch feminists, Indonesian feminists, Chinese men and women, and Indonesian nationalists. Each group was concerned about the sexual use of Indonesian, Chinese, and Japanese women, although most framed the issue along racial and ethnic lines. Organized anticolonial nationalist pressure, in addition to feminist efforts, played a role in the Dutch government's responses to trafficking and prostitution in the Dutch East Indies.

In addition, Dutch officials' own reports to the League of Nations show that they too used anti-trafficking measures to control imperial borders. Officials not only voluntarily repatriated foreign women in prostitution, for example, but also deported them, refused women suspected of being prostitutes entry into Dutch territories, and even deported women who were not prostitutes on the basis of their "immorality" in having sexual relations outside of marriage or for lacking proof of a viable income. The implementation of anti-trafficking measures inevitably detoured state officials away from humanitarianism and toward social control.

Contemporary Trafficking

After the United Nations' initial but truncated attempt to address trafficking in the 1950s, the traffic in women for prostitution faded from international politics until global trends against it placed the issue on center stage some forty years later. Political and economic transition, the growth of neoliberal economic policies, and the expansion and proliferation of the global sex trade have contributed to an increase in contemporary trafficking, again making it a concern for the United Nations and for a variety of national and international nongovermental organizations who have taken up anti-trafficking work since the 1990s.

The international traffic in women today has familiar characteristics: it has resurged with the current wave of globalization, prompted by state transition (now post-socialist), war, and poverty instead of by imperialism. The contemporary traffic still typically involves the movement of women from poorer countries to comparatively wealthier ones. Women are moving not only from the countries of the Global South to the Global North, but also within regions, from countries with more poverty and insecurity to those with less. Central and Eastern European women as well as Russian women are still found in the international sex trade.[15] Southeast Asian women have taken the place of Chinese and Japanese women trafficked for prostitution in Asia.[16]

The international sex trade continues to capitalize on and reinforce gender, class, racial, ethnic, and national hierarchies. Women are still marginalized within countries, and their status can leave them more vulnerable to trafficking than men.[17] Gender discrimination can exclude women from formal work, concentrate them in the informal economy, prevent them from owning property or other forms of wealth, or marginalize them within families. In such cases, they may not only be more vulnerable to trafficking, but may also agree to exploitative sexual labor as part of a family economic strategy, or because they perceive it to be a better alternative to abuse within the home. Racism and poverty continue to lead to the overrepresentation of poor women and women of color at the bottom, most dangerous levels of the international sex trade, and in many countries ethnic and national distinctions create hierarchies even within groups.[18]

The methods of traffickers have remained much the same, though they have been expanded and updated with the times. Recruitment through employment agencies, returning migrants sent to find new candidates in their home areas, and promises of marriage are still mentioned in the trafficking literature, but women and girls can now travel via automobile and airplane rather than ship. The experiences of women, then and now, have much to do with the economics of prostitution, the continued operation of trafficking and smuggling networks through underground processes, and the ongoing efforts of states to control their borders.

There are also some clear differences. Women are moving no longer from metropolitan to colonial or frontier areas but to already established nation-states that are facing pressures to control or limit immigration. This pattern will contribute to the possibility that states will use anti-trafficking measures as migration control. Also, women are now trafficked not only into brothels but also to other parts of the international sex industry, which has professionalized, corporatized, and diversified to a degree surely unimaginable to the participants of the first movement against trafficking.

There also seem to be some differences in the organization of trafficking today compared to the past. Contemporary traffickers are thought to be organized into large underground crime syndicates. Despite the difficulty of documenting underground activities, the League of Nations commission that first studied trafficking and prostitution in the interwar period concluded that most traffickers of the time were individuals or small groups, typically former pimps.[19] There is some evidence that more organized elements were at work in the past, for example, the involvement of Chinese highbinders in trafficking women and girls to the United States, and networks that operated to move Jewish women and girls to South America.[20] On the whole, however, such networks seem to have been a small portion of traffickers. Today, researchers regularly note the involvement of organized crime in trafficking women, sometimes intertwined with trafficking drugs and arms.[21] Such criminal groups as Chinese and Vietnamese triads, the Japanese Yakuza, South American drug cartels, and Italian, Russian, and Albanian mafias are thought to be involved.[22]

State involvement in the organization of prostitution has also changed. Abolitionists were able to stigmatize states' direct and explicit involvement in prostitution markets, and abolition was eventually achieved even in many staunchly regulationist states in the aftermath of World War II. Yet the end result, following the International Bureau agenda, was that state officials coupled abolition with increased state control over the women in prostitution themselves, criminalizing the act of prostitution while tolerating the existence of the sex trade as long as it did not disturb public order. That model has persisted in many countries, with police targeting street prostitution in order to move it indoors and out of the public eye.[23]

A few states have recently legalized prostitution in all or parts of their countries, such as Australia, Germany, and the Netherlands, ironically, given the past activities of Dutch feminist abolitionists. The results have been controversial. Although some hail the system as a success in preventing trafficking and the abuse of women in prostitution, critics disagree. They contend that police corruption, violence against women in prostitution, and trafficking have increased; that organized crime has become more involved in the sex trade; and that legalized brothels have again begun "nationalizing" as white, European women work in them and immigrant women of color work illegally in the underground sex trade, where they are subject to abuse.[24] These criticisms, like those of the past, again point out the important connections between trafficking and institutionalized prostitution markets, and the often blurred lines between them. In light of these connections, some feminists continue to stress the need to include an anti-prostitution agenda in anti-trafficking work.

Even though fewer states now regulate prostitution directly by licensing establishments and by registering the women working in them, many nonetheless still influence the development of prostitution markets within their territories by fostering sex tourism, encouraging or restricting the labor migration of particular groups of women, and working toward neoliberal economic policies that can worsen the vulnerability of poor women. State officials also still encourage sex industries and trafficking during and after situations of conflict.[25] Ethnic and nationalist concerns may still lead state officials to prefer migrant women rather than their "own" women to work in local sex industries.[26]

Contemporary Anti-Trafficking Efforts

What can the study of the early international anti-trafficking movement contribute to our understanding of contemporary trafficking and the movements to combat it? As in the past, concern about the contemporary traffic in women has brought together feminists who want to stop the exploitation of women in prostitution, conservative religious reformers who want to protect the sexual honor of the girls of their nations, and state officials with various interests in women's sexuality. In addition, the contemporary anti-trafficking movement also has the active involvement of sex-work activists interested in decriminalizing or legalizing prostitution worldwide. These groups, each with different motivations and agendas, create unstable alliances that all too easily give way to a focus on migrant women themselves rather than on either the reasons for their migration or their involvement in the sex trade.

The debates in the contemporary anti-trafficking movement are familiar, with contention about the relationship of trafficking and voluntary prostitution at the top of the list.[27] Echoing some aspects of regulationist arguments of the past, sex-work feminists now argue that prostitution should be recognized as legitimate paid labor, implying that some level of state oversight of sex industries is necessary to help ameliorate abuses. They believe that normalizing prostitution markets and allowing women opportunities to migrate legally to work as prostitutes in other countries would help to eliminate the problems of trafficking.[28]

Other feminists adopt a neoabolitionist view, arguing that prostitution should not be normalized and that states should target all third-party organizers of prostitution and criminalize their activities.[29] Both groups agree that women involved in migratory prostitution, whether voluntary or not, should not be penalized by state officials. But their stances are all too familiar given the history of the international trafficking movement, and it is doubtful that state officials will safeguard women's rights as a result of either approach.

Foreign women in prostitution remain a focal point for state officials: whether to repatriate them, and at whose expense; whether as victims of trafficking they have rights that voluntary migrant prostitutes do not; and when and under what conditions they could be granted residency or citizenship in the countries where they are found. As in the past, some feminists stress the sexual exploitation of all women in prostitution as a philosophical perspective and a political strategy. They hope to convince states to treat migrant women humanely, to allow them to stay in their countries of destination, and to allow them to receive a variety of social supports that officials would otherwise be reluctant to provide.

Sex-work feminists have vehemently critiqued this position, arguing that it negates the agency of women who want to work in prostitution, but they too grapple with the distinction between forced and voluntary prostitution. They are concerned about current anti-trafficking legislation that separates "voluntary prostitutes" from "innocent victims of trafficking," because it sets up a harmful dichotomy between "good" and "bad" women.[30] Defined as the latter, as we have seen, migrant women are more likely to be brought under the control of the state or deported than provided with assistance.

As in the past, the debate about the voluntary or involuntary nature of prostitution still places the attention of reformers on the women rather than on the men involved in the global sex trade. It has also led many sex-work feminists to downplay the fact that women do find themselves in situations of coercive or involuntary prostitution, both within and across borders. The portrayal of women as individuals who want the right to prostitute in foreign countries also does little to problematize the relations of power in sex industries around the world, and it obscures the structural bases for women's inequality.[31] In focusing on the individual and her right to work, proponents have tended to ignore the political economy of the international sex trade and the ways that gender, ethnicity, nationality, and class intersect to create particular patterns of trafficking and prostitution.[32]

Yet the focus on women in prostitution as victims of sexual exploitation, as we learned from the earlier movement, does not guarantee that state officials will not turn anti-trafficking measures against women themselves. Moreover, although this approach does focus attention on male sexuality and questions the assumption that men have a "right" to purchase sexual labor, it also tends to privilege a concern with gender exploitation over class, racial and ethnic, and national inequalities.[33] Again, the reasons for the growth of the international sex trade and the conditions that lead women into prostitution are not examined.

There is much more to learn about the organization of prostitution worldwide, the extent of trafficking, the efforts of anti-trafficking groups, and the experiences of women involved in prostitution, both historically and today. The legal status of prostitution—that is, whether it is still regulated by the state, prohibited through criminalization, allowed while third-party involvement is made illegal, or completely decriminalized—may have important effects both on the ways that women enter into prostitution as well as on the exploitation they experience. However, there may also be more similarities in women's experiences under the various types of systems than is commonly assumed. The organization of the sex industries themselves, rather than only the issue of their legalization, needs further investigation.

Comparative studies in particular are necessary if we are to understand more about the similarities and differences between sex industries in different countries and why some countries seem to have much more trafficking than others. Such studies can help us to learn more about the political, economic, and criminal aspects of sex industries in various countries, as well as about the intersections of class, race and ethnicity, nationality, and gender that help to structure them. They can also shed light on the relations among militarization, prostitution, and trafficking, which were such an important component historically and remain so today.[34]

As anti-trafficking reformers work to build international organizations and networks to help women, they need to think clearly about the nation-state and the politics of trafficking in order to avoid the outcomes of the past movement. Some contemporary feminist abolitionist activists in the United States, for example, have collaborated with neoconservative faith-based organizations and conservative state officials to develop anti-trafficking policies and agendas. This approach has alarmed other feminists concerned about the stances of those groups on the criminalization of voluntary prostitution, as well as on migration and women's reproductive rights.[35]

On the other hand, sex-work groups also need to examine critically the support they receive from state officials who stand to benefit from prostitution as a revenue source, and from those men (and women) who provide the capital for, reap the profits of, and implicitly or explicitly participate in the abuses associated with the international sex trade. One thing is certain: the divisions between women leave the door open for state officials to implement anti-trafficking measures that end up being repressive for women. History has shown that without unified feminist efforts, and perhaps even despite them, state officials will often place nationalist concerns above protections for women and girls in the international sex trade, whether they have been trafficked or not.

Notes

Chapter 1

1. The first speaker, Percy Bunting, addressed the 1899 International Congress on the White Slave Trade in London. See National Vigilance Association, *The White Slave Trade: Transactions of the International Congress on the White Slave Trade* (London: National Vigilance Association, 1899), 66–67, GL FAI Brochures, 300(6), 343.545.NVA(758). The second speaker, Henry J. Wilson, a member of Parliament in Great Britain, was associated with the International Abolitionist Federation. See National Vigilance Association, "White Slave Traffic: International Congress Under the Auspices of the National Vigilance Association Held at the Westminster Palace Hotel on Wednesday June 21, Thursday 22nd, Friday 23rd, 1899," *The Vigilance Record*, 1899 (July):6–7, WL.

2. I use the term *globalization* to refer to the worldwide expansion of material and symbolic infrastructures that increase global connectedness. This expansion entails the transformation of social relations and power. The nineteenth century experienced a massive wave of globalization, generally understood to have continued until 1914. See, for example, Held and McGrew 2000 for an overview of contemporary debates about globalization.

3. See, for example, Offen 2000 and Rupp 1997 on the history of European and international feminisms and their efforts on these issues.

4. In using the term *sexuality,* I am referring to socially constructed meanings, expectations, practices, and identities pertaining to sex.

5. Kligman 1998; Mosse 1985; Stoler 1997b; Yuval-Davis 1998.

6. Clancy-Smith and Gouda 1998; Gal and Kligman 2000; Nagel 2003; Stoler 1989; Yuval-Davis 1998.

7. Nagel 1998:255–256.

8. Mosse 1985.

9. Nagel 1998.

10. See Cynthia Enloe 1990; 2000; and 2005 on masculinity, nationalism, and militarization.

11. See Nagel 1998. See also Connell 1987:183-188 and Connell and Messer-schmidt 2005 on the concept of "hegemonic masculinity."

12. Enloe 1990; 2000.

13. Nagel 2003.

14. Stoler 1997a:226.

15. Stoler 1997b.

16. Phillips 2006.

17. Gal and Kligman 2000:18.

18. Phillips 2006.

19. Phillips 2005:291.

20. Enloe 2000; Nagel 1998.

21. Conklin 1998; Stoler 1997b.

22. Bryder 1998; Levine 1994.

23. Howell 2005; Lester 2002.

24. Stamatov 2006.

25. Boli and Thomas 1999; Iriye 2002; Rieff 2002; Tarrow 1994.

26. See Mumm 2006 on abolitionists and trafficking. Margot Badran 1995:192 identifies the origins of the term with French writer Victor Hugo, who wrote to the founder of the International Abolitionist Federation, Josephine Butler, that "the slavery of black women is abolished in America, but the slavery of white women continues in Europe."

27. See, for example, Hyam 1990; and Nadelmann 1990.

28. Compare Berkovitch 1999a; Doezema 2000; Hyam 1990; Jeffreys 1985; Nadelmann 1990; Sharma 2005.

29. Lester 2002:290.

30. See Mann 2005:62 on statist projects in Europe during this period.

31. The League of Nations' mandate system granted administrative authority over particular territories, under the agreement that the mandatory powers had to attend to the well-being and development of the people in the mandated areas. The intent was to develop and implement a new moral and legal responsibility in the international realm on behalf of colonized people, though there was no way to enforce it (Abernethy 2000:105–106). Pedersen 2005 argues that the mandate system was little more than window dressing but was still an ideological effort undertaken by liberals and humanitarians to reconcile continued imperial rule with popular ideals of self-determination.

32. See for example, Burton 1994; and Grever and Waaldijk 2004.

33. Kaplan 1997.

34. See, for example, National Vigilance Association, "International Conference on the Suppression of the White Slave Traffic Held at Zurich, September 15th and 16th, 1904," *The Vigilance Record*, 1904, 10(October):1–6, WL.

35. International Agreement for the Suppression of the White Slave Traffic, signed at Paris, May 18, 1904 (London: His Majesty's Stationery Office, 1905), WL 4/IBS/ Box 128/LN.1.

36. International Agreement for the Suppression of the White Slave Traffic, signed at Paris, May 4, 1910 (London: His Majesty's Stationery Office, 1912), WL 4/ IBS/Box 128/LN.1.

37. League of Nations 1921b.

38. League of Nations 1926a.

39. For the 1904 agreement, see the International Agreement for the Suppression of the White Slave Traffic, signed at Paris, May 18, 1904 (London: His Majesty's Stationery Office, 1905), WL 4/IBS/Box 128/LN.1. For the text and status of all subsequent anti-trafficking conventions, see chapter seven of *Multilateral Treaties Deposited with the Secretary-General*, http://treaties.un.org/Pages/Treaties.aspx?id =7&subid=A&lang=en (accessed September 12, 2009).

40. The United States did sign the 1904 agreement but did not adhere to the 1910 or 1921 accords. On anti-trafficking efforts in the United States, see Donovan 2006.

41. Reanda 1991.

42. United Nations, *Convention for the Suppression of the Traffic in Persons and of the Exploitation of the Prostitution of Others* http://treaties.un.org/Pages/ViewDetails .aspx?src=TREATY&mtdsg_no=VII-11-a&chapter=7&lang=en (accessed September 12, 2009).

43. Imperialism is "the process by which an expanding state dominated the territory, population, and resources of less powerful states or regions" and can take a colonial form involving "the imposition of direct military and administrative control, the influx of settlers from the imperialist country, and the systematic subordination of indigenous peoples" (Conklin and Fletcher 1999:1).

44. Conklin and Fletcher 1999:4.

45. Gal and Kligman 2000.

46. Stoler 1997a; 1997b; 1989.

47. Clancy-Smith and Gouda 1998; Gal and Kligman 2000; Levine 2003; Yuval-Davis 1998.

48. See, for example, Orloff 1996 for sociologists on gender and the welfare state. See Bock and Thane 1991 for an example of historians. For a list of sociologists who study empire, see http://www.bu.edu/sociology/grad/Empire/People .html (accessed February 28, 2009).

49. Cooper and Stoler 1997:29.

50. The International Bureau collection is at the Women's Library, London Metropolitan University, London, England. The British Library and the London School of Economics' British Library of Political and Economic Science in London hold materials related to both the International Bureau and the International Abolitionist Federation. The International Abolitionist Federation archives, which are not catalogued, are at the Geneva Library in Switzerland. Most of the documents retain their original catalogue numbers from when they were housed in the International Abolitionist Federation's library; I have noted these numbers in each reference. The League of Nations archives are also in Geneva, at the library of the United Nations Office. Materials were collected at the Women's Library, the British Library, and the London School of Economics library in 2002, and at the Geneva Public and University Library and the United Nations in 2002 and 2003.

51. Kligman and Limoncelli 2005.

52. Kelly 2005; Laczko 2005; Tyldum and Brunovskis 2005.

53. Gilfoyle 1999.

54. For an exception, see Bernstein 1995, which includes letters written by women in Russian lock hospitals. These hospitals were for the treatment of venereal diseases, and women were detained in them until authorities deemed them well enough for release.

55. See, for example, Hirata 1979; League of Nations 1927a; and Warren 1993 on trafficking and the coercive aspects of prostitution historically.

56. Ibid.

Chapter 2

1. This view that has often been and continues to be contested, especially by feminists who see it as a form of sexual exploitation or who point out the class aspects of prostitution and how it results from and reinforces inequalities for poor women especially. See Barry 1979 on prostitution as sexual slavery. See Walkowitz 1983 and Fischer-Tiné 2003 on the class aspects of prostitution historically, and Kligman and Limoncelli 2005 and Limoncelli 2008 and 2009 on the political and economic conditions fostering trafficking and prostitution today.

2. Weeks 1989.

3. This is true today as well. State officials have been implicated in trafficking schemes in some countries. See, for example, Human Rights Watch 2002 on the complicity of judges and prosecutors and on the active involvement of police in trafficking women in Bosnia.

4. Stoler 2002:48.

5. Barrera 1996; Iyob 2000; Stoler 2002:48.

6. Stoler 1997a; 1997b; 1989.

7. Levine 2006:134–135. Fischer-Tiné 2003 also notes that interracial contact be-

tween white men and Indian women was tolerated, but mixing between lower-class Indian men and white women was not.

8. Manderson 1997; Stoler 1997b.

9. Abalahin 2003:406–407.

10. Hui 2003:5

11. Bullough and Bullough 1987; Gronewold 1985; Roberts 1992.

12. Akyeampong 1997; Howell 2004b; 2005; Kumar 2005; Phillips 2005; 2006.

13. Gilfoyle 1999.

14. Barrera 1996:25; Spaulding and Beswick 1995.

15. See Henriot 1994 and Hershatter 1992 on Chinese courtesans in Shanghai. See Whitehead 2001 on the influence of local elites in shaping the regulation of prostitution.

16. Whitehead 2001.

17. Scully 2001.

18. Warren 1993.

19. Kumar 2005.

20. Naanen 1991.

21. Enloe 2000.

22. Bristow 1982.

23. Lazreg 1994.

24. Berque 1967:305.

25. Barrera 1996; Berque 1967; Howell 2004b; Iyob 2000; Jones, Sulistyaningsih, and Hull 1995; Kumar 2005; Sbacchi 1985; Surkis 2006; Taraud 2003.

26. Harsin 1985.

27. See, e.g., Walkowitz 1983:80; and Gibson 1986. This left abolition to an assortment of evangelical, Quaker, Unitarian, and other reform groups. In Japan, Christian and progressive reformers, politicians, and educators took up abolition (Garon 1993).

28. Ogborn 1993 suggests that medical doctors were even more supportive of regulation than were military officials.

29. Butler 1898.

30. See Mann 1993 on the increased infrastructural power of states during this period.

31. Howell 2004a:176.

32. Harsin 1985:13.

33. Fujime 1997.

34. Gal and Kligman 2000.

35. Foucault 1979.

36. McMillan 1981:175–176.

37. See, e.g., Bernstein 1995:172–174 on Russian women in brothels.

38. Andrew and Bushnell 1899:59.

39. See Jordan 2006 on Butler's biographical sketches of women in prostitution and on the issue of authentic representation.

40. Andrew and Bushnell 1899.

41. See Bernstein 1995:68–69 on Russia; Corbin 1990:328–330 on France; and van Heyningen 1984:183–184 on the Cape Colony in 1893.

42. The historical literature on prostitution, much of which addresses the issue of regulation, is small but geographically expansive. The most helpful country-based historical narratives on prostitution are Guy 1991 on Argentina; van Heyningen 1984 on the Cape Colony; Corbin 1990 and Harsin 1985 on France; Evans 1976b on Germany; Walkowitz 1983 on Great Britain; Miners 1988 on Hong Kong; Levine 1994 on India; Gibson 1986 on Italy; Fujime 1997, Garon 1993, Lie 1997, and Youn-ok 1997 on Japan; Bernstein 1995 on Russia, Henriot 1995 and Hershatter 1989 and 1992 on Shanghai; Warren 1993 on Singapore; and Rosen 1982 and Hirata 1979 on the United States.

43. Levine 1994; 2001. See Lee 2003 on racialization in state- and nation-building. She traces this process for Chinese and Japanese immigrants to the United States from 1870 to 1924.

44. Levine 1994:593.

45. See Strobel 1993 on the masculinity of empire.

46. Levine 1994.

47. I define trafficking in this paragraph as the movement of women across territorial borders for the purposes of prostitution; I do not make a distinction as to the voluntary nature of this movement because the sources of data for the trends noted here do not make this distinction. See also Chapter One on sources and definitions of trafficking, and Chapter Three on the historical difficulties of defining what is meant by the term *trafficking* and on its use by international voluntary associations.

48. Data collected by state officials and international voluntary associations did not include clandestine prostitution, but because regulation systems were implemented and maintained in many countries, there is some information on registered women in prostitution, most often in brothels but sometimes independent. Some inferences can be drawn from these data. The nationalities of clandestine prostitutes may well have been different from those of registered ones, but because the practice of banning foreign prostitutes from registration was not commonly accepted until the late interwar period, we cannot assume that foreign prostitutes would necessarily avoid it more than others.

49. League of Nations 1927a.

50. See Doezema 1998 on the forced/voluntary distinction.

51. Corbin 1990.

52. Corbin 1990; Gibson 1986; see Torpey 2000 on the state surveillance of movement.

53. League of Nations 1927a.

54. Bristow 1982; League of Nations 1927a.

55. Guy 1991.

56. Scully 2001.

57. Fischer-Tiné 2003.

58. League of Nations 1927a.

59. League of Nations 1927a.

60. Alison Neilans, *Report on Activities in Syria* (London: Association for Moral and Social Hygiene, 1931), WL 3/AMS/64.4.

61. Association for Moral and Social Hygiene, *Letter to All Societies Concerned with Social Welfare: Regarding the Russian Women in China*, with flyer entitled *The Tragedy of the Russian Women Refugees in China, 1935*, WL 4/IBS/Box 129/L.N. 3.7; Association for Moral and Social Hygiene, *Notes/Report on Russian Women in Far East*, 1935, WL 4/IBS/Box 129/L.N. 3.7; British National Committee for the Suppression of the Traffic in Women and Children, Extracts from Minutes of the British National Committee held Monday, May 16, 1938, WL 4/IBS/Box 129/LN 3.7; F. Sempkins, *Traffic in Women and Children: Russian Refugees in the Far East* (London: International Bureau for the Suppression of Traffic in Women and Children, 1935), WL 4/IBS/Box 129/LN 3.7.

62. League of Nations 1933a.

63. See, for example, Joachim Joesten, *"Prostitution and the White Slave Traffic in 'French' North Africa,"* 1955, WL 4/IBS/8/B/3/19/Box FL353.

64. International Bureau for the Suppression of the Traffic in Persons, *Conference of the International Bureau for the Suppression of the Traffic in Persons*, 1958, WL 4/IBS/124.

65. Barlay 1969.

66. O'Callaghan 1965.

67. United Nations 1948; 1949 and 1950. See also, for example, United Nations 1955 and 1959 on trafficking patterns after World War II.

68. Ibid.

69. Abernethy 2000:94.

70. Abernethy 2000:95.

71. Howell 2004b.

72. Association of Moral and Social Hygiene, *The Regulation of Prostitution in Hong Kong*, 1923, 1, WL, 4/IBS/115/28.

73. Manderson 1997.

74. Association for Moral and Social Hygiene, *The Shield* 1948, 11(1):49–50, GL Fax 51.

75. Association for Moral and Social Hygiene, *The Shield* 1937, 5(1):7–8, GL Fax 51.

76. Association for Moral and Social Hygiene, *Letter to All Societies Concerned*

with Social Welfare: Regarding the Russian Women in China, with flyer entitled *The Tragedy of the Russian Women Refugees in China*, 1935, WL 4/IBS/Box 129/L.N. 3.7.

77. See also Leppänen 2007 on the trafficking of Russian women.

78. F. Sempkins, *Traffic in Women and Children: Russian Refugees in the Far East* International Bureau for the Suppression of Traffic in Women and Children, 1935), 2, WL 4/IBS/Box 129/LN 3.7.

79. Nelson 1970.

80. Marks 1983:321.

81. The pamphlet was filled with blatantly racist assumptions about the sexuality of black men, although Morel's main target was French militarism and conscription.

82. E. D. Morel, *The Horror on the Rhine* (London: Union of Democratic Control, 1921), GL: IAF Brochures, Box 300(17), 351.76 Mor.

83. German National Committee for the Suppression of Traffic in Women and Children, *Verbatim Report of the Speech Held on Sept. 19, 1924 at the Congress in Graz Against the White Slave Traffic (Point 3 of the Agenda) by the President of the German National Committee*, 1924, LON 12/42959.

84. Marks 1983:303–304.

85. League of Nations 1927a. Contrast this with the traffic in Chinese women to the United States and Shanghai, where they were specifically imported for the Chinese community (Henriot 2001; Hershatter 1989; Hirata 1979; Lee 2003). There was a definite class component at work in these cases. Some Chinese women who were trafficked were reserved only for well-to-do Chinese men, while those considered less desirable serviced laborers and sailors of different nationalities.

86. Levine 1994; 2000.

87. Fischer-Tiné 2003.

88. Levine 2000.

89. Howell 2004a; 2005.

90. Abalahin 2003.

91. O'Callaghan 1965; Spaulding and Beswick 1995.

92. Fischer-Tiné 2003:181.

93. Harsin 1985:17–18.

94. Whitehead 2001:161–162.

95. Ballhatchet 1980:66.

96. Phillips 2006.

97. See Mann 1993, chapters 13 and 14, on nineteenth century bureaucratization and the expansion of civilian scope in the rise of the modern European state.

98. This question is still central in trafficking debates today.

99. Association for Moral and Social Hygiene, Letter to Sir J. Eric Drummond, May 22, 1920, LON 12/647.

100. Harsin 1985:11–13.

101. Mumm 2006.

102. Sbacchi 1985:172.

103. Lazreg 1994:32–33.

104. Fischer-Tiné 2003:179.

105. Salvation Army, *The Salvation Army and the Abolition of Licensed Prostitution*, no date, LON; U. G. Murphy, *The Social Evil in Japan and Allied Subjects with Statistics and the Social Evil Test Cases and Progress of the Anti-Brothel Movement* (Tokyo: Methodist Publishing House, 1904), GL Varia 1124.

106. Association for Moral and Social Hygiene, *The Regulation of Prostitution in Hong Kong*, 1923, 1, WL 4/IBS/115/28.

107. League of Nations 1927b.

Chapter 3

1. Limoncelli 2006.

2. See, e.g., Doezema 2000 and Hyam 1990 for criticisms.

3. The International Abolitionist Federation had fewer members who overlapped with International Bureau members than visa versa; only 6 percent of its 1898 congress attendees also attended the 1899 International Bureau congress, while 17 percent of International Bureau's attendees also took part in the International Abolitionist Federation congress. See British Committee of the Federation for the Abolition of State Regulation of Vice, "International Congress of the British, Continental, and General Federation for Abolition of State Regulation of Vice," *The Shield*, 1898, (16):129–150, GL New Series, No. 1-51, 1897–1901; and National Vigilance Association, *The White Slave Trade: Transactions of the International Congress on the White Slave Trade* (London: National Vigilance Association, 1899), GL FAI Brochures, 300(6), 343.545. NVA(758).

4. See Bannerji, Mojab, and Whitehead 2001 for a critique of postcolonial and post-structuralist approaches to colonialism, including the tendency to create binary categories of colonizer and colonized, and to obscure the gender and class components of anticolonial nationalist movements.

5. Bristow 1982.

6. Marcelle Legrand-Falco, *History of the Abolition of State Regulation of Prostitution with Special Relation to France and the Position Today*, 1946, GL FAI Brochures 300(8), 351.764(44).Leg.

7. Jordan 2001 writes, "Under English law, the seduction of a child under twelve years of age was a felony; between the ages of twelve and thirteen it was a misdemeanour; yet above the age of thirteen it was not a legal offence, although it was a misdemeanour to abduct a girl under the age of sixteen with intent to seduce." In Belgium, women were supposed to be twenty-one to register as prostitutes.

8. Mumm 2006.

9. Bristow 1977.

10. British Committee of the Federation for the Abolition of State Regulation of Vice, "The Abolitionist Federation and the White Slave Traffic," *The Shield*, 1909, 11(105):57–58, LON 12/4919/647.

11. For example, in Russia in 1899, the age of consent was reportedly fourteen; in parts of Denmark it was only twelve, while in Holland it was twenty-three. See National Vigilance Association, *The White Slave Trade: Transactions of the International Congress on the White Slave Trade* (London: National Vigilance Association, 1899), 98, GL FAI Brochures, 300(6), 343.545.NVA(758). In many British colonies in 1912, the age of consent was sixteen. See Dr. H. M. Wilson, *Law and Administration in Regard to the Social Evil* (Westminster, UK: British Committee of the International Federation for the Abolition of the State Regulation of Prostitution, 1912), GL Varia 79.

12. Maurice Gregory, *Facts Used in Japan and Australia in 1911 and 1912* (Perth, W. Australia: V. E. Jones, 1912), GL Varia 2096; Salvation Army, *The Salvation Army and the Abolition of Licensed Prostitution*, no date, LON; U. G. Murphy, *The Social Evil in Japan and Allied Subjects with Statistics and the Social Evil Test Cases and Progress of the Anti-Brothel Movement* (Tokyo: Methodist Publishing House, 1904), GL Varia 1124. See also Lie 1997 and Warren 1993.

13. Methodist missionaries and, later, white and Japanese Salvation Army workers described in detail their often futile efforts to assist Japanese women and girls in prostitution who had run away from brothels precisely because of their lack of individual rights under the law and outside of their family systems. Police and brothel keepers worked in conjunction to return women and girls to the brothels involuntarily to finish their contracts. Family members also helped police and brothel keepers, because they had contracted the women and girls to the brothels in the first place. See Salvation Army, *The Salvation Army and the Abolition of Licensed Prostitution*, no date, LON. See also Garon 1993; Sone 1992; and Hiroshi 1992.

14. See e.g., Walkowitz 1983 and Butler 1898:85–92, on the Federation's efforts in England; and Miller 2000:72, on police repression during Butler's first visit to France.

15. British Committee of the International Abolitionist Federation, *Our Army in India and Regulation of Vice* (Westminster, UK: Office of the British Committee of the International Abolitionist Federation, 1912), GL FAI Brochures, 300(27), 351.764(54).Bri.

16. Josephine E. Butler, *Mrs. Butler's appeal to the women of America, addressed to the International Council of Women* (New York: The Philanthropist, 1888), 12, GL Varia 218.

17. See Rupp 1996 and 1997 on the International Council of Women and the International Women's Suffrage Alliance, both of which internationalized quite extensively, particularly in the interwar period.

18. Women in the United Kingdom did not receive the right to vote until 1928; in the Netherlands, until 1919; in France, until 1944; and in Italy, until 1945 (Seager 2009).

19. British Branch of the British Continental and General Federation for the Abolition of State Regulation of Vice, *Report* (London: J. Cox, 1887), GL Varia 263.

20. See Walkowitz 1983 on this trend in England.

21. British Committee of the Federation for the Abolition of State Regulation of Vice, "Rescue and Preventive Work in Germany," *The Shield*, 1899, 2(27):64, GL New Series, No. 1-51, 1897–1901; Josephine E. Butler, *A Second Letter of Appeal and Warning* (Westminster, UK: British Committee of the Federation for the Abolition of State Regulation of Vice, 1895), GL 351.764.BUT. See also Butler 1897.

22. Maurice Gregory, *Facts Used in Japan and Australia in 1911 and 1912* (Perth, Australia: V. E. Jones, 1912), 29, GL Varia 2096.

23. Marchant 1908:235–236.

24. Association for Moral and Social Hygiene in India, *The Association for Moral and Social Hygiene in India: A Brief Survey of Its Origin and Development Prepared for the Nineteenth International Abolitionist Congress, Paris, May 1953* (New Delhi, India: Association for Moral and Social Hygiene in India, 1953), GL IAF Brochures, Box 300(29), 351.764.5. See also Joardar 1985.

25. Johnson and Johnson 1928:215.

26. British Committee of the Federation for the Abolition of State Regulation of Vice, "Discussion Concerning Infractions, &c., of the Law Caused by Prostitution," *The Shield*, 1899, 2(27):63, GL New Series, No. 1-51, 1897–1901; National Association for the Repeal of the Contagious Diseases Acts, *The Shield*, 1884, 15(477):51–52, GL Fax 51.

27. Johnson and Johnson 1928.

28. From the National Association for the Repeal of the Contagious Diseases Acts, *The Shield*, 1884, 15(477), 51—52, GL, Fax 51. See also the British Committee of the Federation for the Abolition of the State Regulation of Vice, *The Shield*, 1899, 2(27), 64, GL, New Series, No. 1-51, 1897—1901.

29. Helen Wilson, *Prostitution and the Law* (London: Association for Moral and Social Hygiene, 1926), 4–5, GL IAF Brochures, Box 300(8), 343.544 WIL.

30. Alison Neilans, International Congress of the International Abolitionist Federation, Paris, 1937, 3–4, GL IAF Brochures, Box 300(10), 351.764.5 FAI.

31. Maurice Gregory, *Facts Used in Japan and Australia in 1911 and 1912* (Perth: V. E. Jones, 1912), 29, GL Varia 2096.

32. Ibid.

33. See, for example, Corbin 1990:33–35, on such requirements in France.

34. Ogborn 1993.

35. See Burton 1990 and 1994 on the imperialism of British feminists.

36. Ladies National Association, "Modern Heathenism Caused by Christian Faithlessness": A paper read at the Christian Women's Union Conference (London: Dyer Brothers, no date), 10, GL Varia 92.

37. Depictions of interracial rape were common in British novels about the uprising, perhaps reflecting English male concerns about English women's increasing independence (see Paxton 1992).

38. See, for example, Burton 1994 on Josephine Butler, Bosch 1999 on Aletta Jacobs, and Donovan 2006 on Katharine Bushnell.

39. British Committee of the Federation for the Abolition of State Regulation of Vice, "The International Federation for the Abolition of State Regulation of Vice: The 'Assemblee Generale' in London," *The Shield* 1903, 6(65):33–39, GL.

40. Butler, Josephine E., *The Revival and Extension of the Abolitionist Cause*, London: Dyer Brothers, 1887, GL 351.764.BUT.

41. Butler 1898:1–2.

42. See, for example, Elizabeth Andrew and Katharine Bushnell, *Reply to Certain Statements in a Published Letter Addressed by Lady Henry Somerset to a Correspondent on the Regulation of Vice in India* (London: British Committee for the Abolition of State Regulation of Vice in India and Throughout the British Dominions, 1897), GL Varia 89(2054).

43. Even in their social work approaches, feminists sought to cross the racial, ethnic, and religious boundaries that separated women from one another. For example, in 1924, feminists at the League of Nations asked for formal coordination between all international voluntary associations dealing with the traffic, including the International Bureau, the Jewish Association, and all travelers associations for the protection of girls. They complained that the work was not occurring in the locations in which it was needed, and that some areas had hostels or homes for girls that were not filled, while others that had girls in need of such homes had none. They wanted homes for girls that crossed religious lines, which would entail coordination between Protestant, Catholic, and Jewish reformers. The Catholic and Jewish associations dissented, preferring to maintain their religious and ethnic identities (League of Nations 1924a:28–30).

44. Andrew and Bushnell 1899:73–74, emphases in original.

45. Burton 1990; 1994.

46. Andrew and Bushnell 1899:14.

47. It was under this act that Oscar Wilde was charged and tried.

48. National Vigilance Association, *Ninth Annual Report of the Executive Committee* (London: National Vigilance Association, 1894), WL.

49. The works of Richard Francis Burton and Émile Zola were of particular concern to British purity reformers, who persuaded Burton's widow to give them his books to burn and who successfully fought to have the publisher who was translating Émile Zola's books convicted of indecency.

50. National Vigilance Association, *Sixth Annual Report: Foreign Traffic Subcommittee* (London: National Vigilance Association, 1891), GL.

51. Coote 1910.

52. National Vigilance Association, "Verbatim Report of the Fifth International Congress for the Suppression of the White Slave Traffic," *The Vigilance Record*, 1913, 7/8(July and August):49–68, WL. See also Bristow 1977; 1982.

53. National Vigilance Association and International Bureau for the Suppression of the White Slave Traffic, *Work Accomplished by the Association* (London: National Vigilance Association and International Bureau for the Suppression of the White Slave Traffic, 1907), 6, LSE Pamphlet Collection, 35034.

54. National Vigilance Association, *The White Slave Trade: Transactions of the International Congress on the White Slave Trade* (London: National Vigilance Association, 1899), 66–67, GL FAI Brochures, 300(6), 343.545.NVA(758).

55. Ibid.

56. International Bureau for the Suppression of Traffic in Women and Children 1924:107.

57. Ibid.:104–105.

58. National Vigilance Association, "Fourth International Congress for the Suppression of the White Slave Traffic Held at Madrid from October 24th–28th, 1910," *The Vigilance Record*, 1910, 82–88, WL.

59. Ibid.

60. Offen 2008:244. See also Leppänen 2007 on the change in terminology.

61. National Vigilance Association 1913:115.

62. International Bureau for the Suppression of Traffic in Women and Children 1924, 104.

63. Sybil Neville-Rolfe, letter to Dame Rachel Crowdy dated September 28, 1920, LON 12/9780/7260.

64. C. B. Davenport, letter to Dame Rachel Crowdy dated November 25, 1920, LON 12/9780/9789; Dr. Inazo Nitobe, commentary dated December 24, 1920, LON 12/9780/7260.

65. Ibid. Nitobe continued: "German scientists under the lead of Gobineau and Stewart Chamberlain tried to find [a] scientific basis to demonstrate the absolute superiority of the 'Hun.' I hope America will not follow the German example. —I hail all scientific researches: but I am doubtful of their hasty application to social politics as was done by 'Politische Anthropologische Revue' set. —I.N."

66. Coote 1910:151.

67. F. Sempkins, 1931, report on Egypt, WL 4/IBS/Box 112/Co. 6CB/Egypt, italics in original.

68. Josephine E. Butler, "Which Are the Greatest Criminals?" *The Storm Bell*, 1899, (May):179–183, LSE.

69. British Committee of the Federation for the Abolition of State Regulation of Vice, "The Abolitionist Federation and the White Slave Traffic," *The Shield*, 1909, 11(105):57–58, LON 12/4919/647.

70. Association for Moral and Social Hygiene, letter to Dame Rachel Crowdy dated June 14, 1921, 1, LON 12/13873/13793.

71. Coote 1910:149.

72. F. Sempkins, letter to Dr. Karveliene, 1933, WL 4/IBS/Box 115/Co.32/ Lithuania.

73. International Bureau for the Suppression of Traffic in Women and Children, *What It Is and What It Is Not*, no date, WL.

74. F. Sempkins, letter to Miss McCall dated March 18, 1930, WL 4/IBS/112/ 6CA.

75. F. Sempkins, letter dated December 12, 1928, WL 4/IBS/Box 128/File 3.3.

76. League of Nations 1927a and 1927b.

77. League of Nations 1927a:43.

78. Reanda 1991.

79. This was the case in the United States, as Luker 1998 notes, and in many other countries as well.

80. Alison Neilans, letter to Miss Higson dated March 8, 1935, WL 3/AMS/62.2.

Chapter 4

1. Crowdy 1928; League of Nations 1926a.

2. Levine 1994.

3. Leppänen 2007:528 argues that the League of Nations took a nonmoralising stand on the issues of prostitution and trafficking, but debates about the necessities and harms of regulated prostitution (that is, its moral implications) were at the center of the work of the Traffic in Women and Children Committee.

4. This point is contra Leppänen 2007, who sees prostitution as transitioning from being a national interest to being a matter of international concern in the interwar period, and contra Gorman 2008, who suggests that the League of Nations's anti-trafficking work was a case of successful internationalization. It is important to separate out trafficking and prostitution, which were defined and treated differently in the international anti-trafficking movement. Furthermore, the internationalization of the movement happened prior to the League of Nations and a kind of "re-nationalization" of prostitution actually occurred as a result of interwar anti-trafficking efforts.

5. See Miller 1994 on interwar feminists at the League of Nations.

6. For details on the International Council of Women's resolutions transmitted to the League of Nations, see League of Nations, *Resolutions Adopted by the International Council of Women*, letter dated September 24, 1920, LON 20/31/82. The British Com-

mittee of the International Abolitionist Federation also corresponded with League of Nations officials to ask that regulation be addressed. See Association for Moral and Social Hygiene, letter to Sir Eric Drummond dated July 28, 1920, LON 12/4616/647; letter to Sir Eric Drummond dated October 7, 1920, LON 12/7352/647LON, Assembly Document 36A; Association for Moral and Social Hygiene, letter to Sir J. Eric Drummond dated May 22, 1920, LON 12/647.

7. Miller 1994:238.

8. League of Nations, correspondence on abolition from Dame Rachel Crowdy to F. P. Walters, 1920, LON 12/3628/647.

9. See League of Nations, report of meeting between the secretary general and a deputation of the International Women's Suffrage Alliance, at Sunderland House, on 16th July 1920, LON 23/5579/3554; *Resolutions Officially Transmitted to the Secretariat by a Deputation from the International Women's Suffrage Alliance*, 1920, LON 23/5359/3554 (Council Document G2).

10. See the full text of the covenant at http://avalon.law.yale.edu/20th_century/leagcov.asp; accessed March 1, 2009.

11. For correspondence on initial efforts to organize a League of Nations conference, see Malcolm Deleveigne, letter to Drummond dated August 7, 1919, and October 9, 1919, LON 12/1439/647; Bishop Herbert E. Ryle, letter to the Home Office dated October 7, 1919, LON 12/2117/647; F. P. Walters, letter to S. W. Harris dated October 11, 1919; LON 12/1439/647; S. W. Harris, letter to F. P. Walters dated November 14, 1919, LON 12/2117/647; Home Office (London), report of visit with Mr. Coote dated July 24, 1919, LON 12/1439/647; Correspondence on white slave traffic between Sir Eric Drummond, Dame Rachel Crowdy, and others dated October–December 1919, LON 12/2117, 2118, 2086, 1439/647; Dame Rachel Crowdy, unofficial conversation between Dame Rachel Crowdy and Miss Baker dated November 21, 1919, LON 12/2086/647; Dame Rachel Crowdy, memo Dated March 31, 1920, LON 12/647; and International Bureau, report of Mr. W.J.H. Brodrick on his return from the continent in September 1920, LON 12/7963/647.

12. Lady Ishbel Aberdeen, letter to Sir Eric Drummond dated April 14, 1921, LON 12/12477/647; Sir Eric Drummond, letter to Lady Aberdeen dated June 16, 1921, LON 12/12477/11024.

13. League of Nations 1921a; 1921b.

14. League of Nations 1921b:135–137.

15. Metzger 2007:59.

16. A. Colin, Memo to Captain Walters, 1929, LON 11B/10216/77.

17. See Offen (1984; 2000) and Miller (1994) on "difference" and equality feminisms.

18. League of Nations 1924a:37–38.

19. League of Nations 1925a:13.

20. League of Nations 1925a. From all accounts, trafficking in Argentina *was* much worse, but what is interesting here is the struggle of the delegate, Paulina Luisi, to reconcile her national and feminist identities. In her defense, she was often placed in the position of educating others on the committee about the differences between Latin American countries and the importance of distinguishing between Argentina, Brazil, and Uruguay. See also 1925b.

21. League of Nations 1923:61.

22. League of Nations 1927a; League of Nations 1927b.

23. S. W. Harris, letter to Dame Rachel and her reply, May 19, 1923, and June 16, 1923, LON.

24. League of Nations 1927b:5–9.

25. League of Nations 1927b:5–9.

26. For a digest of the report, see Harris 1928.

27. League of Nations 1933a.

28. Henriot 2001:320; League of Nations 1938.

29. Henriot 2001:320.

30. Lie 1997.

31. The countries that voted against the extension of the definition of the traffic were primarily regulationist: Brazil, Chile, Czechoslovakia, France, Greece, Italy, Monaco, Romania, Portugal, Siam, and Uruguay. Supporters of the proposal included Austria, Belgium, Canada, China, Denmark, Germany, Great Britain, Hungary, India, Japan, Netherlands, Norway, Poland, South Africa, Spain, Sweden, and Switzerland— a mix of abolitionist and regulationist countries.

32. Historian Christine Ehrick (1999) says that from 1903 to 1929 Uruguay was a model of progressiveness, social reform, political democracy, and feminism. Feminist leader Paulina Luisi, who was the Uruguay representative to the League of Nations Traffic in Women and Children Committee, was very active in the international realm.

33. League of Nations 1923.

34. The National Council of Women in Great Britain was actually divided on the issue, with aristocratic women (a few of whom were associated with the purity reformers and the International Bureau) supporting the measure. The council's vote just barely missed the necessary two-thirds majority, so they did not officially support it, and many feminists in Great Britain actively campaigned against it, writing to the League of Nations to voice their concerns (League of Nations 1923:19).

35. League of Nations 1923:24.

36. Association for Moral and Social Hygiene, *Prohibition of Foreign Women in Licensed Houses* (London: Association for Moral and Social Hygiene), 1923, WL GB106/3/AMS/65.1.

37. Alison Neilans, Memorandum on Prohibition of Foreign Women in Tolerated Houses, 1922, LON 12/25172/647.

38. League of Nations 1924a:27–28.

39. International Bureau for the Suppression of Traffic in Women and Children 1924:109.

40. Ibid.

41. Ibid.:107.

42. In this case, the League of Nations delegate from Great Britain, although abolitionist, did not side with the feminists on the resolution.

43. League of Nations 1925a:14.

44. League of Nations 1925a:15.

45. See reports on repatriation based on each country's self-reported cases, provided to the League of Nations. League of Nations 1924b; 1925c; 1928b; 1931; 1934.

46. League of Nations 1925a:15. See also Lee 2003 on this point.

47. Hiroshi 1992; Sone 1992; Warren 1993.

48. League of Nations 1933a:69

49. Ibid.

50. Hiroshi 1992; Sone 1992.

51. National Vigilance Association, "The Seventh International Congress," *Vigilance Record*, 1927, 6–7(June-July):48, WL.

52. National Vigilance Association, "The Eighth International Congress for the Suppression of Traffic in Women and Children," *Vigilance Record*, 1930, 6:56, WL.

53. See Brubaker (1996) on nationalizing states such as Poland in interwar Europe.

54. International Bureau for the Suppression of Traffic in Women and Children, *Repatriation of Prostitutes: A Memorandum on the Proposals of the International Bureau*, 1930, WL 4/IBS/Box 102-103/File 22T.

55. Ibid., 13.

56. Ibid., 9.

57. Alison Neilans, *Compulsory Repatriation of Prostitutes: Position Paper and Report of Conference Held at Caxton Hall, Westminster, Tuesday, March 3, 1931* (London: Association for Moral and Social Hygiene), WL 3/AMS/B/11/08.

58. Ibid.:3, emphasis in original.

59. Association for Moral and Social Hygiene, *Some Arguments Against the Compulsory Repatriation of Prostitutes* (London: Association for Moral and Social Hygiene, a.k.a. La Branche Anglaise de la Federation Abolitionniste Internationale, no date), 3–4, WL 3/AMS/B/11/08, emphasis in original.

60. Ibid.:5.

61. Association for Moral and Social Hygiene, *Compulsory Repatriation of Prostitutes* (London: Association for Moral and Social Hygiene, 1931), WL 11B/26359/3293.

62. League of Nations, *List of Organisations Who Have Sent in Resolutions Concerning the Compulsory Repatriation of Prostitutes*, 1931, LON 11B/26359/3293.

63. The accounts were gruesome. Greece, Czechoslovakia, Poland, Russia, and

Yugoslavia reported cases of forced prostitution, forced labor, rape, forced pregnancy, murder, and mass murder of women and girls by German troops. See International Bureau for the Suppression of Traffic in Women and Children, minutes dated March 25, 1942, WL 4/IBS/Box 192/Vol. 4. The Japanese were also implicated. An International Abolitionist Federation contact from Hong Kong reported that "in the prison camps there had been rumours that 1,000 girls had been procured for the Japanese." See International Abolitionist Federation, *Conference with the International Abolitionist Federation Delegates on November 8, 1945*, WL 3AMS/D/8/4/52.2. See also Grossman 1997; Naimark 1995, particularly chapter 2; and Hicks 1995 on violence against women in World War II.

64. United Nations 1948; 1949; 1950.

65. United Nations 1959:6–7.

66. International Bureau for the Suppression of Traffic in Women in Children, A Series of Lectures Delivered on the Occasion of an International Meeting Convened by the International Bureau for the Suppression of Traffic in Women and Children (London: International Bureau for the Suppression of Traffic in Women in Children, 1943), GL IAF Brochures, Box 300(22), 351.764 International.

67. United Nations 1959:20.

68. United Nations 1959:21.

69. United Nations 1955.

70. United Nations 1958b.

71. United Nations 1958a.

72. Association for Moral and Social Hygiene, letter from Secretary to M. de Felice, 1944, WL 3/AMS/52.2.

73. Association for Moral and Social Hygiene, *The Shield*, 1948, 11(1):50, GL Fax 51.

74. International Bureau for the Suppression of Traffic in Persons, executive meeting minutes dated February 3, 1954, WL 4/IBS/Box 193/Folder 10.

75. Association for Moral and Social Hygiene, *The Shield*, 1950, 12(1):16–19, GL Fax 51.

76. In a letter to Sir Eric Drummond about her contract, Crowdy refers to her nationality, "which seems to handicap me so heavily." See letter dated August 29, 1928, LON. In response, a flood of letters sent to the League from feminist and women's organizations noted that men's contracts were being extended for longer periods than Crowdy's and asked for an extension of five to seven years rather than one.

77. See, e.g., political scientists Finnemore 1996; Keck and Sikkink 1998; Risse, Ropp, and Sikkink 1999; and Khagram, Riker, and Sikkink 2002, who have adopted the approach from sociology and the work of John Meyer and John Boli. Meyer and Boli see the emergence and development of "world culture," i.e., global ideas or principles, as creating isomorphism among states in everything from their organizational

structures to their educational curricula. In the absence of a central state, they argue, world social control takes the form of global normative values and rules promoted by expert consultants in intergovernmental organizations or diffused even without such agents as long as the principles are "theorized"—i.e., developed into cultural models that can be adopted by distant others even without interaction (Boli and Thomas 1997; Meyer 1999; Meyer, Boli, Thomas, and Ramirez 1997). For an analysis of the anti-trafficking movement from such a perspective, see Berkovitch 1999b.

Chapter 5

1. Stokvis 1994; Swierenga 1993.

2. Swierenga 1993.

3. League of Nations 1926c.

4. League of Nations 1927b.

5. League of Nations 1927b. This finding had been foreshadowed by Paulina Luisi's words several years before at the International Bureau's 1924 congress, where she argued that the prohibition of foreign women in state-regulated brothels would result in nationalizing them and in protecting "homegrown" prostitution against foreign competition. What she did not perhaps anticipate was that it could be women nationals in prostitution themselves who supported such measures.

6. Stoler 2002:49–51

7. Stoler 2002:51

8. British Continental and General Federation for the Abolition of Government Regulation of Prostitution, *First Annual Report, 1875–1876* (Liverpool, UK: T. Brakell, Printer, 1876), WL 3/AMS/S1.1.

9. Maurice Gregory, *History of Regulation and Abolition in Holland from 1795 to the Present Time* (Capetown: South African Branch of the International Federation, 1913), GL Varia 2096; see also Butler 1898:180. See van Drenth and de Haan 1999 on the Dutch Réveil movement, which was part of an international Protestant religious revival, and on its ties to philanthropic activities in the Netherlands.

10. de Vries 2001; van Drenth and de Haan 1999.

11. Butler 1898:181.

12. van Drenth 2006:86.

13. van Drenth 2002.

14. de Vries 2008.

15. Ibid.

16. Maurice Gregory, *History of Regulation and Abolition in Holland from 1795 to the Present Time* (Capetown: South African Branch of the International Federation, 1913), GL Varia 2096.

17. de Vries 2008.

18. Ibid. The Dutch Association for the Protection of Young Girls did not develop

a feminist viewpoint and remained a "womanist" association while the Dutch Women's Union and the van Hogendorp sisters moved toward feminism and equal rights for women (van Drenth 2006; van Drenth and de Haan 1999:150).

19. British Committee of the Federation for the Abolition of the State Regulation of Vice, "The International Federation for the Abolition of State Regulation of Vice: The 'Assemblee Generale' in London," *The Shield*, 1903, 6(65):33–39, GL; Josephine E. Butler, *New Abolitionist Work Throughout the World*, 1885, GL Varia 258.

20. Bosch 2004:62.

21. van Drenth 2006; van Drenth and de Haan 1999:150.

22. de Vries 2008.

23. Bosch 2004:57.

24. de Vries 2005:13.

25. van Drenth 2006:86; van Drenth and de Haan 1999:151.

26. British Committee of the Federation for the Abolition of State Regulation of Vice, "International Congress of the British, Continental, and General Federation for Abolition of State Regulation of Vice," *The Shield*, 1898, 1(16):138, GL New Series, No. 1-51, 1897–1901.

27. Houkes 2005:332.

28. Jacobs 1996.

29. Butler 1898:183.

30. Coote 1910:45.

31. de Vries 2005; de Vries 2008:268.

32. Coote 1910; de Vries 2008:14.

33. de Vries 2008:13.

34. National Vigilance Association, "Third International Congress for the Suppression of the White Slave Traffic Held at the Hotel Continental, Paris, from the 22nd to the 25th October, 1906," *The Vigilance Record*, 1906, 11(November):85–92, WL.

35. International Bureau for the Suppression of the Traffic in Women and Children, minutes of meeting held December 3, 1909, p. 240, WL 4/IBS/Boxes 192, Vol. 1.

36. de Vries 2008:16.

37. de Vries 2001.

38. International Bureau for the Suppression of the Traffic in Women and Children, minutes of meeting held May 11, 1908, 201, WL 4/IBS/Boxes 192, Vol. 1; League of Nations 1924b.

39. British Branch of the International Abolitionist Federation, letter to M. de Graaf dated October 23, 1928, WL 3/AMS/51.2.

40. League of Nations 1921b:69.

41. See, e.g., National Vigilance Association, "The Graz Congress, September 18–20th, 1924," *The Vigilance Record*, 1924, 9(October):65–67, WL.

42. Dutch National Committee for the Suppression of the Traffic in Women and

Children, *Report to the Seventh International Congress in London*, 1927, GL IAF Bro-chures, Box 300(11), 343.545 Dutch.

43. League of Nations 1924b; 1925c; 1928b; 1931; 1934.

44. Lucassen 2002b.

45. Lucassen 2002b:330.

46. Henkes 2001.

47. Lucassen 2002a; 2002b.

48. Lucassen 2002a.

49. See, e.g., League of Nations 1934:16.

50. Clancy-Smith and Gouda 1998; Lammers 2003.

51. Betts, 1985:106.

52. Wesseling 1980:133.

53. Stoler 1997a:221.

54. Stoler 2002:53.

55. See, e.g., Gouda 1995:163–165; Betts 1985:96.

56. Betts, 1985:96.

57. Wertheim 1990.

58. Ingleson 1986; Jones, Sulistyaningsih, and Hull 1995:3.

59. Abalahin 2003:87–90.

60. Jones, Sulistyaningsih, and Hull 1995:3.

61. Jones, Sulistyaningsih, and Hull 1995.

62. Hiroshi 1992.

63. Hiroshi 1992:24–25 writes that Singapore was the main distribution center. Surabaya and Makasser were two major redistribution centers, for Java and the Cele-bes respectively. From the port of Surabaya, women in prostitution were redistributed to the neighboring islands and elsewhere.

64. Hesselink 1987; Hiroshi 1992.

65. Hiroshi 1992:19–20.

66. They did, however, maintain separate facilities for them when they needed treatment (Abalahin 2003:131–132).

67. Abalahin 2003:389.

68. Ingleson 1986.

69. See Coté (1999) for a postcolonial critique of Dutch feminism.

70. Grever and Waaldijk 2004:212.

71. Abalahin 2003; British Committee of the Federation for the Abolition of the State Regulation of Vice, "Abolitionist and Rescue Work in Holland and Java," *The Shield*, 1901, 4(49):71–72, GL New Series, No. 1-51, 1897–1901.

72. Maurice Gregory, *History of Regulation and Abolition in Holland from 1795 to the Present Time* (Capetown: South African Branch of the International Federation, 1913), 7, GL Varia 2096.

73. It is interesting to note that at this time Dutch women were also forming suffrage associations in the Dutch East Indies. The first, established in 1908, was a branch of the Dutch Women's Suffrage Association. Comprising Dutch women initially, these associations nonetheless argued that educated indigenous and Chinese women in the colony should have the right to vote. After achieving little success, they began recruiting Indonesian women's organizations in the 1920s, and some Indonesian women joined these associations. The relationship between the Dutch suffragists and the Indonesian women's movement was not smooth, given the latter's interests in independence; but together they successfully pressured the government to provide limited voting rights for Indonesian women in the late 1930s (Blackburn 2004a).

74. Gouda 1995.

75. Blackburn 2004b:17–18.

76. Hiroshi 1992:32.

77. Abalahin 2003:267.

78. Jones, Sulistyaningsih, and Hull 1995:6.

79. Ming 1983.

80. International Bureau for the Suppression of Traffic in Women and Children 1927:95; Jones, Sulistyaningsih, and Hull 1995.

81. Hiroshi 1992.

82. International Bureau for the Suppression of Traffic in Women and Children 1927.

83. National Vigilance Association 1913.

84. See S. Sutarman, "The Suppression of the Traffic in Persons etc.: A Summary of the Work of the International Bureau for the Suppression of the Traffic in Persons, etc. in Indonesia," November 1951, WL 3/AMS/62.3. See also Abalahin 2003:359.

85. Abalahin 2003:360.

86. See M. Velthusin, talk to the 1930 International Bureau congress, LON 11B/627/179. Abalahin's characterization (2003:279) suggests that Van Walsem maintained pressure on brothel keepers rather than target women for prostitution.

87. International Bureau for the Suppression of Traffic in Women and Children 1927

88. Abalahin 2003:276.

89. Abalahin 2003:374–376; League of Nations 1933a:249–254.

90. League of Nations 1933.

91. Abalahin 2003:388–389; League of Nations 1933a:247–248.

92. League of Nations 1924b:63.

93. Abalahin 2003:409; League of Nations 1933a:245.

94. League of Nations 1933a:245.

95. Abalahin 2003:398.

96. League of Nations 1933a:245.

97. Ingleson 1986.

98. Martyn 2005:40–43.

99. Blackburn 2004b; Blackburn and Bessell 1997; Martyn 2005.

100. Martyn 2005.

101. Blackburn 2004b; Blackburn and Bessell 1997; Locher-Scholten 2000.

102. Abalahin 2003.

103. League of Nations 1921b:54–57; National Vigilance Association 1913:337–339.

104. League of Nations 1921b:56–57.

105. Abalahin 2003:268.

106. Hiroshi 1992:34.

107. See M. Velthusin, talk to the 1930 International Bureau Congress, LON 11B/627/179.

108. See, for example, League of Nations 1924b; 1925c; 1928b; 1931; 1934.

109. League of Nations, 1924b.

110. League of Nations, 1925c:65.

111. League of Nations 1933a:254.

112. League of Nations 1938:53.

113. League of Nations 1933a:246–248.

114. International Bureau for the Suppression of Traffic in Women and Children 1927:97.

115. Ibid.

116. League of Nations 1927a; 1933a.

117. Gouda 1995:26.

118. Ingleson 1986.

119. Breman 1990:137.

120. Houkes 2005.

121. Mann 2004:187.

122. Abernethy 2000:85.

123. See Cooper and Stoler 1997:25 on morality and imperial regimes.

Chapter 6

1. Pedersen 1998.

2. Sassen 1999:65–66. She notes that until 1890, 45 percent of French emigrants went overseas, 20 percent to French colonies and the rest to other European countries. After 1890, overseas migration dropped, and there were fluctuations in migration to colonies (10 to 30 percent), as well as an increase in emigration to other European countries.

3. League of Nations 1927b.

4. Corbin 1990:287.

5. Sassen 1999.

6. Noriel 1996:139–140.

7. Corbin 1990.

8. Corbin 1990:282–283.

9. Ibid.

10. Corbin 1990:285.

11. Harsin 1985:324–325.

12. Harsin 1985:26.

13. Butler 1898:70–84, 136–151; Johnson and Johnson 1928:110, 117.

14. Weston 1979:164.

15. British Continental and General Federation for the Abolition of Government Regulation of Prostitution, *A Question of Life and Death for the Nations: Being a Supplement to the Second Annual Report of the British, Continental, and General Federation for the Abolition of Government Regulation of Prostitution* (Birmingham, UK: T. H. Lakins, 1877), GL Varia 193; and *Second Annual Report, 1876–1877* (Liverpool, UK: T. Brakell, 1877), 13–18, GL Varia 1575.

16. Miller 2000:113; Weston 1979:91–92.

17. Miller 2000:58.

18. British Continental and General Federation for the Abolition of Government Regulation of Prostitution, *A Question of Life and Death for the Nations: Being a Supplement to the Second Annual Report of the British, Continental, and General Federation for the Abolition of Government Regulation of Prostitution* (Birmingham, UK: T. H. Lakins, 1877), 16, GL Varia 193.

19. Offen 2000:155.

20. British Continental and General Federation for the Abolition of Government Regulation of Prostitution, *A Question of Life and Death for the Nations: Being a Supplement to the Second Annual Report of the British, Continental, and General Federation for the Abolition of Government Regulation of Prostitution* (Birmingham, UK: T. H. Lakins, 1877), 16, GL Varia 193.

21. McMillan 1981:24.

22. Weston 1979.

23. Rochefort 2008:187–189.

24. See Offen 2000.

25. Moses 1984:38.

26. Corbin 1990:234–240.

27. Weston 1979:159–160.

28. Bidelman 1982:195; Weston 1979:164.

29. This latter charge was actually from Pastor Tommy Fallot (Miller 2000:127). See Rochefort 2008 on the pastor.

30. Miller 2000:153–158; Watson 2000.

31. Surkis 2006:200. This quote is attributed to French doctor Alfred Fournier.

32. Offen 2005a; 2005b.

33. Offen 2005a:355–356.

34. Offen (2005a; 2008) reports that by 1920 the association was operating three or four centers and had attracted financial aid from U.S. as well as French supporters.

35. Offen 2008.

36. Coote 1910.

37. Corbin 1990:297; National Vigilance Association, *The White Slave Trade: Transactions of the International Congress on the White Slave Trade* (London: National Vigilance Association, 1899), GL FAI Brochures, 300(6), 343.545.NVA(758).

38. Surkis 2006:207.

39. Coote 1910:73.

40. International Abolitionist Federation for the Abolition of State Regulation of Vice, "Report of the Portsmouth Conference, June 15–18, 1914," in *Portsmouth Conference*, 1914, 14, WL 3/AMS/51.2.

41. Offen 2005a:362. On Sainte-Croix's appointment to the League of Nations' Traffic in Women Committee Offen writes, "It has to be said that she owed no thanks to the French government for this distinction! In fact, France continued to refuse ratification of the Geneva Convention of 1921, claiming that the question of the traffic in women and children was strictly an internal matter, and it refused until the early 1930s to appoint a woman to the French delegation to the League."

42. Rene Bérenger, Invitation to the 3rd International Congress for the Repression of the White Slave Trade, Paris, October 22–25, 1906, under the patronage of M. Armand Fallieres, President of the French Republic, INS Records, Folder 2, File 52483/1.

43. Watson 2000:84.

44. National Vigilance Association, "Third International Congress for the Suppression of the White Slave Traffic Held at the Hotel Continental, Paris, from the 22nd to the 25th October, 1906," *The Vigilance Record*, 1906, 11(November):85–92, WL.

45. British Committee of the Federation for the Abolition of the State Regulation of Vice, *The Shield*, 1901, 4(50):74–76, GL New Series, No. 1-51, 1897–1901.

46. McMillan 1981:25.

47. National Vigilance Association, "Third International Congress for the Suppression of the White Slave Traffic Held at the Hotel Continental, Paris, from the 22nd to the 25th October, 1906," *The Vigilance Record*, 1906, 11(November):85–92, WL.

48. International Bureau for the Suppression of the Traffic in Women and Children, minutes of meeting held May 11, 1908, 196–197, WL 4/IBS/Boxes 192, Vol. 1.

49. Watson 2000:72–74, 96.

50. League of Nations 1924a:29.

51. Miller 2000:296–302.

52. Corbin 1990:294–296.

53. League of Nations 1924b; Watson 2000:136.

54. League of Nations Traffic in Women and Children Committee 1932; Watson 2000.

55. Abernethy 2000:112, 432.

56. Betts, 1985:11

57. See, for example, Stovall 1993.

58. Lucassen 2005.

59. McMillan 1981:107–108.

60. Ibid.:174–175.

61. Watson 2000:199.

62. See, for example, League of Nations 1922; 1923; 1924a.

63. League of Nations 1921b:66.

64. League of Nations 1922.

65. International Bureau for the Suppression of Traffic in Women and Children 1924:96.

66. League of Nations 1925c:64.

67. Nelson 1970.

68. British National Committee for the Suppression of Traffic in Women and Children 1940, minutes dated May 23, WL France, File 27-M.

69. Offen 2008:248; Pollard 1998:67.

70. McMillan 1981:177.

71. Pollard 1998:67.

72. Ibid.:68.

73. Miller 2000:525–528.

74. Tambor 2006:134.

75. Miller 2000:550–567.

76. Ibid.:566.

77. Clancy-Smith and Gouda 1998; Lammers 2003.

78. Conklin 1997.

79. Direct control was not limited to the issue of regulation. Associationist policy, which was originally suggested for Indochina and later extended as policy to Africa, was geographically limited as a colonial practice (Betts 1985:68).

80. Lazreg 1994:55.

81. Ibid.:32–33.

82. Ibid.

83. Heggoy 1972.

84. Lazreg 1994, 57.

85. Lazreg 1994.

86. Berque 1967:305.

87. Taraud 2006; Watson 2000:196.

88. Berque 1967:170.

89. Taraud 2006.

90. Berque 1967:304.

91. Miller 2000:371.

92. Cooper 2000.

93. Surkis 2006:224.

94. League of Nations 1933a:213–214.

95. Ibid., 215.

96. Ibid.

97. Proschan 2002.

98. Ibid.

99. Marr 1976.

100. Conklin 1998.

101. Cooper and Stoler 1997:137.

102. Ibid.

103. Miller 2000:368.

104. League of Nations 1927c:87.

105. League of Nations 1928b:78

106. Cooper 2001:160–161.

107. Lazreg 1994:57.

108. Ibid.

109. Association for Moral and Social Hygiene, *The Shield*, 1948, 11(1):49–50, GL Fax 51.

110. Miller 2000:365.

111. Ibid.:366–367.

112. McMillan 1981:52, note 16.

113. Hélie 1995.

114. Kimble 2006.

115. Ibid.

116. Miller 2000:393–394.

117. Ibid.

118. Ibid.:403–405.

119. Ibid.:366–367.

120. Ibid.:401.

121. Ibid.

122. Heggoy 1972.

123. Lazreg 1994:59.

124. Lazreg 1990:763.

125. Miller 2000:406.

126. Chatterjee 1989; Chatterjee 1993; Lazreg 1990.

127. Marr 1976.

128. Enloe 1990:59–60.

129. Lazreg 1994:59.

130. International Bureau for the Suppression of the Traffic in Persons, minutes of meeting held June 18, 1959, WL 4/IBS/Box193/Folder10.

131. Joachim Joesten. *Prostitution and the White Slave Traffic in 'French' North Africa*, 1955:1, WL 4/IBS/8/B/3/19/Box FL353. This was a report presented by the American journalist to the North African and Middle East Committee of the Movement for Colonial Freedom.

132. International Bureau for the Suppression of Traffic in Persons, Executive Meeting Minutes, 1955, WL 4/IBS/Box 193/Folder 10.

133. Lazreg 1994:59.

134. Ibid.

135. Offen 1984.

136. Conklin 1998:169.

137. Watson 2000:195.

Chapter 7

1. Sassen 1999:70.

2. League of Nations 1927b.

3. Gibson 1986:98–99.

4. League of Nations 1927b:111.

5. Gibson 1986:25–26.

6. Ibid.:31.

7. Tambor 2006:133.

8. Gibson 1986:33.

9. British Branch of the British, Continental, and General Federation for the Abolition of State Regulation and Vice, *Report* (London: J. Cox, 1887), 11–2, GL Varia 263.

10. Ibid.:12.

11. Ibid.:11.

12. Wanrooij 2008:3.

13. British Continental and General Federation for the Abolition of Government Regulation of Prostitution, *First Annual Report, 1875–1876* (Liverpool, UK: T. Brakell, 1876), WL 3/AMS/S1.1.

14. British, Continental, and General Federation for the Abolition of Government Regulation of Prostitution, *Second Annual Report, 1876–1877* (Liverpool, UK: T. Brakell, 1877), GL Varia 1575.

15. National Association for the Repeal of the Contagious Diseases Acts, *The Shield*, 1883, 14(451):13, GL Fax 51.

16. Gibson 1986:44.

17. Butler 1898:13.

18. Gibson 1986:43.

19. Birnbaum 1986:19–20.

20. Wanrooij 2008:4.

21. Gibson 1986:59.

22. Wanrooij 2008:164.

23. Ibid.:156.

24. Wanrooij 2008.

25. Coote 1910.

26. Gibson 1986.

27. International Bureau for the Suppression of the Traffic in Women and Children, minutes of meeting held May 11, 1908, 203, WL 4/IBS/Boxes 192, Vol. 1.

28. Gibson 1986:67.

29. National Vigilance Association 1913.

30. Gibson 1986:69.

31. League of Nations 1921b:67.

32. League of Nations 1923:9.

33. International Bureau for the Suppression of Traffic in Women and Children 1924:42.

34. International Bureau for the Suppression of the Traffic in Women and Children, minutes of meeting held June 8, 1923, 165, WL 4/IBS/Boxes 192, Vol. 2.

35. de Grazia 1992:44–45.

36. International Bureau for the Suppression of Traffic in Women and Children 1924; 1927.

37. F. Sempkins, letter to Miss McCall dated September 10, 1929, WL 4/IBS/112/6CA.

38. Association for Moral and Social Hygiene, notes on visit to Italy and on earlier organising efforts in Rome by Mrs. Butler, 1933, WL 3/AMS/62.5.

39. League of Nations 1926c:65. See also 1926b.

40. League of Nations 1925a.

41. League of Nations 1929:91.

42. Ipsen 1993.

43. See Mann 2004:101 on organizing women under fascism.

44. League of Nations 1933b:23.

45. League of Nations 1935:16.

46. Tambor 2006.

47. Alison Neilans, *Rome 1933*, 1933, WL 3/AMS/62.5.

48. Tambor 2006:133

49. Association for Moral and Social Hygiene, *The Shield*, 1948, 11(2):100–104, GL.

50. Tambor 2006:136.

51. Ibid.:140.

52. Barrera 1996:36.

53. Ibid.:37–38.

54. Sbacchi 1985.

55. Ibid.

56. Iyob 2000:228.

57. Pankhurst 1974:177.

58. Sbacchi 1985:172.

59. Ibid.:171.

60. Pankhurst 1974:176.

61. Iyob 2000.

62. Pankhurst 1974:177.

63. Association for Moral and Social Hygiene, *The Shield*, 1937, 5(1):7–8, GL Fax 51.

64. Ibid.

65. Ibid. See also Fischer-Tiné 2003; Levine 2000.

66. Palumbo 2003.

67. Barrera 2003.

68. Ibid.

69. Willson 2007.

70. Josephine E. Butler, *New Abolitionist Work Throughout the World*, 1885, 45–47, GL Varia 258.

71. League of Nations 1927b:109.

Chapter 8

1. Coté 1999:469; Houkes 2005; van Drenth and de Haan 1999.

2. Limoncelli 2006. The International Abolitionist Federation had repeatedly attempted to organize in Germany, prompting police repression and attacks by German Evangelicals, including the noted anti-Semitic leader Adolf Stoecker, who had worked in the Inner Mission. William Coote, in contrast, arrived in 1898 to a cordial reception when he successfully sought to organize a German committee. The committee included prominent state officials, members of the General Conference of German Morality Associations and members of the German-Evangelical Women's League (Bristow 1982; Coote 1910; Evans 1976a:195). On the significance of strong organizational religious networks in fostering early humanitarian efforts in Europe and on the relevance of their relations to states, see Stamatov 2006.

3. Moses 1984; Rochefort 2004:89–90.

4. Offen 1984.

5. Gibson 1986.

6. Cooper 2001.

7. Palumbo 2003.

8. Abernethy 2000:86.

9. See, e.g., Barrera 1996. The Dutch colonial army included indigenous men as well, but it was distinguished from the others by the fact that it housed them with Europeans (Ming 1983).

10. Ming 1983.

11. See, for example, Gouda 1995:165 on the long-term prevalence of interracial unions in the Dutch East Indies. See also Wertheim 1990:73.

12. Taylor 1983.

13. See, e.g., Barrera 1996.

14. Mann 2005:309.

15. Kligman and Limoncelli 2005.

16. Limoncelli 2008.

17. Masika 2002:13.

18. Kempadoo 2001; Kempadoo and Doezema 1998; Lazaridis 2001.

19. League of Nations 1927a.

20. Bristow 1982; Hirata 1979.

21. Kanics, Galster, Steinzor, and Caldwell 1999; Kelly 2007; Monzini 2004; Shannon 1999; Shelley 2007.

22. Miko and Park 2002.

23. Bernstein 2001; Wijers 1998.

24. Altink 1995; Jeffreys 2004.

25. Agathangelou and Ling 2003; Nelson, Guthrie, and Coffey 2004; Talleyrand 2000.

26. Diep 2005.

27. See Outshoorn 2005 for a thorough discussion of the current debates on trafficking and prostitution. See also Wijers 1998 and Ucarer 1999.

28. See, e.g., Berman 2003; Doezema 1998; and Murray 1998.

29. See, e.g., Jeffreys 1997; 2004.

30. See, e.g., Chapkis 2003; and Doezema 1998.

31. Davidson 1998; 2002.

32. Limoncelli 2009.

33. See, e.g., Jeffreys 1997.

34. Enloe 2000; Kligman and Limoncelli 2005; Rathgeber 2002.

35. See Soderlund 2005; and Bernstein 2007.

References

Archival Sources

WL: The Women's Library, London Metropolitan University. Archive collections: Societies for the Abolition of State Regulation of Prostitution; Societies for the Suppression of the Traffic in Persons.

GL: Geneva Library (formerly Geneva Public and University Library), Geneva Switzerland. Uncatalogued collection, International Abolitionist Federation.

LON: United Nations Office at Geneva Library, Geneva, Switzerland. The League of Nations Archives collections: League of Nations Secretariat 1919–1946, Social Questions Section; and Collections (1919–), Printed Documents, Social Questions Bodies.

LSE: London School of Economics and Political Science Archives. Pamphlet collection.

Secondary Sources

Abalahin, Andrew Jimenez. 2003. *Prostitution Policy and the Project of Modernity: A Comparative Study of Colonial Indonesia and the Philippines, 1850–1940.* Ph.D. Dissertation, Cornell University.

Abernethy, David B. 2000. *The Dynamics of Global Dominance: European Overseas Empires, 1415–1980.* New Haven, CT: Yale University Press.

Agathangelou, Anna M., and L.H.M. Ling. 2003. "Desire Industries: Sex Trafficking, UN Peacekeeping, and the Neo-Liberal World Order." *Brown Journal of World Affairs* 10(1):133–148.

Akyeampong, Emmanuel. 1997. "Sexuality and Prostitution Among the Akan of the Gold Coast c. 1650–1950." *Past and Present* 156(1):144–173.

Altink, Sietske. 1995. *Stolen Lives: Trading Women into Sex and Slavery.* London: Scarlet Press.

Andrew, Elizabeth, and Katharine Bushnell. 1899. *The Queen's Daughters in India.* London: Morgan and Scott.

Badran, Margot. 1995. *Feminists, Islam, and Nation: Gender and the Making of Modern Egypt.* Princeton, NJ: Princeton University Press.

Ballhatchet, Kenneth. 1980. *Race, Sex and Class Under the Raj.* London: Weidenfeld and Nicolson.

Bannerji, Himani, Shahrzad Mojab, and Judith Whitehead (eds.). 2001. *Of Property and Propriety: The Role of Gender and Class in Imperialism and Nationalism.* Toronto: University of Toronto Press.

Barlay, Stephen. 1969. *Bondage: The Slave Traffic in Women Today.* New York: Dell.

Barrera, Giulia. 1996. *Dangerous Liaisons: Colonial Concubinage in Eritrea, 1890–1941.* Evanston, Il: Program of African Studies, Northwestern University.

———. 2003. "Mussolini's Colonial Race Laws and State-Settler Relations in Africa Orientale Italiana (1935–41)." *Journal of Modern Italian Studies* 8(3):425–443.

Barry, Kathleen. 1979. *Female Sexual Slavery.* New York: New York University Press.

Berkovitch, Nitza. 1999a. "The Emergence and Transformation of the International Women's Movement." In *Constructing World Culture: International Nongovernmental Organizations Since 1875.* Ed. John Boli and George M. Thomas, 100–126. Stanford, CA: Stanford University Press.

———. 1999b. *From Motherhood to Citizenship: Women's Rights and International Organizations.* Baltimore, MD: Johns Hopkins University Press.

Berman, Jacqueline. 2003. "Unpopular Strangers and Crises Unbounded: Discourses of Sex-Trafficking, the European Political Community and the Panicked State of the Modern State." *European Journal of International Relations* 9(1):37–86.

Bernstein, Elizabeth. 2001. "The Meaning of Purchase: Desire, Demand and the Commerce of Sex." *Ethnography* 2(3):389–420.

———. 2007. "The Sexual Politics of the "New Abolitionism." *Differences: A Journal of Feminist Cultural Studies* 18(3):128–151.

Bernstein, Laurie. 1995. *Sonia's Daughters: Prostitutes and Their Regulation in Imperial Russia.* Berkeley: University of California Press.

Berque, Jacques. 1967. *French North Africa: The Maghrib Between Two World Wars.* Trans. Jean Stewart. London: Faber and Faber.

Betts, Raymond F. 1985. *Uncertain Dimensions: Western Overseas Empires in the Twentieth Century.* Minneapolis: University of Minnesota Press.

Bidelman, Patrick Kay. 1982. *Pariahs Stand Up! The Founding of the Liberal Feminist Movement in France, 1858–1889.* Westport, CT: Greenwood Press.

Birnbaum, Lucia Chiavola. 1986. *Liberazione della donna: Feminism in Italy.* Middletown, CT: Wesleyan University Press.

Blackburn, Susan. (2004a). "Women's Suffrage and Democracy in Indonesia." In *Women's*

Suffrage in Asia: Gender, Nationalism and Democracy. Ed. Louise Edwards and Mina Roces, 79–105. New York: RoutledgeCurzon.

Blackburn, Susan. 2004b. *Women and the State in Modern Indonesia.* Cambridge, UK: Cambridge University Press.

Blackburn, Susan, and Sharon Bessell. 1997. "Marriageable Age: Political Debates on Early Marriage in Twentieth-Century Indonesia." *Indonesia* 63(April):107–141.

Bock, Gisela, and Pat Thane (eds.). 1991. *Maternity and Gender Policies: Women and the Rise of the European Welfare States, 1880s–1950s.* London: Routledge.

Boli, John, and George M. Thomas. 1997. "World Culture in the World Polity: A Century of International Non-Governmental Organizations." *American Sociological Review* 62(2):171–190.

———. 1999. *Constructing World Culture: International Nongovernmental Organizations Since 1875.* Stanford, CA: Stanford University Press.

Bosch, Mineke. 1999. "Colonial Dimensions of Dutch Women's Suffrage: Aletta Jacobs's Travel Letters from Africa and Asia, 1911–1912." *Journal of Women's History* 11(2):8–35.

———. 2004. "History and Historiography of First-Wave Feminism in the Netherlands, 1860–1922." In *Women's Emancipation Movements in the Nineteenth Century: A European Perspective.* Ed. Sylvia Paletschek and Bianka Pietrow-Ennker, 53–76. Stanford, CA: Stanford University Press.

Breman, Jan. 1990. "The Civilization of Racism: Colonial and Post-Colonial Development Policies." In *Imperial Monkey Business: Racial Supremacy in Social Darwinist Theory and Colonial Practice.* Ed. Jan Breman, Piet de Rooy, Ann Stoler, and Wim F. Wertheim, 123–152. Amsterdam: VU University Press.

Bristow, Edward J. 1977. *Vice and Vigilance: Purity Movements in Britain Since 1700.* Dublin, Ireland: Gill and MacMillan.

———. 1982. *Prostitution and Prejudice: The Jewish Fight Against White Slavery, 1870–1939.* Oxford, UK: Clarendon Press.

Brubaker, Rogers. 1996. *Nationalism Reframed: Nationhood and the National Question in Europe.* New York: Cambridge University Press.

Bryder, Linda. 1998. "Sex, Race, and Colonialism: An Historiographical Review." *International History Review* 20(4):806–822.

Bullough, Vern, and Bonnie Bullough. 1987. *Women and Prostitution: A Social History.* New York: Prometheus Books.

Burton, Antoinette M. 1990. "The White Women's Burden: British Feminists and the Indian Woman, 1865–1915." *Women's Studies International Forum* 13(4):295–308.

———. 1994. *Burdens of History: British Feminists, Indian Women, and Imperial Culture, 1865–1915.* Chapel Hill: University of North Carolina Press.

Butler, Josephine E. 1897. *Truth Before Everything.* London: Dyer Brothers.

———. 1898. *Personal Reminiscences of a Great Crusade.* London: Horace Marshall.

Chapkis, Wendy. 2003. "Trafficking, Migration and the Law: Protecting Innocents, Punishing Immigrants." *Gender and Society* 17(6):923–937.

Chatterjee, Partha. 1989. "Colonialism, Nationalism, and Colonialized Women: The Contest in India." *American Ethnologist* 16(4):622–633.

———. 1993. *The Nation and Its Fragments: Colonial and Postcolonial Histories.* Princeton, NJ: Princeton University Press.

Clancy-Smith, Julia, and Frances Gouda (eds.). 1998. *Domesticating the Empire: Race, Gender, and Family Life in French and Dutch Colonialism.* Charlottesville and London: University Press of Virginia.

Conklin, Alice L. 1997. *A Mission to Civilize: The Republican Idea of Empire in France and West Africa, 1895–1930.* Stanford, CA: Stanford University Press.

———. 1998. "Redefining "Frenchness": Citizenship, Race Regeneration, and Imperial Motherhood in France and West Africa, 1914–1940." In *Domesticating the Empire: Race, Gender, and Family Life in French and Dutch Colonialism.* Ed. Julia Clancy-Smith and Frances Gouda, 65–83. Charlottesville and London: University Press of Virginia.

Conklin, Alice L., and Ian Christopher Fletcher (eds.). 1999. *European Imperialism, 1830–1930.* Boston: Houghton Mifflin.

Connell, R. W. 1987. *Gender and Power.* Stanford, CA: Stanford University Press.

Connell, R. W., and James W. Messerschmidt. 2005. "Hegemonic Masculinity: Rethinking the Concept," *Gender and Society* 19(6):829–859.

Cooper, Frederick and Ann Laura Stoler (eds.). 1997. *Tensions of Empire: Colonial Cultures in a Bourgeois World.* Berkeley: University of California Press.

Cooper, Nicola. 2001. *France in Indochina: Colonial Encounters.* Oxford, UK: Berg.

Cooper, Nikki. 2000. "(En)gendering Indochina: Feminisms and Female Figurings in French Colonial Discourses." *Women's Studies International Forum* 23(6):749–759.

Coote, William Alexander. 1910. *A Vision and Its Fulfillment.* London: National Vigilance Association.

Corbin, Alain. 1990. *Women for Hire: Prostitution and Sexuality in France after 1850.* Trans. Alan Sheridan. Cambridge, MA: Harvard University Press.

Coté, Joost. 1999. "'Our Indies Colony': Reading First Wave Dutch Feminism from the Periphery." *European Journal of Women's Studies* 6(4):463–484.

Crowdy, Dame Rachel. 1928. "The League of Nations: Its Social and Humanitarian Work." *The American Journal of Nursing* 28(4):350–352.

Davidson, Julia O'Connell. 1998. *Prostitution, Power and Freedom.* Ann Arbor: University of Michigan Press.

———. 2002. "The Rights and Wrongs of Prostitution." *Hypatia* 17(2):84–98.

de Grazia, Victoria. 1992. *How Fascism Ruled Women: Italy 1922–1945.* Berkeley: University of California Press.

de Vries, Petra. 2001. "'The Shadow of Contagion': Gender, Syphilis and the Regulation of prostitution in the Netherlands, 1870–1914." In *Sex, Sin and Suffering: Venereal Disease and European Society Since 1870*. Ed. Roger Davidson and Lesley A. Hall, 44–60. London: Routledge.

———. 2005. "'White Slaves' in a Colonial Nation: The Dutch Campaign Against the Traffic in Women in the Early Twentieth Century." *Social & Legal Studies* 14(1):39–60.

———. 2008. "Josephine Butler and the Making of Feminism: International Abolition-ism in the Netherlands." *Women's History Review* 17(2):257–277.

Diep, Hanh. 2005. "We Pay: The Economic Manipulation of International and Domestic Laws to Sustain Sex Trafficking." *Loyola International Law Review* 309:309–331.

Doezema, Jo. 1998. "Forced to Choose: Beyond the Voluntary v. Forced Prostitution Dichotomy." In *Global Sex Workers: Rights, Resistance and Redefinition*. Ed. Kamala Kempadoo and Jo Doezema, 34–50. New York: Routledge.

———. 2000. "Loose Women or Lost Women? The Re-emergence of the Myth of 'White Slavery' in Contemporary Discourses of 'Trafficking in Women.'" *Gender Issues* 18(1):23–50.

Donovan, Brian. 2006. *White Slave Crusades: Race Gender, and Anti-Vice Activism, 1887–1917*. Champaign: University of Illinois Press.

Ehrick, Christine. 1999. "Madrinas and Missionaries: Uruguay and the Pan-Ameri-can Women's Movement." In *Feminisms and Internationalism*. Ed. Mrinalini Sinha, Donna Guy, and Angela Woollacott, 62–80. Oxford, UK: Blackwell.

Enloe, Cynthia. 1990. *Bananas, Beaches and Bases: Making Feminist Sense of Internation-al Politics*. Berkeley: University of California Press.

———. 2000. *Maneuvers: The International Politics of Militarizing Women's Lives*. Berke-ley: University of California Press.

———. 2005. *The Curious Feminist: Searching for Women in a New Age of Empire*. Berke-ley and Los Angeles: University of California Press.

Evans, Richard J. 1976a. *Feminist Movement in Germany, 1894–1933*. London: Sage.

———. 1976b. "Prostitution, State and Society in Imperial Germany." *Past and Present* 70(1):106–129.

Finnemore, Martha. 1996. *National Interests in International Society*. Ithaca, NY: Cornell University Press.

Fischer-Tiné, Harald. 2003. "'White Women Degrading Themselves to the Lowest Depths': European Networks of Prostitution and Colonial Anxieties in British India and Ceylon ca. 1880–1914." *Indian Economic Social History Review* 40(2):163–190.

Foucault, Michel. 1979. *Discipline and Punish: The Birth of the Prison*. Trans. Alan Sheri-dan. New York: Random House.

Fujime, Yuki. 1997. "The Licensed Prostitution System and the Prostitution Abolition Movement in Modern Japan." *Positions* 5(1):135–170.

Gal, Susan, and Gail Kligman. 2000. *The Politics of Gender After Socialism.* Princeton, NJ: Princeton University Press.

Garon, Sheldon. 1993. "The World's Oldest Debate? Prostitution and the State in Imperial Japan, 1900–1945." *The American Historical Review* 98(3):710–732.

Gibson, Mary. 1986. *Prostitution and the State in Italy, 1860–1915.* New Brunswick, NJ: Rutgers University Press.

Gilfoyle, Timothy J. 1999. "Prostitutes in History: From Parables of Pornography to Metaphors of Modernity." *American Historical Review* 104(1):117–141.

Gorman, Daniel. 2008. "Empire, Internationalism, and the Campaign Against the Traffic in Women and Children in the 1920s." *Twentieth Century British History* 19(2):186–216.

Gouda, Frances. 1995. *Dutch Culture Overseas: Colonial Practice in the Netherlands Indies 1900–1942.* Amsterdam: Amsterdam University Press.

Grever, Maria, and Berteke Waaldijk. 2004. *Transforming the Public Sphere: The Dutch National Exhibition of Women's Labor in 1898.* Durham, NC: Duke University Press.

Gronewold, Sue. 1985. *Beautiful Merchandise: Prostitution in China 1860–1936.* New York: Harrington Park Press.

Grossman, Atina. 1997. "A Question of Silence: The Rape of German Women by Occupation Soldiers." In *West Germany Under Construction: Politics, Society and Culture in the Adenauer Era.* Ed. Robert G. Moeller, 33–52. Ann Arbor: University of Michigan Press.

Guy, Donna J. 1991. *Sex and Danger in Buenos Aires: Prostitution, Family, and Nation in Argentina.* Lincoln: University of Nebraska Press.

Harris, H. Wilson. 1928. *Human Merchandise: A Study of the International Traffic in Women.* London: Ernest Benn.

Harsin, Jill. 1985. *Policing Prostitution in Nineteenth-Century Paris.* Princeton, NJ: Princeton University Press.

Heggoy, Alf Andrew. 1972. "Cultural Disrespect: Europeans and Algerian Views on Women in Colonial and Independent Algeria." *The Muslim World* 62(4):323–334.

Held, David, and Anthony McGrew. 2000. *The Global Transformations Reader: An Introduction to the Globalization Debate.* Cambridge, UK: Polity Press.

Hélie, Anissa. 1995. "Between 'Becoming M'tourni' and 'Going Native': Gender and Settler Society in Algeria." In *Unsettling Settler Societies: Articulations of Gender, Race, Ethnicity.* Ed. Daiva Stasiulis and Nira Yuval-Davis, 263–290. London: Sage.

Henkes, Barbara. 2001. "Maids on the Move: Images of Femininity and European Women's Labour Migration During the Interwar Years." In *Women, Gender and Labour Migration: Historical and Global Perspectives.* Ed. Pamela Sharpe, 224–243. London and New York:: Routledge.

Henriot, Christian. 1994. "Chinese Courtesans in Late Qing and Early Republican Shanghai (1849–1925)." *East Asian History* 8:33–52.

———. 1995. ""La Fermeture": The Abolition of Prostitution in Shanghai, 1949–58." *China Quarterly* 142:467–486.

———. 2001. *Prostitution and Sexuality in Shanghai: A Social History, 1849–1949.* Trans. Noel Castelino. Cambridge, UK: Cambridge University Press.

Hershatter, Gail. 1989. "The Hierarchy of Shanghai Prostitution, 1870–1949." *Modern China* 15(4):463–498.

———. 1992. "Courtesans and Streetwalkers: The Changing Discourses on Shanghai Prostitution, 1890–1949." *Journal of the History of Sexuality* 3(2):245–269.

Hesselink, Liesbeth. 1987. "Prostitution: A Necessary Evil, Particularly in the Colonies. Views on Prostitution in the Netherlands Indies." In *Indonesian Women in Focus: Past and Present Notions.* Ed. Elsbeth Locher-Scholten and Anke Niehof, 205–224. Dordrecht, the Netherlands: Foris Publications Holland.

Hicks, George. 1995. *The Comfort Women.* New South Wales, Australia: Allen and Unwin.

Hirata, Lucie Cheng. 1979. "Free, Indentured, Enslaved: Chinese Prostitutes in Nineteenth-Century America." *Signs* 5(1):3–29.

Hiroshi, Shimizu. 1992. "Rise and Fall of the Karayuki-San in the Netherlands Indies from the Late Nineteenth Century to the 1930s." *Review of Indonesian and Malaysian Affairs* 26(2):17–43.

Houkes, Annemarie. 2005. "Foreign Examples as Eye Openers and Justification: The Transfer of the Anti-Corn Law League and the Anti-Prostitution Movement to the Netherlands." *European Review* 12(2):321–344.

Howell, Philip. 2004a. "Race, Space and the Regulation of Prostitution in Colonial Hong Kong." *Urban History* 31(2):229–248.

———. 2004b. "Sexuality, Sovereignty, and Space: Law, Government and the Geography of Prostitution in Colonial Gibralter." *Social History* 29(4):444–464.

———. 2005. "Prostitution and the Place of Empire: Regulation and Repeal in Hong Kong and the British Imperial Network." In *(Dis)Placing Empire: Renegotiating British Colonial Geographies.* Ed. Lindsay J. Proudfoot and Michael M. Roche, 175–197. Aldershot, England: Ashgate.

Hui, Tan Beng. 2003. "'Protecting' Women: Legislation and Regulation of Women's Sexuality in Colonial Malaya." *Gender, Technology and Development* 7(1):1–29.

Human Rights Watch. 2002. *Hopes Betrayed: Trafficking of Women and Girls to Post-Conflict Bosnia and Herzegovina for Forced Prostitution.* New York: Human Rights Watch.

Hyam, Ronald. 1990. *Empire and Sexuality: The British Experience.* Manchester, UK: Manchester University Press.

Ingleson, John. 1986. "Prostitution in Colonial Java." In *Nineteenth and Twentieth Century Indonesia.* Ed. David P. Chandler and M. C. Ricklefs, 123–140. Clayton, Victoria, Australia: Southeast Asian Studies, Monash University.

International Bureau for the Suppression of Traffic in Women and Children. 1924. *Sixth International Congress for the Suppression of the Traffic in Women and Children.* London: National Vigilance Association.

———. 1927. *Seventh International Congress for the Suppression of the Traffic in Women and Children.* London: International Bureau for the Suppression of the Traffic in Women and Children.

Ipsen, Carl. 1993. "The Organization of Demographic Totalitarianism: Early Population Policy in Fascist Italy." *Social Science History* 17(1):71–108.

Iriye, Akira. 2002. *Global Community: The Role of International Organizations in the Making of the Contemporary World.* Berkeley: University of California Press.

Iyob, Ruth. 2000. "Madamismo and Beyond: The Construction of Eritrean Women." *Nineteenth-Century Contexts* 22:217–238.

Jacobs, Aletta H. 1996. *Memories: My Life as an International Leader in Health, Suffrage, and Peace.* Trans. Annie Wright. New York: Feminist Press at the City University of New York.

Jeffreys, Sheila. 1985. *The Spinster and Her Enemies: Feminism and Sexuality 1880–1930.* London: Pandora Press.

———. 1997. *The Idea of Prostitution.* Melbourne: Spinifex Press.

———. 2004. *The Legalisation of Prostitution : A Failed Social Experiment.* http://sisyphe.org/article.php3?id_article=697 (accessed March 1, 2009).

Joardar, Biswanath. 1985. *Prostitution in Nineteenth and Early Twentieth Century Calcutta.* New Delhi: Inter-India Publications.

Johnson, George W., and Lucy A. Johnson (eds.). 1928. *Josephine E. Butler: An Autobiographical Memoir.* Bristol, UK: J. W. Arrowsmith.

Jones, Gavin W., Endang Sulistyaningsih, and Terence H. Hull. 1995. *Prostitution in Indonesia.* Working Papers in Demography, No. 52. Canberra: Research of the School of Social Sciences, Australian National University.

Jordan, Jane. 2001. *Josephine Butler.* London: John Murray.

———. 2006. "'Trophies of the Saviour': Josephine Butler's Biographical Sketches of Prostitutes." In *Sex, Gender, and Religion: Josephine Butler Revisited.* Ed. Jenny Daggers and Diana Neal, 21–36. New York: Peter Lang.

Kanics, Jyothi, Steve Galster, Nadia Steinzor, and Gillian Caldwell. 1999. "Capitalizing on Transition Economies: The Role of the Russian Mafiya in Trafficking Women for Forced Prostitution." In *Illegal Immigration and Commercial Sex: The New Slave Trade.* Ed. Phil Williams, 42–73. London: Frank Cass.

Kaplan, Gisela. 1997. "Feminism and Nationalism: The European Case." In *Feminist Nationalism.* Ed. Lois A. West, 3–40. New York: Routledge.

Keck, Margaret E., and Kathryn Sikkink. 1998. *Activists Beyond Borders.* Ithaca, NY: Cornell University Press.

Kelly, Liz. 2005. "'You Can Find Anything You Want': A Critical Reflection on Research on Trafficking in Persons Within and Into Europe." *International Migration* 43(1/2):235–265.

———. 2007. "A Conducive Context: Trafficking of Persons in Central Asia." In *Human Trafficking*. Ed. Maggy Lee, 73–91. Cullompton, Devon, UK: Willan.

Kempadoo, Kamala. 2001. "Women of Color and the Global Sex Trade: Transnational Feminist Perspectives." *Meridians: Feminism, Race, Transnationalism* 1(2):28–51.

Kempadoo, Kamala, and Jo Doezema (eds.). 1998. *Global Sex Workers: Rights, Resistance and Redefinition.* New York: Routledge.

Khagram, Sanjeev, James V. Riker, and Kathryn Sikkink (eds.). 2002. *Restructuring World Politics: Transnational Social Movements, Networks, and Norms.* Minneapolis: University of Minnesota Press.

Kimble, Sara L. 2006. "Emancipation Through Secularization: French Feminist Views of Muslim Women's Condition in Interwar Algeria." *French Colonial History* 7:109–128.

Kligman, Gail. 1998. *The Politics of Duplicity: Controlling Reproduction in Ceausescu's Romania.* Berkeley: University of California Press.

Kligman, Gail, and Stephanie A. Limoncelli. 2005. "Trafficking Women After Socialism: From, To, and Through Eastern Europe." *Social Politics* 12(1):118–140.

Kumar, M. Satish. 2005. "'Oriental Sore' of 'Public Nuisance': The Regulation of Prostitution in Colonial India, 1805–1899." In *(Dis)Placing Empire: Renegotiating British Colonial Geographies.* Ed. Lindsay J. Proudfoot and Michael M. Roche, 155–173. Aldershot, UK: Ashgate.

Laczko, Frank. 2005. "Introduction: Data and Research on Human Trafficking." *International Migration* 43(1/2):5–16.

Lammers, Cornelis J. 2003. "British, Dutch and French Patterns of Inter-Organizational Control of Foreign Territories." *Organization Studies* 24(9):1379–1403.

Lazaridis, Grabriella. 2001. "Trafficking and Prostitution: The Growing Exploitation of Migrant Women in Greece." *European Journal of Women's Studies* 8(1):67–102.

Lazreg, Marnia. 1990. "Gender and Politics in Algeria: Unraveling the Religious Paradigm." *Signs* 15(4):755–780.

———. 1994. *The Eloquence of Silence: Algerian Women in Question.* New York: Routledge.

League of Nations. 1921a. *International Conference on Traffic in Women and Children: General Report on the Work of the Conference.* Geneva, Switzerland: League of Nations. C.227.M.166.1921.IV.

———. 1921b. *Records of the International Conference on Traffic in Women and Children (Meetings Held from June 30th–July 5th, 1921).* Geneva, Switzerland: League of Nations. C.484.M.339.1921.IV.

———. 1922. *Advisory Committee on the Traffic in Women and Children: Minutes of the First Session.* Geneva, Switzerland: League of Nations. C.445.M.265.1922.IV.

———. 1923. *Advisory Committee on the Traffic in Women and Children: Minutes of the Second Session.* Geneva, Switzerland: League of Nations. C.225.M.129.1923.IV.

———. 1924a. *Advisory Committee on Traffic in Women and Children: Minutes of the Third Session.* Geneva, Switzerland: League of Nations. C.217.M.71.1924.IV.

———. 1924b. *Summary of Annual Reports for 1922 Received from Governments Relating to the Traffic in Women and Children.* Geneva, Switzerland: League of Nations. C.164.M.40.1924.IV.

———. 1925a. *Advisory Committee on the Traffic in Women and Protection of Children: Minutes of the Fourth Session.* Geneva, Switzerland: League of Nations. C.382.M.126.1925.IV.

———. 1925b. *Advisory Committee on the Traffic in Women and Protection of Children: Report on the Work of the Fourth Session.* Geneva, Switzerland: League of Nations. C.293.1.1925.IV.

———. 1925c. *Traffic in Women and Children: Summary, Prepared by the Secretariat, of Annual Reports for the Year 1924.* Geneva, Switzerland: League of Nations. C.825.M.282.1925.IV (C.T.F.E. 250(2)).

———. 1926a. *Social and Humanitarian Work.* Geneva, Switzerland: League of Nations.

———. 1926b. *Traffic in Women and Children Committee: Report on the Work of the Fifth Session.* Geneva, Switzerland: League of Nations. C.240.M.89.1926.IV.

———. 1926c. *Traffic in Women and Children Committee: Minutes of the Fifth Session.* Geneva, Switzerland: League of Nations. C.233.M.84.1926.IV

———. 1927a. *Report of the Special Body of Experts on Traffic in Women and Children, Part One.* Geneva, Switzerland: League of Nations. C.52.M.52.1927.IV (C.T.F.E./Experts/55).

———. 1927b. *Report of the Special Body of Experts on Traffic in Women and Children, Part Two.* Geneva, Switzerland: League of Nations. C.52(2).M.52(1).1927.IV (Including C.592.1927.IV).

———. 1927c. *Traffic in Women and Children Committee: Minutes of the Sixth Session.* Geneva, Switzerland: League of Nations. C.338.M.113.1927.IV.

———. 1928a. *Traffic in Women and Children Committee: Minutes of the Seventh Session.* Geneva, Switzerland: League of Nations. C.184.M.59.1928.IV.

———. 1928b. *Traffic in Women and Children: Summary of Annual Reports for 1926, Prepared by the Secretariat.* Geneva, Switzerland: League of Nations. C.28.M.14.1928.IV.

———. 1929. *Traffic in Women and Children: Minutes of the Eighth Session.* Geneva, Switzerland: League of Nations. C.294.M.97.1929.IV.

———. 1931. *Traffic in Women and Children: Summary of Annual Reports for 1929 Prepared by the Secretariat.* Geneva, Switzerland: League of Nations. C.164.M.59.1931.IV.

———. 1933a. *Commission of Enquiry into Traffic in Women and Children in the East: Report to the Council.* Geneva, Switzerland: League of Nations. Ser. L.o.N. P. 1932.IV.8.

———. 1933b. *Traffic in Women and Children: Summary of Annual Reports for 1931 Prepared by the Secretariat.* Geneva, Switzerland: League of Nations. C.857.M.399.1932.IV.

———. 1934. *Traffic in Women and Children: Summary of Annual Reports for 1932–33 Prepared by the Secretariat.* Geneva, Switzerland: League of Nations. C.2.M.2.1934.IV.

———. 1935. *Traffic in Women and Children: Summary of Annual Reports for 1933–34 Prepared by the Secretariat.* Geneva, Switzerland: League of Nations. C.127.M.65.1935.IV.

———. 1938. *Traffic in Women and Children: The Work of the Bandoeng Conference.* Geneva, Switzerland: League of Nations. C.516.M.357.1937.IV.

League of Nations Traffic in Women and Children Committee. 1932. *Central Authorities.* Geneva, Switzerland: League of Nations. C.504.M.245.1932.IV.

Lee, Catherine Y. 2003. *Sexing the Nation: Race, Gender, and Chinese and Japanese Immigration to the United States, 1870–1924.* Ph.D. Dissertation, University of California, Los Angeles.

Leppänen, Katarina. 2007. "Movement of Women: Trafficking in the Interwar Era." *Women's Studies International Forum* 30:523–533.

Lester, Alan. 2002. "Obtaining the 'Due Observance of Justice': The Geographies of Colonial Humanitarianism." *Environment and Planning D: Society and Space* 20:277–293.

Levine, Philippa. 1994. "Venereal Disease, Prostitution, and the Politics of Empire: The Case of British India." *Journal of the History of Sexuality* 4(4):579–602.

———. 2000. "Orientalist Sociology and the Creation of Colonial Sexualities." *Feminist Review* 65(1):5–21.

———. 2001. "Public Health, Venereal Disease, and Colonial Medicine in the Later Nineteenth Century." In *Sex, Sin and Suffering: Venereal Disease and European Society Since 1870.* Ed. Roger Davidson and Lesley A. Hall, 160–172. London: Routledge.

———. 2003. *Prostitution, Race, and Politics: Policing Venereal Disease in the British Empire.* New York: Routledge.

———. 2006. "Sexuality and Empire." In *At Home with the Empire: Metropolitan Culture and the Imperial World.* Ed. Catherine Hall and Sonya O. Rose, 122–142. Cambridge, UK: Cambridge University Press.

Lie, John. 1997. "The State as Pimp: Prostitution and the Patriarchal State in Japan in the 1940s." *Sociological Quarterly* 38(2):251–264.

Limoncelli, Stephanie A. 2006. "International Voluntary Associations, Local Social Movements and State Paths to the Abolition of Regulated Prostitution in Europe, 1870–1950." International Sociology 21(1):31–59.

———. 2008. "Human Trafficking: Globalization, Exploitation, and Transnational Sociology." *Sociology Compass* 3(1):72–91.

———. 2009. "The Trouble with Trafficking: Conceptualizing Women's Sexual Labor and Economic Human Rights." *Women's Studies International Forum* 32(3):261–269.

Locher-Scholten, Elsbeth. 2000. *Women and the Colonial State: Essays on Gender and Modernity in the Netherlands Indies, 1900–1942.* Amsterdam: Amsterdam University Press.

———. 2003. "Morals, Harmony, and National Identity: "Companionate Feminism" in Colonial Indonesia in the 1930s." *Journal of Women's History* 14(4):38–58.

Lucassen, Leo. 2002a. "Administrative into Social Control: The Aliens Police and Foreign Female Servants in the Netherlands, 1918–40." *Social History* 27(3):327–342.

———. 2002b. "Bringing Structure Back in: Economic and Political Determinants of Immigration in Dutch Cities, 1920–1940." *Social Science History* 26(3):503–529.

———. 2005. *The Immigrant Threat: The Integration of Old and New Migrants in Western Europe Since 1850.* Chicago: University of Illinois Press.

Luker, Kristin. 1998. "Sex, Social Hygiene and the State: The Double-Edged Sword of Social Reform." *Theory and Society* 27(5):601–634.

Manderson, Lenore. 1997. "Colonial Desires: Sexuality, Race, and Gender in British Malaya." *Journal of the History of Sexuality* 7(3):372–387.

Mann, Michael. 1993. *The Sources of Social Power.* Vol. 2: *The Rise of Classes and Nation-States, 1760–1914.* Cambridge, UK: Cambridge University Press.

———. 2004. *Fascists.* Cambridge, UK: Cambridge University Press.

———. 2005. *The Dark Side of Democracy: Explaining Ethnic Cleansing.* Cambridge, UK: Cambridge University Press.

Marchant, James (eds.). 1908. *Public Morals.* London: Morgan & Scott.

Marks, Sally. 1983. "Black Watch on the Rhine: A Study in Propaganda, Prejudice and Prurience." *European History Quarterly* 13(3):297–334.

Marr, David. 1976. "The 1920s Women's Rights Debates in Vietnam." *Journal of Asian Studies* 35(3):371–389.

Martyn, Elizabeth. 2005. *The Women's Movement in Post-Colonial Indonesia: Gender and Nation in a New Democracy.* London: Routledge.

Masika, Rachel (eds.). 2002. *Gender, Trafficking and Slavery.* Oxford, UK: Oxfam.

McMillan, James F. 1981. *Housewife or Harlot? The Place of Women in French Society, 1870–1940.* Brighton, UK: Harvester Press.

Metzger, Barbara. 2007. "Towards an International Human Rights Regime During the Inter-War Years: The League of Nations' Combats the Traffic in Women and Children." In *Beyond Sovereignty: Britain, Empire and Transnationalism, c. 1880–1950.* Ed. Kevin Grant, Philippa Levine, and Frank Trentmann, 54–79. New York: Palgrave Macmillan.

Meyer, John W. 1999. "The Changing Cultural Content of the Nation-State: A World Society Perspective." In *State/Culture: State Formation After the Cultural Turn.* Ed. George Steinmetz, 123–144. Ithaca, NY: Cornell University Press.

Meyer, John W., John Boli, George M. Thomas, and Francisco O. Ramirez. 1997. "World Society and the Nation-State." *American Journal of Sociology* 103(1):144–181.

Miko, Francis T., and Grace Park. 2002. *Trafficking in Women and Children: The U.S.*

and International Response. Washington, DC: Library of Congress, Congressional Research Service.

Miller, Carol. 1994. "'Geneva—The Key to Equality': Inter-war Feminists and the League of Nations." *Women's History Review* 3(2):219–245.

Miller, Julia Christine Scriven. 2000. *The 'Romance of Regulation': The Movement Against State Regulated Prostitution in France, 1871–1946*. New York: New York University.

Miners, R. J. 1988. "State Regulation of Prostitution in Hong Kong, 1857 to 1941." *Hong Kong Branch of the Royal Asiatic Society* 24:143–161.

Ming, Hanneke. 1983. "Barracks Concubinage in the Indies, 1887–1920." *Indonesia* 35(April):65–93.

Monzini, Paola. 2004. "Trafficking in Women and Girls and the Involvement of Organised Crime in Western and Central Europe." *International Review of Victimology* 11(1):73–88.

Moses, Claire Goldberg. 1984. *French Feminism in the Nineteenth Century*. Albany: State University of New York.

Mosse, George L. 1985. *Nationalism and Sexuality: Respectability and Abnormal Sexuality in Modern Europe*. New York: Howard Fertig.

Mumm, Susan. 2006. "Josephine Butler and the International Traffic in Women." In *Sex, Gender, and Religion: Josephine Butler Revisited*. Ed. Jenny Daggers and Diana Neal, 55–71. New York: Peter Lang.

Murray, Alison. 1998. "Debt-Bondage and Trafficking: Don't Believe the Hype." In *Global Sex Workers: Rights, Resistance and Redefinition*. Ed. Kamala Kempadoo and Jo Doezema, 51–64. New York: Routledge.

Naanen, Benedict B. B. 1991. "'Itinerant Gold Mines': Prostitution in the Cross River Basin of Nigeria, 1930–1950." *African Studies Review* 34(2):57–79.

Nadelmann, Ethan A. 1990. "Global Prohibition Regimes: The Evolution of Norms in International Society." *International Organization* 44(4):479–526.

Nagel, Joane. 1998. "Masculinity and Nationalism: Gender and Sexuality in the Making of Nations." *Ethnic and Racial Studies* 21(2):242–269.

———. 2003. *Race, Ethnicity, and Sexuality: Intimate Intersections, Forbidden Frontiers*. New York: Oxford University Press.

Naimark, Norman M. 1995. *The Russians in Germany. A History of the Soviet Zone of Occupation, 1945–1949*. Cambridge, MA: Belknap Press.

National Vigilance Association. 1913. *The Fifth International Congress for the Suppression of the White Slave Traffic*. Caxton Hall, Westminster, London: National Vigilance Association.

Nelson, Keith L. 1970. "The 'Black Horror on the Rhine': Race as a Factor in Post-World War I Diplomacy." *Journal of Modern History* 42(4):606–627.

Nelson, Sue, Jeannine Guthrie, and Pamela Sumner Coffey. 2004. *Literature Review and Analysis Related to Human Trafficking in Post-Conflict Situations*. Washington, DC: Development Alternatives Inc./United States Agency for International Development.

Noriel, Gerard. 1996. *The French Melting Pot*. Trans. Geoffroy de Laforcade. Minneapolis: University of Minnesota Press.

O'Callaghan, Sean. 1965. *The White Slave Trade*. London: Robert Hale.

Offen, Karen. 1984. "Depopulation, Nationalism, and Feminism in Fin-de-Siecle France." *American Historical Review* 89(3):648–676.

———. 2000. *European Feminisms: 1700–1950*. Stanford: Stanford University Press.

———. 2005a. "Intrepid Crusader: Ghenia Avril de Sainte-Croix Takes on the Prostitution Issue." *Proceedings of the Western Society for French History* 33:352–374.

———. 2005b. "'La plus grande féministe de France': Mais qui est donc Madame Avril de Sainte-Croix ?" *Archives du Féminisme* No. 9. http://www.archivesdufeminisme .fr/article.php3?id_article=127 (accessed March 1, 2009).

———. 2008. "Madame Ghénia Avril de Sainte-Croix, the Josephine Butler of France." *Women's History Review* 17(2):239–255.

Ogborn, Miles. 1993. "Law and Discipline in Nineteenth Century English State Formation: The Contagious Diseases Acts of 1864, 1866, and 1869." *Journal of Historical Sociology* 6(1):28–55.

Orloff, Ann Shola. 1996. "Gender in the Welfare State." *Annual Review of Sociology* 22(1):51–78.

Outshoorn, Joyce. 2005. "The Political Debates on Prostitution and Trafficking of Women." *Social Politics* 12(1):141–155.

Palumbo, Patrizia (eds.). 2003. *A Place in the Sun: Africa in Italian Colonial Culture from Post-Unification to the Present*. Berkeley: University of California Press.

Pankhurst, Richard. 1974. "The History of Prostitution in Ethiopia." *Journal of Ethiopian Studies* 12(2):159–179.

Paxton, Nancy L. 1992. "Mobilizing Chivalry: Rape in British Novels About the Indian Uprising of 1857." *Victorian Studies* 36(1):5–30.

Pedersen, Jean Elisabeth. 1998. "Special Customs: Paternity Suits and Citizenship in France and the Colonies, 1870–1912." In *Domesticating the Empire: Race, Gender, and Family Life in French and Dutch Colonialism*. Ed. Julia Clancy-Smith and Frances Gouda, 43–64. Charlottesville and London: University Press of Virginia.

Pedersen, Susan. 2005. "Settler Colonialism at the Bar of the League of Nations." In *Settler Colonialism in the Twentieth Century*. Ed. Caroline Elkins and Susan Pedersen, 113–134. New York: Routledge.

Phillips, Richard. 2005. "Heterogenous Imperialism and the Regulation of Sexuality in British West Africa." *Journal of the History of Sexuality* 14(3):291–315.

———. 2006. *Sex, Politics and Empire: A Postcolonial Geography*. Manchester, UK: Manchester University Press.

Pollard, Miranda. 1998. *Reign of Virtue: Mobilizing Gender in Vichy France.* Chicago: University of Chicago Press.

Proschan, Frank. 2002. "'Syphilis, Opiomania, and Pederasty': Colonial Constructions of Vietnamese (and French) Social Diseases." *Journal of the History of Sexuality* 11(4):610–636.

Rathgeber, Corene. 2002. "The Victimization of Women Through Human Trafficking—An Aftermath of War?" *European Journal of Crime, Criminal Law and Criminal Justice* 10(2–3):152–163.

Reanda, Laura. 1991. "Prostitution as a Human Rights Question: Problems and Prospects of United Nations Action." *Human Rights Quarterly* 13(2):202–228.

Rieff, David. 2002. *A Bed for the Night: Humanitarianism in Crisis.* New York: Simon and Schuster.

Risse, Thomas, Stephen C. Ropp, and Kathryn Sikkink (eds.). 1999. *The Power of Human Rights: International Norms and Domestic Social Change.* Cambridge, UK: Cambridge University Press.

Roberts, Nickie. 1992. *Whores in History: Prostitution in Western Society.* London: Harper Collins.

Rochefort, Florence. 2004. "The French Feminist Movement and Republicanism, 1868–1914." In *Women's Emancipation Movements in the Nineteenth Century: A European Perspective.* Ed. Sylvia Paletschek and Bianka Pietrow-Ennker, 77–101. Stanford, CA: Stanford University Press.

———. 2008. "The Abolitionist Struggle of Pastor Tommy Fallot: Between Social Christianity, Feminism and Secularism." *Women's History Review* 17(2):179–194.

Rosen, Ruth. 1982. *The Lost Sisterhood: Prostitution in America, 1900–1918.* Baltimore, MD: Johns Hopkins University Press.

Rupp, Leila J. 1996. "Challenging Imperialism in International Women's Organizations, 1888–1945." *NWSA Journal* 8(1):8–15.

———. 1997. *Worlds of Women: The Making of an International Women's Movement.* Princeton, NJ: Princeton University Press.

Sassen, Saskia. 1999. *Guests and Aliens.* New York: The New Press.

Sbacchi, Alberto. 1985. *Ethiopia Under Mussolini: Fascism and the Colonial Experience.* London: Zed Books.

Scully, Eileen. 2001. "Pre-Cold War Traffic in Sexual Labor and Its Foes: Some Contemporary Lessons." In *Global Human Smuggling: Comparative Perspectives.* Ed. David Kyle and Rey Koslowski, 74–106. Baltimore, MD: Johns Hopkins University Press.

Seager, Joni. 2009. *The Penguin Atlas of Women in the World.* New York, Penguin Books.

Shannon, Sarah. 1999. "Prostitution and the Mafia: The Involvement of Organized Crime in the Global Sex Trade." In *Illegal Immigration and Commercial Sex: The New Slave Trade.* Ed. Phil Williams, 119–145. London: Frank Cass.

Sharma, Nandita. 2005. "Anti-Trafficking Rhetoric and the Making of a Global Apart-heid." *NWSA Journal* 17(3):88–111.

Shelley, Louise. 2007. "Human Trafficking as a Form of Transnational Crime." In *Human Trafficking*. Ed. Maggy Lee, 116–137. Cullompton, Devon, UK: Willan.

Soderlund, Gretchen. 2005. "Running from the Rescuers: New U.S. Crusades Against Sex Trafficking and the Rhetoric of Abolition." *NWSA Journal* 17(3):64–87.

Sone, Sachiko. 1992. "The Karayuki-san of Asia 1868–1938: The Role of Prostitutes Overseas in Japanese Economic and Social Development." *Review of Indonesian and Malaysian Affairs* 26(2):44–62.

Song, Youn-ok. 1997. "Japanese Colonial Rule and State-Managed Prostitution: Korea's Licensed Prostitutes." *Positions* 5(1):171–217.

Spaulding, Jay, and Stephanie Beswick. 1995. "Sex, Bondage, and the Market: The Emer-gence of Prostitution in Northern Sudan, 1750–1950." *Journal of the History of Sexu-ality* 5(4):512–534.

Stamatov, Peter. 2006. *The Religious Origins of Modern Long-Distance Humanitarianism: England, 1780–1880, in Comparative Perspective.* Ph.D. Dissertation, University of California, Los Angeles.

Stokvis, Pieter R. D. 1994. "International Migration from the Netherlands, 1880–1920." In *Connecting Cultures: The Netherlands in Five Centuries of Transatlantic Exchange.* Ed. Rosemarijn Hoefte and Johanna C. Kardux, 155–170. Amsterdam: VU Univer-sity Press.

Stoler, Ann Laura. 1989. "Rethinking Colonial Categories: European Communities and the Boundaries of Rule." *Comparative Studies in Society and History* 31(1):134–161.

———. 1997a. "Sexual Affronts and Racial Frontiers: European Identities and the Cul-tural Politics of Exclusion in Colonial Southeast Asia." In *Tensions of Empire: Colo-nial Cultures in a Bourgeois World.* Ed. Frederick Cooper and Ann Laura Stoler, 198–237. Berkeley: University of California Press.

———. 1997b. "Making Empire Respectable: The Politics of Race and Sexual Morality in Twentieth-Century Colonial Cultures." In *Situated Lives: Gender and Culture in Everyday Life.* Ed. Louise Lamphere, Helena Ragone, and Patricia Zavella, 373–399. New York: Routledge.

———. 2002. *Carnal Knowledge and Imperial Power: Race and the Intimate in Colonial Rule.* Berkeley: University of California Press.

Stovall, Tyler. 1993. "Colour-Blind France? Colonial Workers During the First World War." *Race and Class* 35(2):35–55.

Strobel, Margaret. 1993. "Gender, Sex, and Empire." In *Islamic and European Expansion: The Forging of a Global Order.* Ed. Michael Adas, 345–375. Philadelphia: Temple University Press.

Surkis, Judith. 2006. *Sexing the Citizen: Morality and Masculinity in France, 1870–1920.* Ithaca, NY: Cornell University Press.

Swierenga, Robert P. 1993. "The Delayed Transition from Folk to Labor Migration: The Netherlands, 1880–1920." *International Migration Review* 27(2):406–424.

Talleyrand, Isabelle. 2000. "Military Prostitution: How the Authorities Worldwide Aid and Abet International Trafficking in Women." *Syracuse Journal of International Law and Commerce* 27:151–176.

Tambor, Molly. 2006. "Prostitutes and Politicians: The Women's Rights Movement in the Legge Merlin Debates." In *Women in Italy, 1945–1960: An Interdisciplinary Study*. Ed. Penelope Morris, 131–145. New York: Palgrave Macmillan.

Taraud, Christelle. 2003. *La Prostitution Coloniale: Algérie, Tunisie, Maroc (1830–1962)*. Paris: Payot.

———. 2006. "Urbanisme, hygiénisme et prostitution à Casablanca dans les années 1920." *French Colonial History* 7:97–108.

Tarrow, Sidney. 1994. *Power in Movement: Social Movements, Collective Action, and Politics*. New York: Cambridge University Press.

Taylor, Jean Gelman. 1983. *The Social World of Batavia: European and Eurasian in Dutch Asia*. Madison: University of Wisconsin Press.

Torpey, John. 2000. *The Invention of the Passport: Surveillance, Citizenship and the State*. Cambridge, UK: Cambridge University Press.

Tyldum, Guri, and Anette Brunovskis. 2005. "Describing the Unobserved: Methodological Challenges in Empirical Studies on Human Trafficking." *International Migration* 43(1/2):17–34.

Ucarer, Emek M. 1999. "Trafficking in Women: Alternate Migration or Modern Slave Trade?" In *Gender Politics in Global Governance*. Ed. Mary K. Meyer and Elisabeth Prugl, 230–244. Lanham. MD: Rowman and Littlefield.

United Nations. 1948. *Traffic in Women and Children: Summary of Annual Reports for 1946–1947 Prepared by the Secretariat*. New York: United Nations. E/TWC.1946–47/Summary.

———. 1949. *Traffic in Women and Children: Summary of Annual Reports for 1947–1948 Prepared by the Secretariat*. New York: United Nations. E/TWC.1947–48/Summary.

———. 1950. *Traffic in Women and Children: Addendum to the Summary of Annual Reports for 1947–1948 Prepared by the Secretariat*. New York: United Nations. E/TWC.1947–48/ADD.1.

———. 1955. "Reports from Governments: Existing Conditions with Respect to the Traffic in Persons and the Exploitation of the Prostitution of Others in Six Selected Countries (Australia, Israel, the Netherlands, Pakistan, Singapore, Sweden)." *International Review of Criminal Policy* 6:74–81.

———. 1958a. "Prostitution and Venereal Disease." *International Review of Criminal Policy* 13:67–93.

———. 1958b. "Reports From Governments: Prostitution and Anti-Venereal Disease Measures in Ten Selected Countries: Cambodia, Ceylon, Chile, Denmark, France,

Haiti, Hungary, Ireland, Poland, Spain." *International Review of Criminal Policy* 13:101–111.

———. 1959. "Study on Traffic in Persons and Prostitution." New York: United Nations Department of Economic and Social Affairs. 59.IV.5

van Drenth, Annemieke. 2002. "The City and the Self: The Case of Girls' Protection in the Netherlands Around 1900." *Educational Review* 54(2):125–132.

———. 2006. "Holy Beliefs and Caring Power: Josephine Butler's Influence on Abolitionism and the Women's Movement in the Netherlands (1850–1920)." In *Sex, Gender, and Religion: Josephine Butler Revisited.* Ed. Jenny Daggers and Diana Neal, 73–95. New York: Peter Lang.

van Drenth, Annemieke, and Francisca de Haan. 1999. *The Rise of Caring Power: Elizabeth Fry and Josephine Butler in Britain and the Netherlands.* Amsterdam: Amsterdam University Press.

van Heyningen, Elizabeth B. 1984. "The Social Evil in the Cape Colony 1868–1902: Prostitution and the Contagious Diseases Acts." *Journal of South African Studies* 10(2):170–197.

Walkowitz, Judith. 1983. *Prostitution in Victorian Society: Women, Class, and the State.* New York: Cambridge University Press.

Wanrooij, Bruno P. F. 2008. "Josephine Butler and Regulated Prostitution in Italy." *Women's History Review* 17(2):153–171.

Warren, James Francis. 1993. *Ah Ku and Karayuki-san: Prostitution in Singapore 1870–1940.* Oxford, UK: Oxford University Press.

Watson, Molly McGregor. 2000. *The Trade in Women: "White Slavery" and the French Nation, 1899–1939.* Ph.D. Dissertation, Stanford University.

Weeks, Jeffrey. 1989. *Sex, Politics and Society: The Regulation of Sexuality Since 1800.* Ed. J. Stevenson. London: Longman.

Wertheim, Wim F. 1990. "Netherlands-Indian Colonial Racism and Dutch Home Racism." In *Imperial Monkey Business: Racial Supremacy in Social Darwinist Theory and Colonial Practice.* Ed. Jan Breman, Piet de Rooy, Ann Stoler, and Wim F. Wertheim, 71–88. Amsterdam: VU University Press.

Wesseling, H. L. 1980. "Post-Imperial Holland." *Journal of Contemporary History* 15(1):125–142.

Weston, Elisabeth Anne. 1979. *Prostitution in Paris in the Later Nineteenth Centry: A Study of Political and Social Ideology.* Buffalo: State University of New York.

Whitehead, Judith. 2001. "Measuring Women's Value: Continuity and Change in the Regulation of Prostitution in Madras Presidency, 1860–1947." In *Of Property and Propriety: The Role of Gender and Class in Imperialism and Nationalism.* Ed. Himani Bannerji, Shahrzad Mojab, and Judith Whitehead, 153–181. Toronto: University of Toronto Press.

Wijers, Marjan. 1998. "Women, Labor and Migration: The Position of Trafficked Women and Strategies for Support." In *Global Sex Workers: Rights, Resistance, and Redefinition*. Ed. Kamala Kampadoo and Jo Doezema, 69–78. New York: Routledge.

Willson, Perry. 2007. "Empire, Gender and the 'Home Front' in Fascist Italy." *Women's History Review* 16(4):487–500.

Yuval-Davis, Nira. 1998. "Women, Gender and Nationalism." In *Ethnicity and Nationalism*. Ed. Rick Wilford and Robert L. Miller, 23–35. New York: Routledge.

Index

Note: Tables are indicated by *t* following a page number.

International Bureau for the Suppression of the White Slave Traffic (International Bureau), 12, 56–64, 68–69; aims of, 42; and class, 64; committees by country, 45*t*; delegates to, *59*; in Dutch East Indies, 104–5, 107–9; establishment of, 6, 56–57; in France, 17, 57, 58, 60, 115–18, 121–22, 130; German National Committee, 35–36; in Germany, 57, 58, 61, 186*n*2; International Abolitionist Federation vs., 43, 63, 64–67, 69, 91–92, 117; issues addressed by, 56–58; in Italy, 136–38, 143; League of Nations and, 63, 74–75, 79, 81–82, 85; and nationalism, 60; and nationality, 61–62; in the Netherlands, 57, 58, 98–99; organization of, 58, 60; primary sources from, 14; and race/ethnicity, 61–62; and repatriation of foreign prostitutes, 85–87, 89; on state regulation, 8–9, 13, 56–58, 60, 62–63, 65–67, 91, 144–46; state relations with, 56, 58, 62–63, 68–69, 99, 117–18, 144–46; and trafficking, 57, 66–67; universalism resisted by, 61; and World War II abuses, 89

International Catholic Association for the Protection of Girls, 75. *See also* Catholic Association for the Protection of Girls

International Council of Women, 35, 48, 61, 73–75, 79

International humanitarianism, 6–7

International Medical Congress (Brussels, 1867), 26

International Red Cross, 6

International trafficking. *See* Trafficking

International Union of Friends of Young Women, 44

International Union of the Friends of Girls, 106

International Women's Suffrage Alliance, 48, 73, 75, 89, 98, 119

Interracial sex, 20–21, 28, 33–36, 85, 124–25, 128, 140–41, 148. *See also* Intermarriage

Iraq, 32

Israel, 32

Italian Committee Against the White Slave Trade, 136

Italy, 133–43; abolition in, 134–36; anti-trafficking activities in, 2, 3, 12, 17–18, 133–40, 146–47; anti-trafficking activities in colonies of, 140–43; Fascism in, 139–43; feminism in, 135–36, 138–39, 147; and imperialism, 12;

International Abolitionist Federation in, 143; and international anti-trafficking accords, 136–137; International Bureau in, 58, 136–38, 143; and League of Nations, 72, 75; migration from, 133; prostitutes from, 30–31; prostitution in, 30, 32, 40; and race/ethnicity, 140–42, 148; regulation of prostitution by, 23, 25, 133–40; repatriation of prostitutes in, 138–39; and trafficking, 92, 142–43

Jacobs, Aletta, 98

Japan: and League of Nations, 72, 75; police corruption in, 39; prostitutes from, 30–31, 102–3; prostitution in, 47, 166*n*13; regulation of prostitution by, 22–23, 26; repatriation of prostitutes to, 84–85; and trafficking, 29, 104–5

Java: concubinage in, 20; prostitution in, 21, 102–3

Jewish Association for the Protection of Girls and Women, 44, 74–76, 79, 81–83, 168*n*43

Jewish women, in prostitution, 23, 151

Kanpur, India, 53

Khaled, Emir, 129

Klerck-van Hogendorp, Marianne, 97–98, 103, 175*n*18

Korea, 31

Ladies National Association for the Repeal of the Contagious Diseases Act, 44, 46

League for Public Morality, 115

League of Nations, 16; abolition vs. regulation in, 72–73, 75, 78, 82, 93, 100; and international accords, 9; anti-trafficking activities of, 2, 42, 71–78, 92–94; establishment of, 71; International Abolitionist Federation and, 73, 80; International Bureau and, 63, 74–75, 79, 81–82, 85; mandate system of, 158*n*26; organization of, 71; primary sources from, 14; and prohibition of foreign women in prostitution, 79–89; and prostitution, 62; and race/ethnicity, 62; and repatriation of foreign prostitutes, 82–89; Special Body of Experts, 67; and state sovereignty/interests, 73; Traffic in Women and Children Committee, 9, 72, 75–84, 86, 119, 121–22, 137–38; and universalism, 69